C000284048

DWELL
BEING

DWELL BEING

BEING

FINDING HOME IN THE CITY

CLAIRE BRADBURY

For Mum and Dad, tireless adventurers.

First published 2021

FLINT is an imprint of The History Press
97 St George's Place, Cheltenham,
Gloucestershire, GL50 3QB
www.flintbooks.co.uk

© Claire Bradbury, 2021
Cover illustration © Melissa Turland, 2021

The right of Claire Bradbury to be identified as the Author
of this work has been asserted in accordance with the
Copyright, Designs and Patents Act 1988.

All rights reserved. No part of this book may be reprinted
or reproduced or utilised in any form or by any electronic,
mechanical or other means, now known or hereafter invented,
including photocopying and recording, or in any information
storage or retrieval system, without the permission in writing
from the Publishers.

British Library Cataloguing in Publication Data.
A catalogue record for this book is available from the British Library.

ISBN 978 0 7509 9602 0

Typesetting and origination by The History Press
Printed and bound in Great Britain by TJ Books Limited, Padstow, Cornwall.

Trees for LΥfe

CONTENTS

FOREWORD

In 2007, and for the first time in human history, half of the world's then nearly 7 billion people lived in towns and cities. Until that point, and for millennia before, we lived in more natural or rural settings, as hunter-gatherers and then in agricultural landscapes.

The rise of urban areas was driven by economic opportunity, convenience, security and, of course, our highly sociable nature. Urbanisation continues and it is expected that by 2050 about 68 per cent of all people will be living in cities, and by then our population is projected to rise to around 9.5 billion people.

The twenty-first century is thus an urban story, with a process that began in its modern form during the Industrial Revolution now having taken on the dimensions of a fundamental and ongoing global shift, with massive ramifications for all aspects of how we live.

As we look at the nexus of multiple social and environmental challenges that face us today, from the decline of wild species to the rise of chronic illness, it is clear that if we are to resolve these issues then in large part it will be in cities that we will succeed.

In the pages that follow Claire Bradbury takes us on a journey of discovery into the places most of us live where, during our collective Covid-19 trauma, hyper-local living forced many into a kind of familiarity with their urban environments that had not been experienced before. She draws on personal experience, as well as a vast body of evidence and learning, to seize this moment and to paint a vivid picture of how cities can nurture amazing lives for people, if only we draw on collective insight and muster the will to achieve just that.

While some have recently fled the cities in favour of more rural environments, this book is a reminder of why it is vitally important that we fall back in love with our cities, as habitats and hubs for the regenerative future we must create, for if we don't create that in cities, we won't create it at all. This will require us to revisit how we move, eat, interact, play, live and work in our ever-expanding urban areas, and how in that context we can create the green and blue environments that a vast body of evidence now reveals are not only vital in tackling global change, but are so important for people's health and wellbeing.

But what might be good for one city may not be the best for another, so *Dwellbeing* is less of a blueprint and more an engaging fresh perspective on what have become deeply entrenched challenges. It debunks the myth that cities are necessarily frenetic, hostile and rootless places, and reveals instead how the big questions are indelibly linked to why so many of us choose to live in them in the first place.

This highly readable book presents answers, and I am sure will be a major contribution toward securing amazing and sustainable urban futures during the decades ahead.

Tony Juniper CBE
Environmentalist and Chair, Natural England
July 2021

LOVE AND LOATHING
IN THE CITY

What is the city but the people?

William Shakespeare, *Coriolanus* (1623)

THE QUESTION I'M most often asked is, 'Where are you from?' While I'm comfortable with home being a fluid concept, this doesn't always satisfy human curiosity. It's usually safe, as a migrant, to anticipate the follow-up question – 'but where are you actually from?' It can continue like this, quite maddeningly, until you're presented with some kind of ultimatum scenario like, 'If the world was ending tomorrow, where would you call home?'

In a way, the world did end – at least as we knew it – in 2020, and for most of us the notion of home was suddenly pushed to the front of our minds.

I was born in Johannesburg, South Africa, to a British–Austrian father and Irish mother. My parents met in Gauteng where they were united by a sense of adventure, a love of Africa and a life on the move. When the tension of apartheid made spiralling violence an ugly part of everyday life, we made the heartbreaking decision to leave. Over the next few decades, life stretched between England, Australia, France, Democratic Republic of Congo, Ghana, Tanzania and Scotland until, more recently, I returned to England and put down roots in London.

My early life was split between mining towns in the Highveld coal belt, the wild coast of Kwa-Zulu Natal, and deep in the wilderness of South Africa's iconic national parks. I had an idyllic and peaceful upbringing in the bush, where I was the only white kid in my school, life was outdoors, immersion in nature was regular and I slotted in amongst a menagerie of animals. My parents travelled far and wide, and I went with them. As far as I was concerned, this was all entirely normal. It was only when I began the process of making and remaking my home that fielding questions and assumptions about my heritage and sense of belonging became the norm.

I suppose my memories of being a young South African migrant still lurk beneath the surface. Coming from a long line of stoic adventurers, my response to constant moving was just to get on with it. The chance to make and remake myself again with each change in home is simultaneously empowering, disruptive and addictive. Being a chameleon becomes a lifestyle choice, and it's only recently that I've paused to reflect on the enormity of life on the move. As adaptable as I am, I also know only too well the deep ache that comes from displacement, the yearning to be in several places at once and the desire to take a small piece of each home and stitch those pieces together to make a perfect whole. The sunny side of this is that having a multitude of homes is entirely possible, each existing in different pockets of time and place, each special in their own way. As I travelled further and further from my roots in the African bush, I learned that belonging can be a portable concept. Nowhere have I felt it more than in the city. What is it, then, about the seductive warmth of cities that encourages us to find home within them?

Like many things in 2020, writing this book didn't go according to plan. The year certainly got off to a promising start, beginning, for me, on the banks of the Mississippi River in New Orleans – a bewitching, spirited city whose history, music, people, weather, food and art combine to form a complex and soulful mix of urban life.

A few months later, my dad, uncle and I climbed Mount Kenya with our friend and climbing partner Raphael, who had travelled across from Tanzania. We now know, with the benefit of hindsight, that there were huge amounts of luck on our side to be able to complete this trip. At that stage, the true extent of Covid-19 was uncertain but global travel was certainly dwindling. When we summited at sunrise one frosty but calm morning, we were the only ones on the mountain. On the roof of Africa, we felt as we so often feel on the peaks: unstoppable. Little did I know that this wouldn't be the only or even the biggest obstacle to overcome that year. Spending the following week in Kenya's Meru region, I also had no idea that this would be my last dose of wild, untamed nature for a while. It wasn't until later that it became clear we had escaped with only modest disruption to our travel. Across the world, borders were tightening. Raphael, having left us in Nairobi and returned to a remote mine site in Mbeya, became stranded for the next seven months, unable to get back to his wife and family in Johannesburg.

Back in the city, we were lucky enough to have a few last hurrahs; the panic, though settling in, was still sporadic. I went to the ballet and the Banff Mountain Film Festival in packed-out theatres, and my spin classes were fully booked, but cafes, shops and trains were eerily empty. My neighbours and I went to a local supper club, followed by cocktails in the basement bar of a laptop repair shop. What started off as a civilised evening ended up, as most good nights do, in our local and much-beloved pub. This was our last, hallowed night out before we went into the first lockdown, and we still talk about it today.

The deviations of 2020 and 2021 brought some challenges when it came to researching and writing this book. My infinitely patient and becalming editor, Jo, with me every step of the way, witnessed my erratic shuffling across the spectrum of love and loathing for the city. Three months into the first lockdown and I was already grounded in one place for longer than I had ever been in my life, sparking a monumental exercise in self-reflection.

This is a book about living deeply and joyfully in cities, and the fact that the solutions for many of our challenges begin in our neighbourhoods – in our homes and on our streets. My intention is to uplift and inspire, rather than dampen and blame. In researching this book, I've drawn on my travels, my homes and my workplaces – all of which have involved getting under the skin of urban living. I've interviewed experts and city dwellers alike. All the many conversations I've had in the course of living an urban life have been woven into this book: anecdotes, gripes, quips, drunken rants, and stories of heartbreak and hope.

I've decided to dial down the noise surrounding our institutions because we hear enough from them. It's time for some new voices and stories – those that reflect the real, everyday, lived experience of life in cities.

The seven pillars that follow – wilderness, nourishment, movement, connection, dwelling, imagination and love – are what I believe the city (wherever it may be in the world) is built upon. These pillars frame the explorations in this book as they are indelibly bound up in our urban experience. They are what contribute to the resilience, diversity, charisma, creativity, humour, beauty, contrast and magnetism of our city homes. No one understands the city better than the city dweller, and this might yet be the greatest power we have.

1

WILDERNESS

There is a love of wild nature in everybody, an ancient mother-love showing itself, whether recognized or not, and however covered by cares and duties.

John Muir

I'M AN URBAN blow-in. Like millions of others, I've adopted the city as home. In my truest form, I belong in the wild. My soul and deepest sense of place is grounded in the African bush. So, I've often found myself asking: how on earth have I fallen head over heels for the city again and again? The answer isn't so much to do with me as it is to do with being human. As a species, we're remarkably adaptable and it's this ability to remake ourselves that helps us make sense of – and even relish – life in cities despite them being a far cry from our primal origins. Each one offers a unique, vibrant footprint for community or shared existence that keeps us coming back for more.

There's one thing that humans, rural or urban, can't live without, though: the wilderness. Visible or not, it dictates our quality of life. Our traditional model of city living belies the depth and complexity of the lives they support – humans and wildlife alike. As our nature blind spot has got bigger, we've been playing with fire in pushing our habitats to their limits. As Marco Lambertini cautioned in the World Wide Fund for Nature's (WWF) *Living Planet Report* 2020, our current circumstances are 'a clear manifestation of our broken relationship with nature'.

Our intense focus on high-volume, high-speed commerce has cultivated an environment that has conveniently kept nature from view. When we concentrate on buildings and economic capital over the experience of those who live in the city, we create a greyscale version of life.

Cities can be magnificent but, in their current form, they are leaving us depleted. Retreating behind walls, both literally and figuratively, has eroded our environmental wisdom – our innate faculty to observe, understand and live tunefully within nature. When this wisdom disappears, we're left feeling out of kilter, restless and yearning for something 'other' than our urban landscapes. This gives us some indication that the underlying conditions may not have been the most nurturing. The idea of cities as nothing more than relentless centres of commerce is rooted in the shifts brought about by the industrial revolution that have framed city life as the 'daily grind', 'hamster wheel' or 'rat race'. These terms conjure ideas of suffering and lack of autonomy, where life is a matter of surviving rather than thriving. As nature has been forced to retreat, how can we revitalise our connections with the outdoors?

We need wilderness in all forms – parks and median strips, canals and rivers, harbour foreshores and beaches, allotments and guerrilla gardens, street planters and rooftop farms, as the calm *yin* to the frenetic *yang* of city life. When we dilute our high-octane lifestyles with a dose of the outdoors, great or small, we are reminded that we belong in nature and not as its master.

We should see this as a positive: when we loosen the grip on the reins we have less to do and can enjoy ourselves more. We seek solace from urban stress because the city can feel like a daily assault course. We might, for instance, spend hours squeezed in a *dala dala* to travel a few kilometres in Dar es Salaam, wait on a steamy New York platform to shoehorn ourselves into the L train, or breathe dangerous air pollution on the way to and from school in Kampala. With many versions of this scenario playing out for city dwellers daily, it's hardly surprising that we want to dive into the nearest patch of wilderness we can find. When the Covid-19 pandemic hit, our world contracted and our urban greenspaces were the first places we turned to for solace.

There are few silver linings to the turmoil we've all faced in the past year or so, but Covid-19 has shown that we do not always need to travel far for respite from the city grind. Our traditional notion of what holidays should be and how they should look was turned on its head in 2020. We were reminded of how much we had to appreciate at home.

The pandemic has also highlighted the beauty of simpler and more connected ways of living. In the UK, the first lockdown in March 2020 coincided with the sunniest spring on record, and people headed to their local parks or waterways to give themselves a much-needed boost of vitamin D and endorphins. Places that were usually empty and forgotten – like cemeteries or tiny outcrops of parched grass in the middle of the city – became the high points around which our days were anchored. Londoners began noticing common garden birds whose warbling was no longer drowned out by the din of traffic. Taking advantage of the lull, families emerged into uncluttered streets where children played; would-be cyclists became bona fide cyclists, relishing the chance to navigate their city without running the risk of being squashed or verbally abused; and the intrinsic value of natural, open spaces went up.

Wilderness is vital to humanity. Beyond survival, it helps shape our identity, connects us to our instincts, supports our wellbeing and underpins quality of life. When we understand the transformative role of the urban wild on our quality of life, we can think about how our daily behaviours can, do and should breathe life into nature. When it becomes entwined in our daily routines, we will fight to protect it.

OUR NATURAL IDENTITY

Anyone who has lived, worked in, or visited a city can identify with the break in intensity that comes from stepping into a leafy park or taking a moment in a city farm. This is because our systems are pre-programmed to decompress in natural places. We are already seeking them out because we are hardwired to do so.

Yet, somewhere along the line, 'the city' as an institution closed the door on nature. As our pathways to the wilderness have become blocked and our sprawling cities are creating an ecological cul-de-sac, the grey, crowded and built-up worlds we have created leave us thirsty for something that exists beyond the city limits. Whatever we call it: nature, wilderness, greenspace, bluespace, recreation space, gardens, allotments, freedom to roam – it's a must-have. This does not change from season to season, it will not be in vogue and out again. The natural world is our moral, psychological and physical compass so it is no surprise that, without it, we find ourselves floundering. When this happens, it usually doesn't take much digging to find that the web of urban pressures – urbanisation, extreme gentrification, resource shortages and competition for land – have caused our urban wilds to ebb away.

Life in cities can be depleting and unrelenting. They're often unequal, expensive, noisy, dangerous, dirty, crowded and intense. Whether we're conscious of it or not, it takes tremendous amounts of energy to live, work and socialise in these conditions. When we lose time in the wilderness, the symptoms of city fatigue become compounded. What's scary about this is how insipid nature deficit is – it really is a case of use it or lose it. While we're holed up inside forgetting the beauty or calm of our outdoor spaces, they are under existential threat. This is a problem because we spend a considerable portion of our lives indoors. Some cities have a better track record of getting their people outdoors whatever the weather, but globally it's not been a good picture for outdoor lifestyles, although the Covid-19 pandemic has given us the nudge we needed to get outside.

The reality of wilderness in densely built-up urban areas is that it is often found in tiny pockets, and this can make it hard to see the full picture. Because these spaces have traditionally fallen into the camp of 'too small to matter', we tend to think of nature as something 'out there' rather than central to the identity of our urban environments. Big nature, wild and untamed, can feel remote and difficult to tap into. But when we do, it has a way of reaching straight into our hearts to remind us where we come from and grounds us in the present.

I have a penchant for mountains and have been making my way up, down and between summits across Africa and Europe with my dad over the past decade or so. Plans often go awry – our expeditions have seen us stranded in a tin boat in an electrical storm on Lake Victoria, DRC; dangled off the side of Mount Elbrus, Russia; lodged in crevices in the Rwenzori Mountains in Uganda; and charged by wildlife, to name a few. But even the most hair-raising moments in the wilderness are precious. It's here we learn what we're about, testing the depths of our stamina and our ability to read nature's cues. We don't quite need to replicate life or death experiences in cities (let's face it, there's already enough to be stressed about), but we do need nature to expand our horizons, nurture our minds and bodies, and disrupt the 'grey normal' we've come to accept. Wilder cities will be more playful, reflective and enjoyable to be in. They'll also be healthier and more prosperous. It's a win-win and city dwellers are already on board. The shadows of nature – Table Mountain in Cape Town, New Mexico's forests or Vancouver's creeks and inlets – are helpful, visual reminders that nature is right here with us.

When it comes to balancing the nature deficit, most of us are in the red. Acclaimed writer, psychologist and wilderness guide Dr Ian McCallum, speaking at a Power of Resilience event run by ROAR AFRICA in 2020, lamented the physiological and psychological adaptations and stressors that occur when we do not have access to nature. The deficiencies we start to experience when we lose this connection are real and I'm yet to meet a city dweller who doesn't identify with the feeling of disconnection from nature. The question, then, is: how do we rebalance this shortfall?

ESCAPE TO THE CITY

Time in the wilderness does something profound to us, whether we take the active outdoorsy route or prefer to stop and smell the roses. Immersed in it, we find it easier to unplug from our digital lives, breathe deeper and sleep better. This is because getting out into the wild reacquaints us with the natural cadence of the day, connecting us back to our circadian rhythms such as the sleep–wake cycle. These moments are precious kindling for the soul and help us feel able to keep going, to resume the grit and intensity that might await us back home.

Words like 'escape' and 'retreat' have become part of the narrative of city life because we're often living in an environment that feels worth running from. When we leave our urban spaces for time in the country or by the sea, we commonly take with us emptied tanks, frayed nerves and shorter fuses. But what would it be like if city dwellers were already surrounded by nature, so that when we choose to leave the city, we do so already feeling nourished? It would be a truly wonderful thing to get to a point where we don't need to travel into wild nature to resuscitate us, but we start with a fuller tank. To do this, we need to look at how we can create this nurturing experience in our neighbourhoods on a regular basis so that we aren't leaping across the spectrum from frazzled to restored and back again, but instead reaching equilibrium in our urban homes. If connection with the natural world is intrinsic to city life, we are more likely to feel that we belong as part of it. This might mean we make different decisions about where we go, how we spend our time and why.

In the years following the Covid-19 pandemic, travel will be more restricted, and we will be looking closer to home for respite and fun. The periods of lockdown across the world saw us all leaning on our urban wilds for support, kick-starting renewed appreciation for their value and thinking carefully about where we spend our leisure time. Inadvertently, mercifully, we may have spawned the era of conscious travel where now, if we are going to move beyond our cities, we will seek to do so wisely and well.

As nature has become the province of those who can afford to travel, an empathetic city should be asking what happens to those who remain, whether out of love, loyalty or obligation. When Covid-19 hit, for example, the affluent city dwellers and second-homers fled, from New York City to the Hamptons, London to the Home Counties, Johannesburg to the Hibiscus Coast, and so the story went on across the world. But it doesn't need to be this way.

When travel escapes us, there are many ways we can connect with bigger nature from within our cities and sometimes from within the comfort of our own homes. Film festivals like the Banff Mountain Film Festival and Ocean Film Festival transport us to the lives of modern-day adventurers – the people 'living big' out there in the wild – even when we cannot adventure ourselves. On the less adrenaline-fuelled end of the spectrum, we can spend a quiet few hours taking in a photography exhibition like the Wildlife Photographer of the Year, which offers powerful, resonating imagery from some of the further reaches of the planet. At home on our screens, we are lucky enough to have the charisma and dedication of the king of natural history, Sir David Attenborough, bringing nature into our homes, as well as many others.

This is especially important when we consider city dwellers who don't have access to nature that might lie further afield. As we recover from life in lockdown, we need to pay careful attention to how we enable equality of access to nature in cities as it really does feel a luxury to be able to escape. The prescription to 'spend more time out-doors' doesn't go far enough. It's not as simple as just getting outside more; the quality of our natural places, time to enjoy them and their accessibility is critical too. Being aware of some of the visible and invisible obstacles to our urban wilds can help us make them more welcoming. Gender, ethnicity, mobility and socio-economic status, to name a few, can cause city dwellers to shy away from wilderness areas. Beth Collier, of Wild in the City, champions Black leadership and representation in nature because she recognises that Black and minority ethnic groups have not always felt welcome. This is true too of the rural wilderness. The University of Leicester's 2011 *Rural Racism* report looked specifically at how ethnic minorities were made to feel out of place in Britain's countryside. A sense of belonging is not the only issue – it can often be coupled with fear. All too often, the wilderness that exists outside the city boundaries can also seem off limits, the preserve of genuine country dwellers, or a playground for those who are privileged enough to afford to work hard in the city and party hard in the country.

NURTURING OUR INNER WILD THINGS

If urban landscapes are where we spend most of our time because of relationships, work, education, services and social structures, we need to learn how they can nurture us. To be able to enjoy the full advantage of urban wilderness, it helps to major on their recreational value and this means seeing them as less municipal and more playful. By valuing them for their fun and inclusivity, we can make everybody a champion for the wild, regardless of circumstances.

It's rare that time in the wilderness isn't about fun. From playground monkey bars to field sports, it taps into one of our deepest human needs: playfulness. Stuart Brown, managing director of the National Institute for Play, describes play as a 'deep instinctive fundamental need' that is intrinsic to our heritage. Dr Brown points to our similarities with other animals but, despite the fact we get immense pleasure from watching the antics of our children and pets, grown-ups seem to do a lot less playing, perhaps because we are more self-conscious and strapped for time. This might be one of the reasons why we enjoy taking dogs to the park so much – we're almost living vicariously and experiencing joy through them. But as soon as we shed these shackles, we're in for a treat. In my outdoor bootcamps, I always make sure we play a game or two in the session just to break up the intensity and give us the chance to be silly. It could be something as simple as tag, a wheelbarrow race or a riff on duck-duck-goose, but it is guaranteed to spark joy. My clients, ranging in age from their early twenties to late sixties, are soon in fits of infectious laughter and not a weekend goes by without a passerby sidling up and asking how they can get involved in the fun. I'm sure that the dose of silliness, developing those social bonds and the chance to roll around in the grass are all as beneficial as the workout itself.

One evening in 2020, finding myself in Belfast for work, I ran around the city's Titanic Quarter and happened upon the industrial play park at the river's edge. My first response was an inward moan about the absence of green. But what it lacked in vegetation, it made up for with water, and there was something so captivating about this expanse of hard-standing ground in the middle of a port. Surrounded by freight containers and in the shadow of *Samson* and *Goliath* – the iconic shipyard cranes – the former Harland & Wolff shipyard is something of an amphitheatre to the hubbub of port life. As the sun faded and was replaced by the twinkling city lights, the shipyard became a magnet for people. It was a large open space and well lit, which meant that even on a long winter's evening there were families, youngsters and the elderly enjoying the safe openness of the space while a colony of seals snoozed at the water's edge. Being relatively flat and paved, it was also a paradise for skaters, cyclists and roller bladers. Something about the combination of the port activity, which awakened in me a sense of familiarity with the cities of Sydney and Cape Town, and the visibility of people using a post-industrial space as their playground reminded me of the alternative forms of beauty we can find in our built environment and city infrastructure. At its best, it is enhanced by greenspace or bluespace.

Some cities have been innovative in changing the story of their existing natural assets. The Paris *Plage* project has done just that by transforming the Seine into an aquatic playground. Each year, since 2002, the banks of the Parc Rives de Seine and Canal de l'Ourcq switch from functional and pretty-enough towpaths into a seaside-inspired playground. Against the backdrop of Paris' iconic architecture are beach huts, sunbeds, planted areas and terraces, which encourage visitors to linger. In the Quai de Loire, a network of swimming pools becomes part of the everyday flow, including pools to suit children and those with reduced mobility. Revellers can also canoe, ride a zipline, learn first aid, take an art class or kick back with a book available from a satellite library. Perhaps being grounded over a particularly scorching European summer reminded us all of the need – not to mention the pleasure – of being outside. Paris is greenspace and garden light, as is typical of many European cities, so the Paris *Plage* isn't just a gimmick – it has also provided essential outdoor space and a forum for residents of all ages to connect, blow off some steam and have a little fun outside of the usual four walls. This example shows the raft of creative possibilities to enjoy the city's natural and artificial public spaces. Blue or green, they should be inviting and safe for us all to play in.

Examples like the Paris *Plage* also spark collective curiosity about forgotten places – those that may have been relegated to the purely municipal or industrial. This is especially true of waterways, and London Waterkeeper's campaign for a Thames 'Fit to Swim' shows that the health and wellbeing benefits of a river that is fit to swim in could be transformational for Londoners. Not only would attitudes towards the river change if it is viewed as a public amenity rather than an industrial artery, but the possibility for increasing physical activity is huge. Swimming and all manner of water sports would also increase if people felt able to venture into the water without fear of getting sick. Rivers that are healthy for people are also healthy for wildlife. Generally, we want to be in places that support fish, birds, amphibians, insects and mammals because they are fundamentally lovelier and far more interesting to be in and around. We also know that they can protect our cities from the effects of our rapidly changing climate.

A LANDSCAPE OF LEARNING

As we move along the spectrum from concrete jungle to the real jungle, we experience a sharpening of the senses. This is because natural landscapes were the nucleus of human activity before we adapted to the urban environment. The primal role of nature is what brings us that sense of internal quietness, letting us tune into our surrounds and soften the internal dialogue of 'what if' and 'what next'. Deborah Calmeyer, of inspirational travel company ROAR AFRICA, speaks beautifully of the wilderness as 'the cathedral for our souls'. When I spoke to her in the midst of the Covid-19 pandemic in 2020 – Deborah in New York and me in Belfast – we both lamented our absence from Africa, especially at a time when going outside was off the cards. Perhaps it was unfair to pass judgement on the city then – barely anyone was enjoying life! But she observed that it's only when we stepped away from the noise that we realised how much our traditional city lives were dulling our senses. Wild places, Deborah says, feel profound and transformative because they are. They renew our sense of place in the world, give perspective and down-regulate our nervous systems. They also help us process new ideas and tap into new ways of interacting with our urban worlds.

To understand the impact of the wilderness on our souls, we can draw on our experiences in deep nature. Time in the wilderness is often as much about the psychological journey as the physical. Climbing in the mountains, for instance, is a surefire way to re-energise and restore my mental energy. The empowerment and courage I felt after reaching my first summit of over 5,000m returned with me to the city and fundamentally changed my approach to my career and the workplace from then on. Where things like office politics, bureaucracy and power play might once have taken up considerable energy, returning from playing in the mountains sharpened my problem-solving, sense of perspective and ability to quell panic. The mountains are also a crash course in gratitude and humbleness, as we learn to appreciate being at the mercy of a force we cannot control. Some of the lessons are hard – poor weather, gear failure, sickness and loss of nerve can mean that summit attempts are canned at the last minute. But, up there, above the clouds and gulping thin air, we become grateful for every life that we share the trail with. The mountains are, I recognise, an extreme example; not everyone relishes the thought of using precious holiday time to chase difficult summits, live under canvas and have the occasional brush with death. More importantly, not everyone is able to do so either. The appeal of the wilderness is highly dependent on character, experience, mobility and socio-economic status, but whatever shape they take, visits to wild places plant the seeds for the next generation of environmental champions. So, in order to inculcate a sense of protectorship over the city wilderness, we have to adapt these experiences to the urban context. After all, we can't expect our city dwellers to protect what they can't see or feel.

Our psychological and physical distance from the wilderness poses a real challenge to stemming the collapse of global biodiversity. The vulnerable wild places that we hear about can feel very far from us and become even more removed when we can't relate to a local proxy for wild places on our doorstep. Without this proxy, it can be hard to connect with the plight of our critically endangered species, many of which live a world away from the city. But all is not lost. As we become more curious and learn more about what nature can do for us, we're more likely to invite it into our lives, becoming attuned to how everyday actions can have an impact beyond our immediate field of vision. The growing number of city dwellers aligning their values to consumption choices and patterns (like reducing plastic, opting for high-welfare meat and campaigning for climate action) can often be dismissed as the furthering of an elitist lifestyle but, in reality, the campaign for regenerative, natural cities is one that can improve the urban lived experience for all of us.

Not everyone has the means or inclination to immerse themselves in the wildest of places, but those who do can have a lasting impact on the everyday spaces they inhabit once they return from their adventures. In tapping into the immense generosity and philanthropic psyche of her guests, Deborah has created a model where clients, having made the connection with nature, will continue to invest in and protect it long after their journeys to Africa have ended. Learning from the wilderness and taking its lessons home to the city is not something we can mandate but, Deborah muses, it's often inevitable. If we feel like a nudge is helpful, we can 'sew it into the experience so that people feel it in their own way'. One of the questions she often asks her clients is what luxury means to them; the answers are perhaps unsurprising but poignant: hearing the sounds of the bush, sleeping well, being able to see green and experience natural light. They are all a pretty damning reflection of the acuteness of our nature deficit. No wonder we often return from time in the wilderness and reflect that our lives have been changed. But if we need deep pockets just to see the sky or sleep well, something has gone seriously awry.

The world over, there are huge inequalities of access to these transformative experiences, particularly for children and young people. In the wake of the second wave of Covid-19, funding was reduced or withdrawn from outdoor centres across the UK. In an article in the *Cambrian News* in October 2020, Sara Jones, who runs an outdoor centre in North Wales, reflected that for some inner-city children, school trips to the centre may be the only chance they get to leave the city and experience nature first-hand. Time in nature connects us to our sense of wonder, awakening our curiosity and the desire to explore that is so woven into our heritage as a species. This is why we should be doing everything we possibly can to make high-quality natural places available and accessible in our cities. Where they aren't on our doorstep, we need to recognise what the barriers look like, especially for under-represented groups. Los Angeles-based Community Nature Connection has observed that lack of transportation to Los Angeles' incredible natural spaces is one of the biggest obstacles to access. Their Transit to Trails programme runs free trips, led by naturalists, from the heart of urban communities to the parks, mountains and oceans fringing Los Angeles.

Our hunch that nature is important for learning is correct, and compelling evidence supports the power of nature-based learning. In 2019, the *Frontier Psychology Journal* reviewed the robust body of studies on this score, all showing that hands-on learning in and about natural habitats improves academic performance compared with conventional methods of teaching, and boosts 'critical life skills like critical thinking, leadership, teamwork and resilience'. Just as importantly, the evidence shows that establishing an emotional connection to the natural world inspires environmental stewardship. Their conclusions press for bringing nature into the mainstream education system. There are plenty of examples, such as the Danish concept of forest schools, which has been widely adopted across the globe, the eco schools programme in Tanzania, Uganda and Malawi, bush schools in Brisbane, Australia, and Nature Kids/*Jóvenes de la Naturaleza Lafayette* in Colorado, USA.

While researching this book, it became increasingly clear that we still don't do enough to teach children about nature and humanity's place within it. If, from a young age, we establish a deep connection to wilderness as our life-support system, would we rewire our ingrained habits and even change the aspirations of the young? In recent years, we've certainly seen the impact of young voices like those of Greta Thunberg and others, amplifying critical issues such as climate change. Armed with the knowledge of what nature in all its forms gives us (protection, food, medicine, essential services, recreation and so on), it's likely that the curiosity of our children would spark a return of personal responsibility for our wild spaces. The effects of engaging our children stand to engender liveable, lovable spaces that help both humans and wildlife thrive.

DESIGNING NATURE-RICH CITIES

Biophilia is an elegant term that recognises our innate need for nature. It means, quite literally, love of nature, and is believed to have been first used by Erich Fromm in the 1970s. In his 1973 *The Anatomy of Human Destructiveness*, Fromm described biophilia as 'the passionate love of life and all that is alive'; the term was later popularised by American biologist Edward O. Wilson.

As we've become increasingly urbanised, we have drifted away from our natural roots, and the built environment that seals us indoors in order to protect us and make us more productive has also severed our connection to our most primal life-support system. Urban buildings represent the most visible manifestation of the walls we need to put up to protect ourselves in cities, cocooning us from the outside world so we can work, train, learn, love and heal. Yet, all these activities stand to benefit from rewilding our souls and, if you are a numbers person, these more than stack up. Research by Terrapin Bright Green LLC in 2015 shows that biophilic design can impact job performance (10 per cent of employee absences are linked to buildings with no access to nature), healing rates (hospital stays are more likely to be 8.5 per cent shorter if the patient can view nature), learning rates (children learn 20–26 per cent faster in natural daylight) and violence statistics (areas with access to nature have reported 7–8 per cent less crime, and can add a premium to properties ranging from 4 per cent to 127 per cent).

Thought leader in city greening, Dr Timothy Beatley, uses the phrase 'natureful', and he is clear that for a city to truly embrace a love of nature, it can't just contain it; nature must be woven into its residents' daily experience. Elements of biophilic design are on show in cities across the world.

Singapore has established its supertrees – colossal organic structures that emerge from the ground to provide shade during the day and a spectacular light show at night, which is visible from across the city. The living skin of the eighteen trees is also home to over 158,000 plants. Singapore's prioritisation of access to nature is manifest in its public spending, and mental-health charity Dose of Nature reports that 0.6 per cent of Singapore's annual budget (US$150 million per year) is spent on increasing greenspace. Interestingly, even as its population expands, its proportion of nature is increasing – proving that greening can go hand in hand with urbanisation.

Atlanta, one of the highest density commercial cities in America, has focused on welcoming its migratory birdlife by creating more habitat and nesting sites for birds such as the chimney swift (which are, incidentally, crucial natural mosquito controllers) in Piedmont Park.

Perth, Australia, turned a 1960s brutalist and broken-down water feature into a freshwater urban wetland that has invited the return of wildlife lost when the area was drained for development. The Native Wetland, designed by garden designer and television host Josh Byrne as part of the Perth Cultural Centre project, cost A$100,000 – half the cost of replacing the original fountain. The centre now also includes a civic space for local workers, residents, school children and visitors to interact with the wetland, an urban orchard and a play space. In an article in *Biophilic Cities Journal*, Josh Byrne reflects on the centre as 'a great example of where a bit of inner urban biophilia and civic space can go hand in hand'. Underpinning the business case for creating and managing public assets in a positive way, the wetland also alleviates risks from urban stormwater. Essentially, it acts as a set of kidneys, treating rainwater – which in an urban context is often polluted by hydrocarbons and other chemicals from vehicle runoff – before it ends up in storm drains and flows into the river basin.

A city woven into nature is a disarming and inspiring sight. But biophilia goes beyond beauty; it is also incredibly functional.

Copenhagen's 'cloudburst projects' emerged because of the increase in sudden, heavy storms (for context, in 2011 one storm resulted in 6 inches of rain in less than three hours; the bill for the damage was US$1 billion). We know that these 'freak' storms are now less freak and more standard. By designing parks that turn into ponds to redirect floodwater from the streets, Copenhagen shows us that we can have playful spaces that have alternative purposes. In apocalyptic rain, no one will be playing outdoor sport anyway, so why not let a hockey or basketball court double as a reservoir? Successful biophilic design encourages us to understand, and sometimes recover, a city's natural roots so that we can make the best use of our space.

Whether we look at this through the lens of improving public health, growing social capital, attracting wildlife or designing places to work, relax or contemplate in, the case for biophilia in cities comes out on top. The only thing missing is our understanding of the city's natural ecosystem to grasp these benefits, which might explain why biophilia is far from mainstream in the urban environment.

Roof space and walls are worth a special mention, too. According to a 2021 article in *Circular Economy and Sustainability*, in most developed cities, roofs take up 40–50 per cent of hardstanding surface area, and buildings make a hefty contribution to carbon emissions (45 per cent in the UK). So, turning our roofs from grey to green can lessen the environmental impact of buildings by 1–5.3 per cent. They also provide quieter places for our wildlife to get on with life without interruption.

The suggestion levelled by Dutch evolutionary biologist Menno Schilthuizen, a professor at Leiden University and author of the 2018 book *Darwin Comes to Town*, is that we should create spaces for adaptive species to colonise of their own accord rather than engineering complete ecosystems. In architectural terms, this means designing spaces where biodiversity can flourish. Bioaugmented materials, such as the 'living concrete' being piloted by University College London's Bartlett School of Architecture, can enable colonisation by airborne algae, moss and lichen spores – effectively mimicking tree bark. These innovations are game-changing in helping our urban wilds to thrive, and we need to invest more in making them accessible across our inner-city neighbourhoods.

We also need immersive natural spaces because physical and mental exposure to other species is critical to our sense of ecological happiness. As reassuring as a living wall might be, we cannot simply disappear into it when things get stressful. Nature wraps us up in a cocoon – it soothes the senses by intensifying natural colours, patterns and textures, giving us the scent and sight of greenery and a blast of fresh air, and absorbing unwelcome sounds while amplifying the natural cacophony, such as birdcall and insect chatter. By default, places that are welcoming to nature will be welcoming to us. This doesn't necessarily work the other way around, so we need to seek places that offer reciprocal benefits and are not designed from an exclusively human-centric perspective.

Where original wilderness areas have been built over, reintroduction of the wild is possible and, as city dwellers, we have the chance to shape this. Biophilia shows us the potential for pockets of land, when left to take their own course, to breathe life back into depleted areas. Property developers and asset owners have proliferated doubt around whether there is space and budget for nature in the middle of the city. The real question is: is there space for a city without nature? If we can dig up anything hopeful from the Covid-19 pandemic, it is that it has rewired the hearts and minds of city dwellers who found themselves yearning for, leaning into or finding meaning in the great outdoors. By all accounts, the cities we want for our current and future selves are replete with nature.

SHARED SPACES

Aside from neighbourhood parks, some of our most recognisable wild spaces are community gardens or allotments. I'll elaborate on their significance to our relationship with food later, but for now we can get stuck into the ecological realities underlying these small but mighty powerhouses. In their modern iteration, they have also taken on a new significance as places that are therapeutic, creative, social and even medicinal. From them, we get back to both our ecological and our social hardwiring.

Sadly, when it comes to recognising and protecting natural spaces, size does matter! If you live in a neighbourhood with a community garden or an allotment area, you will notice that these individual patches of land are tiny and increasingly dwarfed by surrounding development. The space allocated to allotments has shrunk considerably; they often fall between the cracks in the municipal system of managing greenspace because they have become too small to count. Dr Tilly Collins, ecologist, urban environment expert and senior teaching fellow at Imperial College, is leading the charge in this field in the UK. When I asked for her thoughts, she observed that endless subdividing and selling off portions of this greenspace to balance increasingly lopsided local authority books neither quells the appetite of developers nor benefits the community. In fact, it does precisely the opposite and, as long as our attention is diverted away from them, we stand to keep losing these remarkable areas that not only help us out but also provide much-needed corridors for urban plants and wildlife to travel around the city.

When it comes to wildlife, our minds often leap first to the furry or feathery variety, but our planet's tiny species are suffering too. Out of the spotlight, insects are quietly propping up the ecosystem services we depend on. As well as pollination, they control pests and weeds, cycle nutrients back into the soil, and purify water, so their wellbeing is essential to our own and to the planet's. In the WWF's *Living Planet Report 2020*, they ask the question, 'Are "the little things that run the world" disappearing?' And it seems in many cases that the sad answer is, yes. The report maps some dramatic declines in insect populations (for example, to quote the report, 'In Germany, insect abundance declined by 78% and biomass by 67% between 2008 and 2017 in grassland sites'). In 2021, the *Proceedings of the National Academy of Sciences* journal published a compelling volume of studies on global insect decline. Thankfully, due to tireless campaigning about the vital role these tiny creatures play in our lives, pollinators have won our hearts.

Once the connection had been made that our ecological security hinges on their future, bees and butterflies moved back into our consciousness. Bug and bee houses (alongside more ambitious city hive projects) are becoming de rigueur on balconies, terraces and courtyards. By nurturing a thriving population of pollinators in cities, we can strengthen our food system and bigger natural habitats that are vital to support all species. After all, as the Royal Botanic Gardens, Kew, reminds us, some 75 per cent of our crop plants (many that we eat every day) depend on pollination.

This comes back to our understanding of how nature works. With our frenetically charged city heads on, we tend to miss the value of what is right in front of us. Allotments and community gardens are a case in point. These higgledy-piggledy-looking spaces – often a little scruffy with their assemblage of ramshackle sheds, bath troughs, repurposed household waste like windows that become cold frames or old floorboards tracing pathways around plots – are more cherished and valuable than appearances might suggest. They are a mosaic of habitats – islands in a storm for our urban wildlife that make the city their home. It is precisely the hotchpotch of habitats that makes them so hospitable to wildlife. Their hedgerows and ponds provide feeding, nesting and breeding habitats for wildlife like bees and butterflies, hedgehogs and bats.

As a result of abundant birds and other native wildlife in Melbourne, Australia, The Nature Conservancy has partnered with Resilient Melbourne (part of the 100 Resilient Cities movement) to spearhead a process of 'greenprinting' – an urban forest strategy that aims to protect and increase access to nature, habitat connectivity and corridors, and natural infrastructure on private land. When I chatted to Tony Juniper CBE, Chair of Natural England, he commented, 'We should be putting as much nature as possible where the people are, and that is in and around cities. We must of course also restore nature in the remote wilds, where fewer people go, but the biggest bang for our buck in terms of social benefit comes when natural green space is made available close to where we live.' The effect of integrating nature in cities, he suggests, should be like 'green fingers': a network of cycleways, paths and nature corridors that stretch across our cities, actively improving our health and well-being and reinstating lost wilderness.

Greenspace of all scales gives us access to other critical services that developers are very quiet about. The grey infrastructure that characterises our cities makes them substantially hotter places to be, and not in a good way. Have you noticed how heat bounces up from the pavement on a hot day? Cities radiate heat on an enormous scale, and it's called the 'urban heat island effect'. So, parks, gardens and any form of outdoor wilderness help to moderate the urban temperatures, which is good because nobody wants to live in an oven.

They also give us somewhere to retreat to when temperatures soar, and they support floodwater management (pavements, roads and buildings are not absorbent!). Greenspace acts like a sponge and can prevent sewers from being overwhelmed in a deluge, as the Danes have proven with their water parks. Tilly expands on the list of ecological benefits of allotments and community gardens: beyond supporting pollination, water purification, nutrient cycling, local climate, air quality, soil fertility and wildlife corridors, they also assist in seed dispersal and pollination of crops at urban–rural boundaries. The fact that these tiny habitats can do so much shows that we do not always need to convert large expanses of land into greenspace to make a difference.

Almost as fast as we have been losing our urban gardens, demand for them has increased. Tilly and MSc student Ellen Fletcher collaborated on a paper examining the situation with London's allotments, concluding that they were more important and yet scarcer than ever, with, in 2020, more than 30,000 people on waiting lists and waiting four to five years to gain access to a sacred patch of land. For the lucky few who own them, they ground us in the present moment, are therapeutic and are a source of food.

The increase in demand for urban gardens has coincided with the increase in mental ill health in cities. Mental- and physical-health benefits are the most valued aspect of allotment gardening. Tilly refers to the growing appetite for hobbies that counteract poor mental health as one of the drivers of demand. Meanwhile, our health systems are buckling under the strain of urban ill health. The *Lancet Global Health* journal reported in 2020 that the cost of poor mental health to the global economy was US$2.5 trillion in 2010. The prediction is that this will rise to US$6 trillion by 2030. According to the Healthy London Partnership, in 2018 75 per cent of cases of depression and anxiety in the city remain untreated, so making the economic link between the health benefits of greenspace and reducing the strain on health services seems more important than ever. A joint report by British Land and WPI Economics in 2018 suggested that modest improvements in the way public spaces in London are designed could save the government in the region of £329 million in reduced costs of health and associated social care by 2040. In Australia, a 2016 study in *Nature* journal, 'Health Benefits from Nature Experiences Depend on Dose', found that depression costs the country A$12.6 billion each year, but visiting greenspace for at least thirty minutes a week can lesson depression and high blood pressure 'by up to 7% and 9% respectively'.

Developers have a formidable appetite for these patches of urban greenspace. Tilly pointed out that their non-toxic soil, accessibility and minimal need for land clearance makes these spaces ideal for buildings, but it is this very set of rare qualities that makes them even more perfect for the communities and ecosystems that rely on them. There is scant evidence that developers who build on former allotments understand the true value of greenspace for existing communities or future residents; if they did, our new buildings would be adding greenery rather than eroding it. Crowding more people into living quarters with fewer gardens or means of escape from grey infrastructure will result in communities that are fragmented, ecologically illiterate and removed from nature. Instead, we should be using every chance we get to elevate community gardens and shared greenspace. They're a powerful way of generating social resilience, creating opportunities for neighbourhood interaction, promoting new skills and knowledge, and keeping nature in sight and mind.

On a neighbourhood level, it is easy enough for city dwellers to monitor where we sit on the grey-to-green spectrum because we see the changes by the day. To stop this critical loss of inner-city habitat, we need to account for the wider benefits (not just monetary land value) of shared greenspace. Earthwatch Europe has come up with a 'super tiny, super powerful' solution in their Tiny Forests, which occupy a space the size of a tennis court. The woodlands they create 'bring the benefits of a forest – reconnecting people with nature and raising awareness, helping to mitigate the impacts of climate change, as well as providing nature-rich habitat patches to support urban wildlife – right into the heart of our cities and urban spaces'.

Measuring wellbeing changes as a result of development is increasing in traction, although, at the moment, the focus is on the wellbeing of the future occupants rather than on the pre-existing communities surrounding developments. We have the chance to change this and show the primacy of greenspace by responding to local development applications. For developments that do go ahead, our local authorities should be mandating what's called post-occupancy analysis (asking how people feel after a building is completed). This would allow them to assess the impacts on existing communities so that they understand the implications of encroaching on or eliminating greenspace.

One of Tilly's central arguments is for a landscape level approach to managing urban greenspace – meaning that councils talk to one another and adequate central resources are made available. She points out that it's become so common for councils to delegate management of urban gardens that there are no central records showing vacancies, demand, loss and subdivision at city level. Without a landscape approach, we stand to lose something so fundamental to the health and future vibrancy of cities. Tilly is firm in her recommendation that allotments up for closure shouldn't be decided on a case-by-case basis, but instead with reference to the overall landscape and with the understanding of the suite of benefits they deliver.

For councils or local authorities, stronger links are needed between policy makers and local administrations who deliver allotments to allow for co-operation, co-ordination and flow of resources. She argues for mapping out allotment sites so the effects of the distribution of allotments as a whole can be considered. For this to work, we also need effective communication between boroughs and councils. Community champions are one way of getting there as they can act as knowledge brokers and reflect the civic needs. When it comes to community gardens or allotments, evidence-based decision-making that reflects the experiences of the communities dependent on them has been absent. Now, academics like Tilly and her associates in other cities are paving the way for nuanced decision-making, but they cannot do it alone.

If we want to live in neighbourhoods that reflect our value of the natural environment, a sense of community and a life well lived, we need to try to rise above the infectious apathy of thinking that our voices do not count. We can help by joining local wildlife trusts, supporting allotment and urban garden trusts, and making even our smallest spaces greener. Our food shops, cafes and restaurants can play a crucial role in supporting community gardens and ensuring that provenance of ingredients means that we can eat well and make our places wilder at the same time, which we'll explore further when we come to look at nourishment in the city. Our schools can also help by integrating nature in the curriculum.

Education, systems thinking when it comes to food and energy, engagement in local decision-making, and economic understanding of the complex co-benefits that urban nature gives us – we need all of this now more than ever. If all else fails, we are constantly reminded not to waste a crisis; each one jolts us a little further along the spectrum of empathy. Championing this empathetic approach in people is difficult and we tend to get just as tired of being politely implored as we do of the doomsday world-is-ending approach. The Covid-19 pandemic was an interesting shake-up because it united city dwellers across the world in their desire for wilder cities.

URBAN CATHEDRALS FOR THE SOUL

Cities without nature can be an assault on the senses. There are many fundamental things we miss in our high-rise and hyper-stimulated built-up world, like the sky, the sun, the stars. Often, we need to escape street level just to be able to see the sky properly. When we spoke, Deborah Calmeyer reflected on the mission that most people face if they want to see the sunset in New York City. Even to get to an open rooftop is often the privilege of those who can afford to stump up for an exclusive club membership, unless you are fortunate enough to have a public park nearby that affords a skyward view, uncluttered by buildings.

This desire to experience wild nature has already caused a shift in the way we present our greenspaces. The cache of manicured, pristine lawns is being gently replaced by soft, imperfect, rewilded landscapes. It seems that when we allowed the bee to win our hearts and minds, we also permitted our urban sensibilities to adapt to new notions of wild and beautiful. The fact that this is a monumental paradigm shift is not lost on the Germans, who in 2016 created a dedicated campaign, *Städte wagen Wildnis* (broadly translated as Cities Dare Wilderness), to improve species diversity and quality of life for residents across Hanover, Frankfurt and Dessau-Rosslau.

The city of Dessau bought corridors of abandoned industrial sites to the tune of 120 hectares, which weave through the city and offer an extended garden for existing housing estates. Commenting in *Deutsche Welle*, Christiane Jahn, head of the city planning department, observed that the project attracted songbirds, hedgehogs, butterflies and endemic bees. Upkeep is minimal, the meadows in the centre only need mowing a few times a year and the outer edge of the site is being left to return to woodland.

The ideas aren't all new – in 1841, Wellington, New Zealand, set aside Te Ahumairangi Hill as a protected area for recreation and the city has continued to lead the way with its ecosanctuary, Zealandia, first tabled by local residents Jim and Eve Lynch in 1990. An area of 225 hectares on the urban fringe is being carefully restored to its pre-human ecosystem (no mean feat as New Zealand's pre-human ecosystem had no predatory mammals). The sanctuary supports some forty species of indigenous wildlife like the tīeke, little spotted kiwi and tuatara. So successful have they been in reinvigorating these vulnerable species that Wellington is one of few cities in the world reporting increasing native birdlife, as set out in their 2020 Annual Report. The enviable dawn chorus that Wellingtonians have the benefit of seems to be making life that much sweeter; studies of local residents have found reduced depression, anxiety and stress.

Rowan Kilduff of Rewilding.org sums up the right approach to city wilding: 'To rewild a city we will pore over maps and plans, go out and walk the land and feel it, talk to the people, look at where and how children play, take note of where the deer trails go, and then we just set aside places. We start small, and add to it.'

Wildflower meadows – also a form of rewilding – can help us make the ugly beautiful again. Because they can thrive in degraded soils, they are often perfect for brownfield sites (land that isn't pristine). The reasons that people shun wildflower meadows are normally aesthetic because they're a departure from what we're used to. In the autumn, they can look overgrown and neglected when they have gone to seed. Come the spring and summer, of course, their beauty is dazzling as they explode into bloom, and once they have gone through one or two seasons, public support for them tends to be warm. Allowing these wilder pockets into the fringes of our parks and gardens represents an important shift as we start to see the beauty in their imperfections and lack of uniformity. Where they would previously have been deemed unkempt, we now see that they perform both aesthetic and ecosystem services.

The Knepp Estate, in south-east England, is an acclaimed example of bold and successful rewilding. Isabella Tree's account of the rewilding project in her book *Wilding* struck a chord when she spoke of her newfound appreciation for how England's wild oak trees grow; they depend on the detritus of fallen branches to be broken down by the soil and reabsorbed into the tree as nutrients (this speaks to the Victorian obsession with clearing up and making new, and also translates through to our development in cities). As the tree grows older, it will gradually reach its lower, heavy branches down towards the ground to support itself. When we come along with our blinkers on, we have a fixed view of the way things should be done and have been done before, believing that we are doing the right thing by cleaning up and clipping the branches, but all the while we are destabilising the habitat and shortening the lifespan of the tree.

As city residents, if we want to maximise the joy we get from our waterways and greenspaces, we need to be vocal. Thankfully, there are organisations aplenty to help us out on this score, like the local wildlife trusts or similar environmental stewardship groups that can be found in most cities across the world. If we feel unsure about who to talk to or how to go about starting, socially minded companies such as Patagonia have done considerable legwork for us. The Patagonia Action Works network connects individuals to grassroots activists in the same community (in the launch film in 2018, Yvon Chouinard described it as 'a kind of dating site') across Europe, North America, Chile and Brazil. This kind of collaborative approach can accelerate real momentum for change within our urban spaces that benefit us all.

GUERRILLAS IN THE GARDEN

As well as adapting our ideal of what beauty is, we also need to think beyond the natural areas that fall under municipal control. When it comes to our own, private spaces we can do a lot with the little we have. This might be a private or shared garden, a terrace or balcony, a driveway that we can convert from paved desert to rewilded habitat (and still fit a car), or even an indoor room.

If the sales of indoor plants are anything to go by, city dwellers are showing a commitment to greening their indoor spaces. In 2019, the Royal Horticultural Society reported a 10–15 per cent year-on-year increase in houseplant sales since 2013 and, according to a *Guardian* article, Patch, an online plant store in the UK, noticed a 10 per cent rise in plant sales for 25–34-year-olds.

His Royal Highness, The Prince of Wales, an avid gardener, speaks often about the therapeutic benefits of gardening. His gardens in Highgrove (Gloucestershire) and Birkhall (on the Balmoral Estate in Scotland) incorporate the values of wild gardening honed over some seventy years. The stumperies, for example, which are made up of planted logs and tree stumps, provide a rich habitat for wildlife and His Royal Highness has been tenacious in upholding their ecological value. It can seem an unlikely shape for a garden to take and stumperies, particularly His Royal Highness', have been the source of much aesthetic debate over the years, but passing through them it's all too clear that they teem with life. As the unearthed stumps decompose, they offer a vital home for insects and fungi, a refuge and food for small garden wildlife and birds, and they are both beautiful and becalming spaces to be in.

And outside our home, there are plenty of other opportunities to recreate this. Small public spaces like station gardens are a wonderful example, which I first came across in the outdoor waiting room at Paris Bercy Bourgogne–Pays d'Auvergne station in 2013. My journey to Clermont-Ferrand that day was fairly unremarkable, but the garden made quite an impression. I remember feeling enormously glad that I'd arrived at the station with time to spare, as it allowed me to bask in the dappled sunlight and decompress from the traffic-ridden taxi trip. This couldn't compare to the usual sense of huffy impatience I feel when waiting in most of my regular stations – indoors, surrounded by crowds and the predictably dull line-up of retail and fast-food chains. That time pre-journey has become something to be endured rather than being a moment of pleasure in the day. In London, we are fortunate to have a man addressing just this, with awesome success.

Agamemnon Otero MBE of Energy Garden, known as Aga, has been steadily recruiting communities across the city to transform London's overground stations into garden oases that brighten up grey transport corridors, produce food and solar energy, im-prove urban biodiversity and make communities, volunteers and commuters happier. As an urban hero, this Uruguayan-born, New York-raised south Londoner has taken it upon himself to reimagine how we can form meaningful connections to the infrastructure that quite literally energises our everyday existence. Through his work with not-for-profit energy co-operative Repowering London, he has established community-owned renewable energy power stations across London, weaving them into the places that we engage with every day, whether it be on social-housing sites or rail and transport networks. With the creativity of individuals and the clout of the collective, we have the opportunity to create true ecological variety in our cities, which means that wildlife won't feel squeezed into islands of parkland but will be able to use a network of corridors. If ever there was a time to let go of the manicured and stifling notion of traditional city greenspace, it is as we emerge from a global pandemic and contemplate the future.

NATURE'S PHARMACY

If there was a supplement for nature, we would have been prescribed it long ago. But there is no pill to substitute the fulsome nourishment that comes from time spent dwelling in the wild. As we've seen, connection to nature brings a host of benefits to our health and happiness. To recap, we can refer again to Terrapin Bright Green's research, which reminds us that the benefits include lower systolic blood pressure, lower heart rate, lower cortisol production and much higher activity (over 50 per cent) in the parasympathetic nervous system (the system that relaxes us).

Ever ahead of the curve when it comes to wellbeing, New Zealand, which launched the world's first wellbeing budget in 2019, first began using the term 'green prescription' back in the 1990s to formally encourage patients to increase physical activity and healthy lifestyle behaviours by spending more time in nature. Over two decades later, the scheme is still going strong and is internationally recognised and replicated.

In South Korea, forest-bathing (*salim yok*) is taken very seriously indeed. Dose of Nature reports on the government's major capital investments in a National Forest Healing Centre, creation of national legislation for the promotion of forest welfare and a Forest Service responsible for rolling out a blueprint of healing forests across the country so that they are within reach of most urban centres. China and Japan have also long been proponents of forest-bathing (*shinrin-yoku*).

The Victorian government in Australia has estimated that the state's parks could yield savings to healthcare costs to the tune of A$200 million. In Santiago, Chile, the Luis Calvo Mackenna Hospital in partnership with Symbiotica is using Native Islands (also called Miyawaki forests) to disrupt the urban jungle and create room for 'real' jungle in a way that promotes recovery for the hospital's young patients. Miyawaki forests is a method for tree-planting on degraded land. It uses trees native to the specific area, planted at high density to encourage fast growth (the saplings compete for light, water and space then natural selection picks out the winners). In a 2019 *JSTOR Daily* article, Lela Nargi highlights that this method encourages trees to grow approximately ten times faster than in conventional afforestation, making it a viable bit of arsenal in our rewilding kit, especially when we're racing against time and need a quick response while planners and developers catch up. Describing the hospital project in Santiago, co-founder Nicolás Corral said, 'Conventional green areas will be transformed into forests, an inner cement courtyard will be rewilded, and abandoned and exposed soil will be renewed with micro and macro life. During the plantation, everyone will connect with the healing of Mother Earth and bring the experience back into their everyday life at the hospital.'

A 1984 study by environmental psychologist Roger Ulrich, published in *Science*, was one of the earliest on the link between patient recovery and visibility of nature. The test-group patients had rooms with views of either a tree or a brick wall. Patients with tree views healed faster (a day on average), were less dependent on pain relief and suffered fewer post-op complications than those with the brick wall to look at. Clare Cooper Marcus, emeritus professor in architecture and landscape architecture at the University of California, quoted in *Scientific American*, clarifies that, while natural views might not cure disease, 'there is good evidence it can reduce your levels of pain and stress – and, by doing that, boost your immune system in ways that allow your own body and other treatments to help you heal'.

One of the most lauded examples of nature healing in hospitals was the Prouty Garden at the Boston Children's Hospital. Writing about it in the *British Medical Journal*, Elliot Martin, director of medical psychiatry at Newton-Wellesley Hospital in Newton, Massachusetts, and a previous fellow at Boston Children's Hospital, recalls, 'The Prouty Garden was the soul of the hospital. The town green. The public square. The place where people gathered, took deep breaths, and returned to face the day, rejuvenated. The place that helped wonderful people, doing incredibly difficult jobs, want to come to work.' Sadly, the garden fell prey to hospital expansion, and buildings filled the space which had once been a sanctuary for those in need. Others are more tenacious: Health Care without Harm Europe – a non-profit network of healthcare providers championing sustainable healthcare – points to the success of La Leçon Verte's garden at the children's hospital La Citadelle in Liège, Belgium. Since 2003, children have been taught to grow and harvest vegetables there, which are then used in the hospital's meals.

The healing properties of our natural spaces can be directed to even the most acute sources of stress, such as the dislocation and depression associated with forced migration and loss of place. The gardens of Werribee Mansion in Werribee Park, Victoria, Australia, are now home to a significant population of Karen people fleeing persecution in Myanmar (formerly Burma), and have become a tonic and social anchor for the emerging community. According to an *AMES* article, the difficulties facing refugees, such as deep physical and psychological trauma, are thrown into even sharper relief for communities like the Karen: 'A largely agrarian and village-based people, Karen refugees have often encountered difficulties when settled in urban locations around the world. Traditionally, they are gardeners and cultivators and living in an urban environment has left many of them dislocated and suffering depression.'

The mental-health impacts associated with dislocation and displacement are likely to continue to increase in line with migration predictions and will join existing urban pressures on mental health, as well as the prevalence of eco-anxiety. Once again, giving nature room to soothe our visible and invisible wounds will do more to unify and restore us than many of our 'smartest' solutions.

Again, The Prince of Wales has shown good foresight in how human and planetary health has long supported nature-based health interventions – or complementary therapy – and, of course, the idea is not new. Writing for the *Journal of the Royal Society of Medicine* in 2012, His Royal Highness reflected on the need 'not simply to treat the symptoms of disease, but actively to create health and to put the patient at the heart of this process by incorporating those core human elements of mind, body and spirit'.

In 2020, Tilly Collins and Ellen Fletcher reminded us again that green prescription and ecotherapy can be complementary to conventional healthcare. The health benefits immediately available to most people include reduced body mass index (BMI), improved lung function, lower blood pressure and lower cortisol levels. Cortisol is our stress hormone and the chemical that powers a life in 'fight or flight' mode – characteristic of a city-based existence. Having had soaring cortisol in the past, I too have turned to gardening or at least borrowed others' gardens when I've had the chance. I'll admit, I was born without green thumbs but, even so, there's nothing more pleasurable than gentle pottering among the foliage. As well as moving across multiple planes of functional movement, we are also creating, tending to and learning from living things beyond just the human.

The wilderness excites and inspires, stimulates and challenges us. It offers different surfaces to walk on, invites the more complacent muscle groups to do their bit to help us balance or scramble; it can give us open horizons and the ability to see without interruption; it keeps us guessing by showing us a variety of species vastly different to our own; it gives us a colour palette of blues and greens. Deborah Calmeyer points out that the colours and shapes in nature are soothing: 'It's like a spa for our eyes.'

I was a reminded of this on a recent trip to Richmond Park. Never quite knowing who or what I might happen upon next, I was thrilled by every local runner, dog walker or even deer I encountered – especially after so many months in lockdown. The restorative value of these few hours was priceless. The injection of energy from that walk gave me the top-up I needed to keep writing this book at a time when contemplating happiness in the city seemed a bridge too far.

In these small yet hands-on ways, we can offer ourselves a remedy when the city has laid us low.

It's in our power to make cities as habitable and hospitable as possible so that they nurture our health. For it to become a reality, we need our life-support system – nature. Wilder cities that give voice to nature's soft power will help us reclaim lost environmental wisdom.

There are many things to be cheerful about. Given half a chance, all cities can be rewilded – nature is ready to take back control as soon as we loosen our vice-like grip on the reins. Happily, we're already in this process of waking up to the value of the wild. In 2020, for instance, Mexico City's longstanding and ill-fated plans for an airport on a contentious site were ditched in favour of an 'ecological park', and the overwhelming sentiment was that *la gente prefiere un lago* – 'the people would prefer a lake'. In Nottingham, a new version of nature-focused inner-city regeneration has led to a proposal to turn a languishing shopping centre into wetlands, pocket woodlands and wildflower meadows. The outcome of the application is still to be decided at the time of writing, but the point is that where once these ideas would have been fringe, they are now popular and increasingly backed by strong community support.

Through the Covid-19 pandemic, we've been gifted a rare calming of city noise. In the silence that fell, we dared to dream about a future city that might give us a break from the relentless freneticism. If we're grounded in our sense of place in the urban environment, nurtured by the wilds that we share with other species, we might just end up chasing distance less. We might let go of perfection and do what we can with what we have. Wilder cities need to offer us space to breathe, to hit pause and to be thoughtful.

The greatest thing we can do as city dwellers is to notice nature more and bring it into our lives as much as possible. The more we do this, the more normal being immersed in nature becomes; grey is abnormal. The deeper our reattachment, awareness and empathy, the greater our ability is to understand the gravity of obliterating nature and our will to fight off threats to take away this most critical resource.

2

NOURISHMENT

At its very heart, food and eating is (or should be) a communal experience that brings together friends, fortifies families, unites neighbours and acquaints strangers.

Hetty McKinnon, *Community*

FOOD IS BOTH functional and joyful. Its presence, quality and provenance can affect our mood, energy, and public and environmental health. With 60 per cent of food expected to be consumed in cities by 2050, it's little wonder that we are seeing cities grappling with juxtaposed challenges, where ill health from malnutrition often sits alongside obesity. Our urban centres magnify contemporary issues of nutrition, education, employment and income security, and their convergence causes deep inequities. In short, our outmoded food system is long overdue a wholesale ethical makeover.

It's worth a quick historical recap to remind ourselves of how we've ended up in this pickle. Up until the industrial revolution, we were hunting, gathering, growing, harvesting and cooking everything we ate. But as mechanised, agro-chemical food-production methods took hold, our connection with our food sources weakened and faded out of view. As the priorities for growing food became about volume and speed of supply, food production moved behind closed doors, where decisions about efficiencies could be made away from the eyes of the consumers.

I'd like to be absolutely clear here that this is not a blanket attack on farming which, if done well, contributes a rich range of real benefits to our environment; the culprit is the intensive, industrial or 'factory' models, and particularly the farming of sentient animals (otherwise called livestock). These factories mistreat (lawfully and otherwise) billions of animals who are locked into short, unrelentingly miserable lives of confinement (Compassion in World Farming reports that around two in every three farm animals are factory farmed). Not only are they morally deplorable but they are also major emitters of greenhouse gases; they pollute air, water and soil, and decimate biodiversity as vulnerable wilderness areas are given over to grow the crops that feed these animals. Plant-based dietary shifts have become a la mode in recent years, partly as a remedy for these entrenched imbalances, but we have to be cautious that our enthusiasm for this does not create new ones.

To repair the system, the Ellen MacArthur Foundation's *Cities and Circular Economy for Food* suggests that our ambition should be threefold: source food grown regeneratively, and locally where appropriate; make the most of food (use by-products more effectively, prevent waste); and design and market healthier food. The numbers stack up – according to the Food Foundation a nutritionally balanced diet would result in a drop in greenhouse gas emissions of 17 per cent (equivalent to 4.3 billion tonnes of carbon dioxide), and the *Cities and Circular Economy for Food* report highlights that such a dietary shift would lower health costs associated with pesticide use to the tune of US$550 billion, while opening up new economic avenues that optimise the use of food and its by-products could be worth US$700 billion.

When talking about food, we must get over our reticence to speak of it in terms of joy, happiness and comfort. Food is fundamental to our existence and mealtimes are often the highlight of days, joyous interludes between stressful periods and general busyness. Alternative ways of producing and consuming food can breathe life into our streets, neighbourhoods and community spaces. Food also plays a crucial role in the city's cultural melting pot, helping us to create, sustain and celebrate a sense of place and shared heritage.

THE WORLD ON A PLATE

In cities, the world comes together on a plate. In the autumn 2020 *Peddler Journal*, Hetty McKinnon, food writer and cookbook author, wrote, 'When one lives in exile (whether voluntary or involuntary), food is a thread which keeps them connected to their former homeland.'

The notion that we are what we eat is one that speaks to my own sense of identity. My late grandmother was Austrian and escaped Nazi persecution in the 1930s by fleeing to England. Food became a way for her to reconnect to her Austrian heritage, with dishes like Wiener schnitzel, sacher torte, strudel and schmaltz. Indeed, as my family became spread far and wide, food was our common language and the anchor of conviviality. Once or twice a year we would come together from all corners of the world – France, Germany, Chile, Australia, South Africa – to gather in my grandmother's living room in Richmond. The table would be extended, and every form of back-up chair or stool would be recruited from the rest of the house so we could all fit in. She could always feed an army and every meal was an occasion, even if it was just the 'scraps' – her loving term for a supper of leftovers that were so plentiful that the table would groan under their weight. There would be all manner of treats foraged from local markets and delis packed to the brim with products from all over Europe. As a child, I would relish each visit, knowing I'd be stuffed silly with every variety of pastry and cheese – my prime staples of food-based joy, to this day.

Cities are the epicentres of immigration and hold complex histories of communities being remade time and again. Everybody is from somewhere else and there is safety in this. With all the practice I've had, I can bed down very quickly in new cities. Without pre-existing social networks and in entirely new territory, the way I ground myself in the early days of a new city is through food. Food is often one of the first, and most accessible, avenues for settling into our new context, creating new memories and nurturing old ones. It is the taste of that first chapati in Ninyuki, Kenya, flat white in Melbourne, Australia, or pad thai in Bangkok, Thailand, that linger in the recollection; they give expression to the very essence of the place, and our emotional connection to food can often transport us back to the places that still hold pieces of our heart.

Emiko Davies, writing in *Peddler* of her discovery of a Chinese ingredient shop in a Tuscan town, remarks that she almost fainted with joy. This dual sense of choked-up relief mingled with nostalgia is a common feeling for most migrants: the joy of discovering the deeply familiar while being reminded of the gulf of distance. For a moment, we can return to sentimentality and access to the right ingredients lets us cook and eat our way back to our roots. On the flip side, Candice Cheung, writing in the same magazine, provides an alternative view when she talks about homesickness at the sight of a foreign supermarket. Writing about the incomprehensible strangeness of new grocery stores when she moved from Hong Kong to Sydney, she commented that 'no language quite captures the grief of losing access to your favourite snacks and mystery meats'.

MEET ME AT THE MARKET

Nowhere connects us more to food culture and tradition than street-food vendors and markets, which are ubiquitous in cities across the world. Markets are the ancient centres of civic life, strengthening communities by developing social fabric and encouraging people to come together. These public spaces where commerce and community coalesce offer a sensory experience and direct human-to-human interaction that cannot be replicated in sprawling supermarkets.

The resurgence of farmers' markets across the world suggests that we are craving a higher-value experience of grocery shopping. With our precious spare time, we can meet a friend, meander outside, connect to the wild, reduce waste and fill our pantries all at the same time. Markets also draw local investment into the surrounding area and lead to increased spending in nearby shops. Standing in a queue for my local fishmonger, Fin and Flounder, I often observe customers shuttling back and forth between other shops while they wait to be served at the market – nipping to the hardware store, the butcher, the bookshop or the post office. Food markets interweave community with commerce, and hope with action.

As interest in fresh food has risen, markets have increased. In the US, there are approximately 8,000 farmers' markets – a doubling in the last decade. This way of shopping for groceries and consuming food is hugely positive for local economies as it encourages us to spread our spending both temporally and geographically, as we pick up bits here and there.

Street food is a particularly powerful way of connecting with the heritage of a food; vendors typically focus on one cuisine, or one snack, perfected over generations, which is plentiful, cheap, fresh, instant and bursting with flavour. Street food, hawker food, street shacks or night markets are particularly prominent in Asia, and food critic Kf Seetoh likens it to a form of 'cultural export', which often fuses different influences. Writing about fusion food, Hetty McKinnon notes that 'the intermingling of flavours, techniques and ingredients from diverse cultures to create a hybrid cuisine is heavily rooted in colonial expansion and migration'. Fusion food also reflects the roots of immigrants and often involves a blend of flavours. George Town, Penang, in Malaysia, for example, reflects Peranakan, Chinese, European and Indian heritage, while Jakarta's Big Durian food centre is interwoven with Javanese, Balinese, Minangkabau, Chinese and Dutch influences.

The City Fix also highlights that markets can play a part in softly addressing urban-planning challenges by making our cites more lively. In Seoul, for example, the *pojangmacha* (street-food vendors) are celebrated as a way of facilitating urban-planning challenges by encouraging people to stay out late, spend locally and walk rather than drive. The places we find our street-food vendors and markets in across the world certainly suggest that they are able to breathe life into areas that may get less use, like car parks, railway arches and builders' yards. By inhabiting these darker corners, they help to keep cities friendly and inviting through the hours when crime or antisocial activity are also more likely to happen.

Sitting at the centre of commercial and community life, markets are often privy to extraordinary stories of community resilience. Borough Market in London, for example, has bounced back bigger and more vibrant than ever after a series of terrorist attacks in and around it. It also plays a vital role in the community, with surplus produce going to Guy's and St Thomas's hospital and local homeless shelters. In New Orleans, the Crescent City Farmers' Market told the story of the city's loss and recovery as a result of Hurricane Katrina in August 2005. Richard McCarthy, executive director of Slow Food USA and the co-founder of the Crescent City Farmers' Market, reflecting on the emotional return to market trading in 2005–06 in an interview for *National Geographic*, showed how fundamental this community was to the city picking itself back up. In the absence of supermarkets, which took much longer to reopen, the commitment to reopen the market showed what McCarthy describes as a 'rugged, DIY sense of obligation to community, to recovery, and to a return to normalcy. The reopening of a coffee shop, for instance, became an act of love for a city damaged by storm and by thoughtless elected officials.'

His sentiments ring true today, some fifteen years later, as we emerge tentatively from the colossal shared trauma of the Covid-19 pandemic. We can see food, which has been by our side for the duration of the virus as either a source of comfort or concern, as one of the most immediate, tangible signs of hope and love. Even on the worst days, we are hard-pressed to find a restaurant, trader or farmer not working out of a sense of love and dogged determination for the survival of their businesses and their communities. Another quote from McCarthy seems apt here; he says of New Orleans, 'If the city was grey and literally marked with trauma, the farmers market was colorful and it smelled of happy taste memories.' The Covid-19 pandemic has highlighted the deep passion and sense of allyship underlying food. There were a number of powerful examples of food nourishing bodies and spirits during the pandemic, such as Meals for the NHS, in which British food producers worked together to provide nutritious food for hospital staff, frontline workers and those in need, and World Central Kitchen – an inspiring initiative that provides disaster relief and was quick to act when those in St Vincent, Barbados, were impacted by a volcanic eruption. There's an added poignancy to these generous acts of nourishment, in that they were co-ordinated by the very people and industries most economically impacted by the pandemic. With their businesses having been shuttered virtually overnight, they would have been forgiven for being laid low, but better than most they recognised the value of food – and sharing – in times of crisis.

Markets have a vitality and community importance, which makes them an excellent starting point as we look for alternative models to our food systems. They can, because of their relatively low rent, supply cheap, fresh ingredients in abundance. Socially, they are gathering places for people with shared heritage, those with a curiosity for the new, and while they attract foodies and the food-curious, they can even charm and convert the food-ambivalent. They are safe spaces for solo outings, connecting us with the pulse of the city even if we walk it alone. They can cure broken hearts, bad moods and lost appetites by enveloping us in their warmth. Markets also give meaning to the spectacle of food and, if the masses drawn to the likes of Barcelona's La Boqueria or Marrakech's Jemaa el-Fna are anything to go by, visitors and residents alike are attracted to the buzz that these places create.

Rather than being written off as expensive or bougie, we should see markets for what they truly are: a lifeline for farmers, artisans, growers and fishers, who can get a fair price for their products. For customers, we get the kind of quality assurance and buying experience that online or mass retail simply cannot compete with. The way we treasure and preserve them is by shopping in them and spreading our money.

In Italy, which has the largest network of direct-selling farmers' markets, Campagna Amica has shown that farmers' markets are taking centre stage in the food-supply chain. According to Salvo Butera, writing in *EurActive*, the network is made up of some 130,000 farmers, and Italian spending at farmers' markets is over €6 billion. Beyond the economics, their civic function is being celebrated. Elderly urban residents are able to walk to their local market and are guaranteed daily access to fresh products and the social connection that comes with market life. The law can help here, too. In Sicily, a regional law passed in 2018 requires municipalities to push shorter supply chains by mandating direct-sales markets and encouraging products with a direct link to the area of production.

Large urban markets can bring together quality food from all over the world, with an emphasis on ethically farmed, small-batch food, as well as iconic gastronomic treats. One of my locals, Borough Market, like most others, is a cacophony of sounds, smells and tastes. Towers of pungent alpine cheese, hanging cuts of meat from Britain's West Country, delicate handmade dumplings and unearthed vegetables all stand shoulder to shoulder. The core of the market is its produce, but the interwoven street food, with specialities from all over the world, show the staggering possibilities for transforming fresh ingredients into a joyous meal. A wonderful Borough initiative is the Borough Market Cookbook Club, run by the inimitable Angela Clutton, food historian and writer. I was lucky enough to join this marvellous little sub-community one rainy afternoon before lock-down. The idea of the club is to invite groups of strangers regularly on a lottery basis (but, importantly, locals get first dibs) to assemble in the on-site kitchen to share food they have cooked at home based on a particular cookbook. Such initiatives show how markets are so much more than just a place to buy food; the effect of engaging closely with fresh ingredients spills over into a food culture that brings people together and encourages them to experiment with healthy and delicious diets.

Food can also transcend fractious geopolitics and become a cultural common denominator. In post-Brexit, mid-Covid-19 Britain, produce has taken on a new poignance as, without clarity on what the future of travel into Europe will look like, neighbourhood farmers' markets reminiscent of the streets of Lyon or Bologna allow us to feel part of the continental food landscape. Short of a passport and permission to travel, markets give us a precious window into other worlds.

HUNGRY CITIES

Food is our fuel for life, and what and how we eat helps our minds and bodies weather the stresses inherent in city living. With this in mind, no conversation about food can ignore poverty. The rise in the use of food banks in cities globally shows how many people are struggling to feed themselves, leaving communities more vulnerable to economic, environmental and public-health shocks. A study by the Food Banking Network, which covered food-banking organisations in seventy countries, found that in 2019 3.75 million metric tons of nutritious, surplus food was directed away from landfills.

This food reached 66.5 million people worldwide and also prevented an estimated 12.39 billion kilograms of greenhouse gases from food wastage. As a result of Covid-19, the landscape has become more extreme. Prior to the pandemic, Foodbank Australia was responding to the need for emergency food assistance in the wake of the catastrophic bushfires of 2019, which burned over 6 million hectares, destroyed thousands of homes and closed businesses. A year later, in 2020, their data shows that three in ten Australians now experiencing food insecurity had not gone hungry before the pandemic. Covid-19 is the latest catalyst in a chain of negative events and, according to Foodbank Australia, shortage of food is just the beginning 'as bills pile up and income dwindles, stress and unmet physical needs are likely to cause a decline in mental health'.

For deprived inner cities, the challenges of social exclusion, crime and violence are exacerbated by lack of access to nutrition, and the link has been made between hunger and quality of learning and behaviour in inner-city schools. Kimberley Wilson, author of *How to Build a Healthy Brain*, has noted that children who depend on free school meals tend to be from ethnic minorities and socio-economically deprived backgrounds. Hunger matters: these children are three times as likely to be excluded from school because of their behaviour and more likely to head towards the prison system.

To give a sense of the scale of the problem, according to UNICEF research, as many as 1.8 million school-age children in the UK are at risk of hunger. In the US, Feeding America estimates that food insecurity in 2020 could affect more than 50 million, including 17 million children. In the global south, Children International reports that 66 million kids go to school hungry.

In the UK, Magic Breakfast was founded by Carmel McConnell MBE in 2000 after speaking with headteachers in Hackney, London, who told her that many school children were coming to school malnourished and struggling to learn. Unable to abide this, McConnell began taking breakfast into these schools. Twenty years on, Magic Breakfast reaches some 170,000 children in the UK each year for the cost of 34p a meal. If you're wondering what this looks like in breakfast terms: in 2018–19 the charity's website reports that 2,892,096 bagels, 1,481,916 bowls of cereal, 1,672,696 glasses of juice and 251,147 bowls of porridge were delivered. Considering that child poverty is at its highest in our capital cities, and that access to opportunities is one of the barriers facing kids in cities, this is far more than just a meal in the morning. In an analysis of the Magic Breakfast meal's return on investment by Pro Bono Economics in 2021, some pretty astonishing figures were reported. If all the 298,000 kids aged 5–6 at English schools with 'high levels of disadvantage' received breakfast in line with the Magic Breakfast model, the long-term economic value created would be in the region of £2.7 billion. The benefits include less need for extra educational provision to keep kids in school and an increase in lifetime earnings because of higher academic achievement.

As we'll see is the case regularly in this book, action often starts in the community, and city dwellers are showing their willingness to tackle the issue head on with or without formal help. This was certainly the case in the UK during the pandemic when it came to feeding the nation's children during the school holidays. The national outpouring of generosity, elevated by the compassion of 23-year-old footballer Marcus Rashford MBE, who had experienced hunger as an inner-city child, was a heartening example of small businesses and community organisations combining physical, social and financial resources to bridge a gap created by poor policy.

Children and young people are also taking up the mantle for themselves. In the UK, Bite Back, a movement of young people campaigning for a fair food system, has recently succeeded in securing a watershed for television advertising of unhealthy foods. Tasha Mhakayakora, youth board member of Bite Back, has observed that fresh, nutritious food is unaffordable for most. Inner-city children are particularly disadvantaged because all roads lead them to unhealthy food. With the absence of safe, high-quality greenspace to hang out in, they are effectively corralled towards the high streets, which tend to be dominated by cheap, fast and unhealthy food (in London, nearly 40 per cent of children aged 10 and 11 are overweight or obese according to figures from London's City Hall Child Obesity Taskforce).

Solutions are often small and highly localised – certainly to begin with. High-street interventions such as Good Food in Catford and Sydenham, London, which was founded in 2015 by Vicky Skingley and crowdfunded by local residents and businesses, represent this appetite to fight back. Their website explains how they came into being: 'Local residents were tired of losing high street shops to residential conversions and resident surveys identified a real hunger for a better local shopping experience. When we opened, we wanted to put local quality food back on the map in Catford, and create jobs in our local economy.' Good Food is an independent social enterprise that pays the London living wage. It sells organic fruit and veg; artisan breads and pastries; wines from small independent producers; a range of locally brewed craft beer; British cheese and charcuterie; and so the list goes on. They make fresh takeaway food from their zero-waste kitchen and their not-for-profit veg-bag scheme funds weekly donations to local food banks. For any locals with a glut of allotment veg, Good Food will buy this too. This is a small, highly localised example of some of the efforts being made on a grassroots level, but a shop like Good Food on every high street could fundamentally change the values, buying habits and quality of life of its local area.

We may well wonder if we ordinary city folk stand a chance of making a difference, given that the global food and grocery retail market size was valued at US$11.7 trillion in 2019 and is expected to continue to grow in line with the rapid urbanisation and expanding middle class globally. So, why do we have 1 million people in so-called developed nations, like the UK, living in 'food deserts', and how are they falling through the system? To get behind the inequities in access to food, we need to investigate how we look after our lowest-paid workers, and why this is so often insufficient to support a healthy life in urban environments.

Promotions of cheap food influence spending habits, which is why we have such a destructive emphasis on unhealthy options. According to the Food Foundation, more than 60 per cent of our calorie intake comes from highly processed food which uses lower-quality ingredients, has a longer shelf life and delivers higher margins. In deprived inner-city wards, which may not be served by local supermarkets, food delivery is often the only option, particularly for large families who need higher volumes of food and seldom have access to a car. Without physically passing the fresh fruit and vegetable aisles, it's only too easy to be drawn in by low-cost promotions of high-fat, high-salt and high-sugar options.

The food landscape is dominated by a cartel of monopolistic players. In the UK, just five companies control the market. It is no wonder, then, that the pressure building in the supply chain to drive prices down in turn forces producers to scale up. To do this, they have to make what the industry rather innocuously calls 'efficiencies'. Translated, this means that animal welfare, environmental safeguards, labour standards and nutrient density can end up taking the hit.

Food pricing all too often doesn't reflect or account for the true cost of production or the welfare of the animals and people underpinning the food system, nor does it take into account the hidden costs to the environment or the public-health costs that come from bad diet. The Ellen MacArthur Foundation estimates that for every dollar spent on food, society pays two dollars in health, environmental and economic costs.

In an attempt to reform food culture, taxation and labelling have become ways of limiting the damage. In Chile, for example, high-sugar drinks have been taxed at around 18 per cent since 2014 and their labelling system represents some of the most ambitious attempts to reform food culture at a national level. But more research needs to be done to establish how far taxation goes to remedy the root causes of our reliance on unhealthy food in the first place. The problem with taxation alone is that it passes the buck to the consumer.

Unsurprisingly, what is unhealthy for us is also deeply unhealthy for the planet, and we as customers would like to know how to shop for food so that our meals aren't adding to the climate quagmire. The

Danish supermarket chain Netto, owned by Salling Group, is piloting climate-labelling of products in its stores, with the aim being to reach consensus on a common national label. Credibility and the potential volume of labels (on everything from modern slavery and animal welfare to food miles and plastic packaging content) are some of the problems we face in this arena but, as long as we keep chasing high-quality food, the industry and its big retailers will have to take up this mantle.

The Food Foundation's latest report shows some sobering figures: 46 per cent of food and drink advertising goes on confectionery, sweet and savoury snacks, and soft drinks, while only 2.5 per cent goes on fruit and vegetables. Unhealthy foods tend to be significantly cheaper than healthy food, which drives unhealthy diet choices. At the same time, 17.6 per cent of employees of the food industry earn the minimum wage, compared to 7 per cent of workers across the UK. Perhaps most alarming of all the figures: the poorest 10 per cent of UK households would need to spend 74 per cent of their disposable income on food to meet the Eatwell Guide costs – the government's official healthy-eating guide. The fact that governments do not, generally, want to hold those industries responsible for the damage caused by the broken food system means that the environmental and public-health costs are passed on to us as consumers.

In the British Library's 2020 Food Season, Angela Clutton chaired an impassioned panel discussion on whether Covid-19 would change our relationship with food forever. The panel included Patrick Holden, founding director of the Sustainable Food Trust, Jenny Linford, food writer, and Tasha Mhakayakora. The consensus was clear: there is no such thing as cheap food; so, we need to look for a model of market that buys produce from producers at a fair price and sells for a fair price. There is an opportunity for the supermarket model to use existing infrastructure to support the distribution of regional, high-quality products. To the question of whether we need a revolution with disruptive models or an evolution through encouraging supermarkets to shun the stack-them-high, sell-them-cheap mentality, Patrick Holden suggests the answer is that we probably need a combination.

We need diversity of food shops; there is absolutely a place for supermarkets alongside corner shops and markets and online specialist providers, and realigning the incentives of the supermarkets with health priorities could help support a scalable shift towards accessible healthy food for city dwellers. Supermarkets used to source their produce regionally, aided by regional packing centres that gave them proximity to local produce. As these packing centres have closed, the infrastructure to support regional produce in supermarkets is fading, so the role of wholesale markets has become even more important. As the Food and Agriculture Organisation has said, wholesale markets are critical; 'they allow producers to aggregate what they produce and increase their access to markets ... for consumers they provide access to diversified diets at affordable prices'.

The Sustainable Food Trust has identified a lever that we need to use more, which is our local councils, who themselves source a lot of food! They secure the food supply for schools, hospitals, prisons and so on. For local farmers and producers, councils are an ideal customer because they tend to spend a lot of money on a regular, recurring basis. Detaching themselves from the knotty and opaque world of public procurement just needs passion and creativity, and the Sustainable Food Trust points to Dumfries & Galloway council in Scotland as an example on their website. The ability to physically distribute products is one of the barriers to small producers, as they can't deliver their products to all their customers on their own. Dumfries & Galloway has created its own distribution hub by repurposing an empty council building. By championing and prioritising the freshness of food and taking the worry of distribution off the hands of micro-, small- and medium-sized businesses, they have provided a route to market for small, local producers who wouldn't otherwise have the means to distribute their products. Because of this, all Dumfries & Galloway's baked goods, dairy and eggs come from within the region. This is a solution that we as individuals can help along; our local councils and public services are open to all of us to speak to and support.

REGENERATIVE FOOD

We have been given the opportunity to make a paradigm shift. To recreate a system that gives more space to territories and communities. I foresee the issues of sustainability and food sovereignty topping the agenda. We can no longer think that food is produced by one company for all. We have stolen space from the countryside, we must regain it to kick start a primary economy at the service of the local communities.

Carlo Petrini, Slow Food President

The imperative for convenience and cost above all else has shifted over the past few decades and a resurgence of interest in more holistic, morally defensible ways of accessing our food has taken hold. Small-scale producers are generally proud of their artisanal farming or production methods, and when it comes to meat, fish or other animal products, they are open about the primacy of the animals in their system, and willing to provide details about their life, diet, death and preparation.

Urbanisation goes hand in hand with a growing middle class and a profile of consumer that is increasingly value-driven. Grassroots promotion of regenerative food, the growth in nostalgia for the good old days and the re-anchoring of food preparation with social connection has in many ways been helped along by shocks both to our supply chains and lifestyles, such as the Covid-19 pandemic, which shrink our world however momentarily. Initiatives such as Slow Food promote small-scale agricultural production methods that provide us with healthy, high-quality and diverse food. Kiss the Ground, behind the 2020 Netflix film, has created its Farmland Program, which aims to support land stewards in adapting their land-management practices so that they improve soil, watershed health, biodiversity and farmer livelihoods.

Regenerative food systems can help us unpack some of the binary myths that have circulated the periphery of 'unconventional' food-production methods, such as the assumption that local food is good and food that has travelled is bad. Similarly, that plant-based is good; meat is bad. As with so much of our high-speed, high-volume economic model, it is not the product that is wrong, but the behaviour associated with it. When we look at how we feed our cities, we must look at rural and remote regions, too – both in country and out – because they are the hubs of agricultural production. In fact, if we do not support our international food producers, we run the risk of losing out on the abundance of regional gastronomic products they provide us.

Slow Food is trying to bridge this gap in understanding and, since 2010, has been creating a network of community gardens across the African continent that help to guarantee supply of fresh, healthy food and raise awareness of land value and the implications of land grabbing, monocultures and chemical inputs, while also providing routes to market for unique products that are at risk of being lost in the current system of food production and distribution.

Slow Food's Ark of Taste programme is cataloguing those most in danger of disappearing. The catalogue lists over 4,000 products from more than 100 countries, which Slow Food identifies as our 'edible bio-diversity'. By raising awareness of these foods, and encouraging chefs to promote and use these products, they stand a chance of surviving into the future rather than being usurped by cheap, homogenous, high-yield crops on which our mass supermarkets depend.

On the matter of the place of meat in the future, Patrick Holden of the Sustainable Food Trust points to the crucial differentiation that must be made between unsustainable farming practices – the intensive farming of chickens, pigs and dairy cows – versus the contribution that small-scale grass-fed ruminants (cows, sheep and goats), pigs and chickens make to a rotational grazing system.

One of the core elements that we need to look at is reframing how we value our land. When it comes to agriculture, we should be looking at nutrient density per acre, rather than yield per acre. This would emphasise the value of nutritionally dense food produced by artisanal methods. Wildfarmed, an emerging biodynamic grain grower and miller in France (incidentally started by former Groove Armada DJ Andy Cato) has said:

> We've come to know that good soil makes great food. Almost all food plants are now grown in dead soil. That makes them unhealthy, requiring chemicals to survive and without any real nutritional quality. The best, healthiest food is grown from living soil, using knowledge and care for the land – not dozens of E-numbers, emulsifiers and preservatives found in so many processed supermarket loaves.

We can't keep our cities fuelled and nourished without understanding where our products have come from and how they journey from farm to plate. There seems to be a much more dynamic conversation between food producers and their customers emerging – we've gone from restaurants that don't talk about sourcing, to those that do, to those who actively give a platform to the voice of the producer. Wildfarmed grain, for instance, is the basis for David Gingell and Jeremie Cometto-Lingenheim's menus at Jolene and their bakeries and restaurants across north London. The grain is milled on site, and their USP has been making their mantra 'mind, body, soil' something to shout about. So, suddenly, just the simplest act of grabbing a loaf of bread in the morning rush exposes even the most hurried commuter or parent doing the school run to planet-positive eating. We need more of these restaurants bringing the story of our food to life in the city, and more of us choosing places like Jolene to buy from and support.

CITY FARMERS

Urban agriculture has historically shown its potential to make a crucial contribution to food security, particularly during the First and Second World Wars. In my conversation with Tilly Collins, she reflected that in wartime London, urban allotments were a material contributor to our food supply. In 1944, for example, they accounted for 10 per cent of food production in the city. Beyond this, farming in the city can also be a catalyst for renewal of down-at-heel areas.

Urban food production emerges as an important gateway to our rural environments and accompanying the yearning for positive stories behind our food is the rise in demand for allotments and urban gardens. They can add to our environmental and nutritional education and provide access to a version of agricultural knowledge, which for many city dwellers may as well be a foreign language. These spaces, as we saw in the Wilderness chapter, give communities the opportunity to participate in the food system, cultivate ecological awareness, exchange produce and stories, and expand social networks.

Urban gardens in France and Italy have been shown to alter purchase decisions and improve nutrition, while in South America food values reflect social issues as well as the scientific imperative to combat nutrient deficiency and lifestyle diseases exacerbated by poor diet. The South American context shows the possibility for food policy to support regenerative food choices, and the Pan American Health Organization promotes fresh, unprocessed food, encourages nature-derived fats and wholefoods rather than the refined alternatives.

Countries such as Brazil have taken a holistic approach to dietary guidelines, integrating cultural and social values into the broader nutritional picture. The Food and Agriculture Organization has recognised Brazil's dietary guidelines as the first to take social, cultural, economic and other aspects of sustainability into account, and their recommendations signpost to eating in appropriate environments, sharing food preparation and enjoyment with others, and reminding Brazilians of the vital time at home with family that food can catalyse. Taking a values-based approach to food is important if we are to be successful in making our cartel of supermarkets shift to promoting nutrients over calories, and over high-volume, ultra-processed foods that are making people and the environment sick.

Indoor agriculture (also known as hydroponics or vertical farming) is also spawning in cities, proving that if the space is not available at ground level, we can move it above, or even below, ground. Farming vertically in cities can add to our food mix because it allows for year-round harvesting and is attractive for cities with increasing water scarcity. The inner-city location of these farms changes the landscape of accessibility, with produce being freshly picked and delivered in a matter of hours. In New York, vertical farms can be found in Tribeca, Brooklyn, Queens and the Bronx. While their target market is primarily direct sales to restaurants, who are dependent on regular supply of the freshest possible produce, some, like Sky Vegetables, which runs an 8,000-square-feet rooftop farm atop a residential building, sell to their immediate neighbours and surrounding communities. Perhaps the most well-established example of urban farming is in Havana, where at least 30 per cent of the available land in the city is farmed and produces 20 per cent of Cuba's fresh food.

Happily, the list of cities giving space to urban farms is growing. Gaya in India is increasing green cover in its urban centre by subsidising rooftop farms, training urban farmers and providing seeds for edible, medicinal and ornamental plants. In Medellin, Colombia, the government's Huertas con Vos programme runs workshops for families to learn how to plant and harvest vegetables in their homes. Paulina Suárez Roldán, secretary for Social Inclusion, notes the improvements to food security, savings on grocery spending and improved social interactions. Residents in Seoul, South Korea, can apply for government support to set up urban farms. The government funds between 80 and 100 per cent of the initial installation fees and city districts run annual programmes to upskill gardeners on soil productivity, pest management and environmental education. As reported in the *Seoul Times* in 2018, the network of city farms in Seoul proved so popular that in seven years, their total area increased six times to about 1.7 million square metres (approximately the size of 238 football fields). In a similar vein, Melbourne, Australia, has created community gardens, street gardens (pockets of wilderness on median strips, for instance) and compost hubs across the city, including several that are reserved for lower-income residents living in public housing.

MAKING A MEAL OF THE CITY

Because food, particularly at the local level, is prepared with love, pride and tradition in mind, food people – producers, traders, chefs and so on – also have a reliable friendliness, and throwing oneself into the local cuisine is often the best crash course we can take on the culture of a people. Our food writers are hugely important in this regard, opening up windows to different food networks often all co-existing in the same city. On the days I might be yearning for a more distant home (it happens from time to time that one wakes up – emotionally – in a former homeland), food is always the remedy. My recipe collection has grown and travelled with me across the world as a small reminder of meals shared, friendships begun and momentous occasions. Cookbooks and assorted recipes hastily scribbled on envelopes or napkins sit on my dresser together – a selection of voices and memories of meals enjoyed in other homes that I can call to mind as I potter about in the kitchen.

We connect with one another through food by cooking, planting and growing produce that drives a respect for the farmers behind it. Food offers us the opportunity to return to the earth and reclaim environmental wisdom, the lost arts of traditional preparation and cooking methods, and the value of thoughtful food. Cities are a spawning ground for cookery innovation and the rise of the eco-chef is attuning culinary sensibilities to high-quality, ethically produced, zero-waste, nose-to-tail or plant-based menus. Writing about the New Nordic movement in *The Guardian* in 2020, Kieran Morris observed that the latest evolution of chefs is as a crusader for a better world.

Post-industrial, gritty areas like Rotterdam, the Netherlands, Brooklyn, New York, and Hackney Wick, London, tend to breed a vibrant food scene, where favourable rents are hospitable to artisans and creatives. Rotterdam's industrial heritage has led to a small empire of food-related heroism: urban farms sit alongside a crowd-funded food-waste programme, Kromkommer, which turns 'ugly' veg into soups; small-batch brewers, bakers, cheese-makers and coffee roasters sit alongside restaurants like Gare du Nord, a vegan, zero-waste, organic restaurant that designs its menu around organic vegetables grown on site and hires local young people. There are many similar examples of food innovators popping up in most cities.

Silo in Hackney Wick, which Doug McMaster opened in 2019, shows the synergies that are possible between fine dining and circularity of resources, including the interior design and furnishings, food-preparation equipment and the food itself. McMaster and his counterparts across the fine-dining business are diverting waste streams by popularising ingredients that would previously have been thought of as waste. The meat from dairy cows is one example; in the UK they reach the end of their 'productive life' at about 7 years old, yet their meat is still delicious. Silo is part of a small but high-profile network of restaurants and chefs who aim to work in harmony with nature, but cafe culture is also showing its pioneering spirit.

Rob Green, of the Pavilion in London and Cornwall, has trailblazed the way for others to follow. His bakeries champion small-scale products and, while primarily plant-based, also make use of Cornish fish and produce, creating a channel for isolated regional produce to become accessible to coast-starved Londoners. Rob is on a mission to rewild his customers through beautiful food. His cafes gently educate customers by celebrating food that nourishes the land.

Through thoughtful eating, we can venerate the ingredients, passion and lives that go into producing our meals. And once we have finished what is on our plate, there are community-led organisations waiting in the wings for our waste too. In cities, we compost or repurpose less than 2 per cent of the valuable biological nutrients in food by-products and organic waste. Enter Pashon Murray, whose company Detroit Dirt has shown the possibilities of mainstreaming urban composting habits by collecting and composting restaurant food waste, then selling this to gardeners and urban farmers. Since 2010, Detroit Dirt has diverted more than 90 million pounds of waste from landfill and the funds support the Detroit Dirt Foundation in its research on soil quality, community networks and zero-waste solutions.

Jenny Linford, food writer, who spoke at the British Library's event on the future of food, talks of time as the critical invisible ingredient in home cooking. In general, time is a scarce resource for city dwellers. On a slow weekend day, there can be nothing more soothing than a pootle around local shops gathering ingredients for an evening meal. The reality, though, is that this is a luxury that cash-poor, time-poor city folk can't always afford. Often, cooking and feeding ourselves and our families nutrient-rich food becomes a chore and another thing to add to the cognitive load. It's little wonder, then, that we lean on the quicker, cheaper options that lessen the burden of time in the kitchen. However, thanks to the 'MasterChef generation', more people than ever before are carving out time to return to the kitchen, acknowledging the worthwhile health and social benefits of doing so.

Home cooks need good ingredients, and independent food shops in the city tend to be very diverse and therefore the food culture tends to be strong. We can feel a cuisine through its food shops and begin to understand its culture through food. When I was first learning to cook, I recall reading Yotam Ottolenghi's warm and vivid descriptions of his local Turkish grocers in north London. At the time, living in regional New South Wales, Australia, I could only imagine what these treasure troves looked like. Fifteen years later, I was living around the corner from Ottolenghi with my own well-trodden paths between local Asian, Turkish, French and Italian grocers. These culinary outposts, often small and unassuming, always friendly and packed to the rafters, offer us direct portals to other places.

As cities tend to have the highest concentration of migrants (the Migration Data Portal estimates that 19 per cent of the world's foreign-born population live in cities), it is no surprise that food also becomes a valuable tool to give creative voice to the linguistic, cultural and ethnic diversity of foreign-born groups. In Melbourne and London, whose migrant population is 35 per cent and 37 per cent respectively, Free to Feed and Migrateful run cookery classes led by refugees, asylum seekers and migrants, which help to build confidence and access to employment, and promote natural integration with the wider community. In Brussels, where some 62 per cent of the population are foreign-born, Our House serves as a community-based integration project that facilitates respectful culinary and cultural exchange between refugees and their arriving community. The revenue from the project now also funds an open-access psycho-social service for refugees arriving in Belgium.

Aside from the functional role of food, we shouldn't forget to make room for the comfort and joy it offers us. The emotions associated with food are complex. Kimberley Wilson offers insight into the psychological value of kitchen-based activities such as baking in her conversation on the Food Medic podcast in 2019. With reference to the Great British Bake Off generation (Wilson is a former finalist), she suggests that interest in dwelling in the kitchen has blossomed because we're creating something different to the norm. A sourdough loaf or banana bread (the hallmark of kitchen survival during lockdowns in many cities), for example, offers us the opportunity to feel proud of ourselves, and inspire others to give us positive feedback – something we do not ritually gift to one another. Kimberley also comments on the psychology of making our way through a recipe, where weighing and blending ingredients can help us sequence our thoughts and give us structure and method. By using our hands, cooking and particularly baking provides us with the meditative pleasure that we may also get from other gentle activities like gardening. We can take advantage of its therapeutic and absorbing qualities, taking our time to create something that cannot be rushed. This is a rarity in city life, where so often we want to slap food on the table quickly so we can race to the next thing.

If mealtimes are important for connection with wilderness and heritage, it is interesting to consider the implications of the rapid rise in food delivery. App-based interventions have transformed the accessibility of food, making both good- and poor-quality food available with the swipe of a finger. While we may still be able to enjoy the conviviality of sharing a meal that we did not have to toil over, delivery services can hamper our attempts at being ethical consumers. In the UK, Just Eat, Deliveroo and Uber Eats – the largest delivery platforms – are inundating homes with plastic. The market is worth £8 billion and, once again, this is an example of environmental and public-health costs being externalised in favour of convenience. While we have gone big on eradicating the plastic straw in the past five years, the bulk of delivery packaging is still plastic based or single use.

At the other end of the spectrum to this high-speed access to food is a small but growing movement for urban foraging. Danish-based VILD MAD ('Wild Food') was launched in 2012 by René Redzepi (co-owner of two-Michelin-star restaurant Noma) to help people find what's edible in their local landscapes. In the section on cities and towns, users are told that 'where asphalt meets greenery, you'll find herbs, berries, and fruits, and along the water's edge, you'll find salty herbs'. The guide lists plant availability by season – in December, oyster mushroom and garlic mustard; in May, morel, sorrel and horseradish – and reminds users that the higher temperatures in the city mean that the urban foraging season starts earlier and finishes later than in the countryside. Once you have foraged your bounty, you can filter for seasonal recipes using Denmark's wild produce.

While VILD MAD is aimed at Danish foragers, foraging is evident across the world and, as Next City Equitable Cities fellow Valerie Vande Panne points out, we have a global shared heritage of foraging. No matter who our ancestors were, the chances are they were foraging 100–150 years ago so, although our environmental wisdom has been all but extinguished, it can be reclaimed relatively quickly.

Paul Bauder, a Belgian wild edibles specialist living in Los Angeles, gives foraging tours in the city that highlight edible, nourishing uses for invasive species like black mustard which is highly flammable.

This is a problem for cities like Los Angeles which face increasingly virulent wildfires at their fringes. Instead of spending public money to drench invasive species in weedkiller, Bauder argues that they should be harvested and preserved for use.

Changing the narrative of how we view wild plants and weeds in our city can create micro-industries that support the local economy, promote food equity and expand our sense of connection to the land. In Albuquerque, New Mexico, Karlos Baca, an Indigenous foods activist (he is Tewa, Diné and Nuche), uses foraging as a way of fighting back against the loss of indigenous knowledge stemming from colonisation. Through storytelling, wild plants can move out of the shadows and into common usage where their value is understood. As Wross Laurence, UK-based forager observes, edible plants can be found growing all over cities and towns, 'pushing out of the cracks in concrete, climbing a park fence, overhanging a cemetery gateway, edging a waterway. Once you begin to notice them, you start to see them everywhere.'

Foraging is one way the desire to tap into our surroundings manifests itself, but this yearning for connection to the land is showing itself in many ways. One weekend in 2020, finding myself between lockdowns, I visited an emerging vineyard in Surrey – a region of Britain that now experiences climate and soil on par with the Champagne region in France. There are few silver linings to the world's changing climate, but this is one place where the havoc, at least, has been tempered with a blossoming wine industry. The resident viticulturist was not necessarily born to farm and had spent stressful decades in a 'city' career in finance before the drive to get back to the land became too loud to ignore. Tending the vines takes over the soul; while the stakes are high (vines are notoriously fickle and yields are at the mercy of British weather), these winemakers had become part of the land. By all accounts, the deeply physical, outdoor lifestyle that depends on listening to the land and creating a product that people will treasure was compelling.

City dwellers want a piece of this, too. Unthinkable Drinkable in north London arose from a spontaneous chat in the local park. While walking around his neighbourhood, co-author of *The Turnaround Challenge* and head of PwC's Disruption practice Leo Johnson had begun to notice the presence of vines, wilting and unattended, seemingly out of place in their urban context. After a chance encounter with an elderly Italian resident, who fortuitously turned out to be a former viticulturist, Leo and his neighbours united around the story of the vines. The project snowballed and the Unthinkables discovered that not only could the vines be salvaged, they could also be turned into wine, which was even – eventually – quaffable. Aga Otero, who we met earlier and we'll hear more about later, has also started brewing beer from hops grown and harvested on London overground platforms. In these inventive ways, every part of the urban landscape can stand to contribute to our dietary needs and desires, if we just allow ourselves to reframe what these spaces can be.

GROWING THE FUTURE

How we treat our emerging generations says a lot about the type of future we want to create. It seems unsurprising that the conventional education syllabuses, which follow siloed disciplines and steer clear of essential life skills, are failing our children – particularly those in inner-city or socio-economically deprived areas. Happily, there is also evidence that an inclusive, holistic curriculum can instil social connection, care and responsibility from a young age, and is creating quality of life for children and their families.

GROW – an initiative set up by TV and radio presenter George Lamb in partnership with the Totteridge Academy in north London – is an excellent example of the benefits of 360-degree learning. According to staff, students and their families, the transformation in the school's culture has been palpable. Offering a testimonial on GROW's website, the school's principal, Chris Fairbairn, credits GROW with helping transform the school's culture 'by encouraging our pupils to ask bigger questions and understand their place within the world'. Students spend quality time outdoors, learning about food, farming and natural life cycles, and take part in extra-curricular activities including yoga, boxing and mindfulness. The aim is that these activities become a core part of the daily routine for young people, who are then more likely to ask the serious questions, engage with their communities and invest in their sense of place as they get older.

This rise in 'empathy education' is a serious piece of good news. As Friends of the Earth noted in their report on the 'empathy effect', this is probably our greatest hope for creating a new generation of political and environmental activists. Food is a powerful anchor for knowledge of our relationship with the planet, and Chefs in Schools, in east London, has created a community garden and cookery school to do just that. Their ethos is that the 'best chance children have to understand the importance of a good diet is by eating, and learning how to make, delicious food, cooked from scratch', and who better to do this than chefs – and a leading chef, at that. Chefs in Schools was co-founded by Nicole Pisani, formerly head chef of Ottolenghi's res-taurant Nopi, in Soho. Taking over the Gayhurt Community School kitchen, Nicole began a programme of retraining school cooks, mean-ing everything was cooked daily from scratch, and created a cooking curriculum through which children learned how to butcher meat and cook over firepits. The programme is open to children and their fami-lies from across London; together they are learning how to grow their own produce and cook affordable, healthy and balanced meals.

The Hackney School of Food, which provides the facilities for the Chefs in Schools programme, has a vegetable garden, orchards, beehives, woodfired oven and cookery classroom. The syllabus on the school's website includes everything from prepping raw ingredients to knife skills and growing food. In a similar vein, the Food for Life programme of the Soil Association works not just with schools, but also with hospitals and care homes to change the landscape of food and poverty by reconnecting people with how ingredients are sourced, grown and cooked. By introducing school farmers' markets – one of their initiatives – pupils and their families get to know small, local producers and business owners. When doing subsequent careers work at school, children have established an affinity with food, and identify with food careers or aspirations of small business ownership.

Food is at the heart of our ability to enjoy fulsome city lives. Our individual and collective efforts to produce, source and share food thoughtfully are critical to remedying the inequities and untruths proliferated by our traditional food system. Happily, in many ways the trends we see playing out are already changing our relationship with food and land. The alternatives available to us, through markets, corner shops, vertical farms, urban gardens, or ingredients that have been foraged or rescued from the waste heap, play directly into the long-term health and resilience of cities. As we saw in the Wilderness chapter, healthy populations save millions in terms of public-health services spending. The question is not, is it expensive to put health first; instead, the question should be what is the cost of *not* putting health first? Entrenched inequality in access to food – one of our most fundamental determinants of health and welfare – is something worth getting angry about.

Adaptations to our food system are already under way and they show that our cities can nurture and feed us while also strengthening the bonds created by empathetic, engaged consumers. Animal welfare and environmentally sensitive production methods often go hand in hand, so food can be an important way of using our purchase power to choose a kinder way of being. With Covid-19 having accelerated this affinity with food and the wilderness, we are in a unique moment in time when we are more interested in our food than ever before. What we do with this momentum is key.

We don't have to be the victim of the multipliers; we can eat a more natural, seasonal diet that is tastier, healthier and does not cost us the earth. The prescription for buying food should support a production system that reconnects with citizens. As the cells of the food system, we have a few powerful cards we can play for change. Firstly, we can buy better and, secondly, we can use our electoral power to demand the realignment of incentives so that all city dwellers can access high-quality food. The rise of food markets reflects our desire to feel connected with the food we are eating to create memories and ground ourselves in our surroundings. Growth in small-scale producers has helped our ailing farming industry and given small, ethical, family-run businesses and co-operatives the chance to access the market.

In a world where there is so much to worry about, and contemporary challenges often leave us feeling dubious about our institutions, city dwellers are looking for a happier story. Food – a hallmark of a city's spectacle – can help us get there. The growing emphasis on artisanal products leads us gently to a place of curiosity. Naturally, we slow down as we pause to appreciate the makers and celebrate the animals behind our produce, and understand the connection between food and land. A population that understands how the food system supports livelihoods, wildlife, and public and ecological health is equipped to make sound decisions. By buying only what we need, buying from local suppliers and embracing diverse ingredients, we can ensure that food not only nourishes us, but nourishes nature too.

3

MOVEMENT

I move, therefore I am.

Haruki Murakami

CITIES ARE THE epicentres of movement. Each day, movement of people, money, products and property all happens at breakneck speed, and it can be hard for us to keep track of where, when and how we carve out time for ourselves to move. In this chapter I'm interested in how our bodies move in cities and, by movement, I mean any form of physical activity, fitness, exercise or sport. It looks different for all of us, depending on our preference, mobility and age. It can be intentional or incidental, sports- or gym-based, solo or in a group, gained in the home while doing housework, looking after children or others needing our care, or squeezed in on our way to, from or during work.

For many of us, our means of generating an income depends on a large portion of time spent not moving. As we're being increasingly bombarded with declarations that sedentary lifestyles are the enemy to our health, working out how to balance sufficient physical activity within the limitations of city living can be a challenge. Currently, much of our physical activity is spent in fits and starts, rather than weaving its way incidentally through our day. We tend to shoehorn movement into concentrated increments while our bodies may check out for the rest of the day, perhaps languishing at a desk or, in the new world, at our dining tables and in chairs that were never designed to support our bodies for longer than a meal.

Even if our jobs require us to be on our feet, the chances are that we might not really be making movement work for us. Amid the urban hubbub, it's surprisingly easy to forget to tend to our minds and bodies; the traditional pace of cities can make us feel like movement is a nice-to-have, a treat or maybe even slightly self-indulgent. In reality, our bodies are our most critical vehicles for survival; to thrive in the urban environment, they need to move in order to regenerate, keep us happy and carry us through stress and disruption.

This was never intended to be a book about the Covid-19 pandemic but, if ever there was a time to take stock of the importance of physical activity to our health and happiness, it is surely now, as we reconcile threats to the health of our urban populations. Periods of confinement have shown us the combined value of public space, physical recreation and social engagement. For me, the curtailment of freedom threw the importance of daily movement outdoors into sharp relief. Getting up and out with the sun, even just for a walk, became an unshakeable pillar in the day, and it's definitely true that most productivity dips or mood funks can be traced back to a day spent indoors and sedentary.

Putting the world into lockdown also required a total revolution of training regimes. While I often trained on my own in the lead-up to climbs or competitive events, not being able to train among friends or even strangers sat heavily on me. Without our physical 'tribe', the taps were turned off on an important source of energy, intensity and fun, and we've had to learn new habits. The technological support systems to get us through lockdown life have been phenomenal and I, along with many of my fitness friends and colleagues, have been bowled over by the strength of the community that has rallied around movement recently. In normal circumstances, we could all do with time away from our screens, but in the face of extreme disruption, virtual platforms showed their value. They helped us to stay connected to our active communities, whether we were using Strava or wearable tech, or were joining workouts by Zoom, Instagram Live or YouTube.

When I leave the city, it is normally in pursuit of a big, wild and highly physical adventure: difficult, sometimes dangerous and often the kind I need to ever so slightly downplay to my mum. So urban life, for me, is a constant yet delicate balance between being match-fit for adventure – being supple, energised, flexible, strong, rested and permissive – and feeling able to judge whether my body most needs a stretch and a sweat, or a pause and a glass of wine.

Life in cities has fundamentally changed my most ingrained movement habits, inviting me to try new things when the opportunity to surf or hike isn't available. In the latter stages of this book, I took the plunge and decided to learn tennis – the first ball sport I've played since school – which filled me with dread. For the first few weeks, I played in the heat of the South African sun with monkeys whooping and hollering in the trees, before heading back to London to an inner-city court surrounded by theatre students and street art. Although my hand–eye co-ordination isn't as woeful as I thought it was when I was a teenager, I can't say by any measure that I'm proficient. But therein lies the beauty, and there are some days when I feel like my greatest achievement is getting outdoors on the court for an hour to laugh at myself.

Movement is about joy, curiosity and discovery; it unlocks creativity, sharpens our senses and helps us to set personal goals. So often, when the body is moving the mind is relaxed and open.

WHY MOVE?

Despite our endless list of daily tasks, city dwellers neither move enough for health nor for happiness. Our days are disproportionately weighted towards being indoors and sitting down, in the car or on public transport, at our desks, in restaurants and on our sofas. Part of remedying this will be in how we value movement. We're often quite strict when we talk about movement – we confine it to health terms (disease prevention, calories burned, step count and so on) – but it's important not to forget that it is also fulfilling and fun. It triggers our internal reward systems, connects us to family and friends, binds communities and creates all-round happier humans.

Exposing ourselves to diversity of movement stimulates our brains, bringing adventure and discovery to busy city lives. No matter what kind of a day we are having, it is extremely rare to 'regret the sweat'. Exercise, as well as giving us a dose of endorphins – which keep us feeling physically and mentally healthy – also tends to bring us into contact with others, meeting our needs as social creatures.

The melting pot of activity in cities can offer us an enormous range of physical outlets. Glossy and immersive indoor studios, for instance, are havens for the active and privileged. They're spotless, occupy some of the most luxury real estate in town, the sound systems are pumping and the lights are dizzying. Their effect of shielding us from the city outside is complete and successful. Meanwhile, outdoor exercise lets us explore our neighbourhoods freely and flexibly. Whether we run, cycle, skate, blade or float, getting a sweat on outside helps to situate us in our homes and offers us a window into our neighbours' lives.

I always enjoy running through the theatre or market districts of cities, for instance, where at sunrise fresh produce and flowers are offloaded from all over the country, or sets are being bumped in or out of theatres. Hitting the pavement can also take us past new artwork and pop-ups, or draw our attention to development applications, lost pets or community institutions that need support – as Leo Johnson showed when the simple act of walking began a neighbourhood wine co-operative. Getting out and about into our neighbourhoods tells us a lot about the people and wildlife we share our homes with. We might not directly socialise or work with each other, but walking by one another, and perhaps making eye contact or even throwing a smile, is an important if subtle reminder that to be a city dweller is a fundamentally shared experience.

It's worth looking closely at the value of different forms of physical activity in our urban areas. While there are perks to both indoor and outdoor movement, each suits different budgets, abilities and tastes. As we adapt to public-health and climate disruptions, urban parks and recreational spaces need to become part of our everyday lives rather than just an occasional treat. As well as being much more affordable and often a lot more fun, they give us a bundle of other benefits. By looping them into our routines, we can create a relationship with our greenspaces and the people we share them with. By using them we are exposing ourselves to daylight and the elements and stimulating our senses by giving them something different to see and smell, diverse textures and colours to focus on and varying terrain to navigate.

Sadly, the reality is that the playing field for physical activity in cities is far from even, and gender, ethnic and socio-economic barriers are at play here too. Poorly wired systematic structures (education, financial and healthcare systems, for example) sit behind many of the issues of city living, particularly for under-represented groups. It's important to recognise and remedy this because physical activity is unique in its ability to unite communities and make city living safer, healthier and happier. Juan Lopez of Steel Warriors (who we will meet properly later) summed this up in a sentiment that seems to be shared by the people behind community movement initiatives. He says:

> Yes, we are suffering mass institutional let-down and, yes, we might not be able to stop this today. But what we can do is to work individually and in our communities to empower vulnerable groups – particularly young people, to navigate their way through the riskiest aspects of city living, providing them guidance and support until they have a strong internal compass to live by.

When it comes to movement, community-led initiatives are more likely to uplift and provide safe spaces that are accessible to everyone, because they have direct insight into what's going on locally. With strong local roots, we are able to get under the skin of who is moving, where, when and how; and if not, why not.

To make movement work for us, we need to understand why it is so vital and what some of the barriers look like. Once we are equipped with this knowledge, we can take action by looking at and pushing for the civic ingredients we need to support a healthy, happy urban lives.

STANDING UP TO THE SIT-DOWN CITY

For 2.5 million years, our ability to store fat for times of scarcity served us in the high-stakes game of survival. Today, though, our lifestyles are almost unrecognisable from their primal origins. Where once our nomadic existence was fuelled by hunting and gathering, plus the occasional run-in with toothy predators, our urban lives are instead shaped by static dwellings, constant availability of food (often the kind that is energy dense but nutrient deficient), unrelenting and evolving sources of stress, and a lack of exercise. JustStand points out that our sedentary lifestyle, dubbed the 'sitting disease' by scientists, has become one of the most unanticipated health threats of our modern time.

The World Health Organization (WHO) has recently amplified its physical activity campaigns because of the severity of the impacts of the sitting disease. According to WHO, a lack of physical activity (alongside poor diet, tobacco use and harmful consumption of alcohol) is one of the leading risk factors for obesity, type-2 diabetes, cardiovascular disease, chronic respiratory illness and some cancers. These noncommunicable diseases – or lifestyle diseases – have followed patterns of globalisation and are the leading cause of death in most regions of the world. The burden is heavier for low- and middle-income countries, whose health systems are already dealing with communicable diseases like malaria, HIV/AIDs and many others that are threatening their populations. Expert in sports and nutritional immunology Dr Jens Freese notes in his co-authored paper *The Sedentary Revolution* that urbanisation and its accompanying population growth has spurred increases in motorised transport in low- and middle-income countries, with travel patterns shifting away from public transport and walking and cycling in favour of cars.

Ultimately this means that we are living longer but unhealthier lives. Alongside diet and other interventions, movement is one of the most powerful levers we have to improve our mental and physical health; and every movement matters – whether it is in the home (household chores or care labour), at work (getting up from the desk and stretching), while travelling (commuter-based walking or cycling) or for leisure (such as boxing or dance). WHO recently published a two-minute film clip setting out almost every movement you can think of to accompany its refreshed suite of recommendations; the overarching message is simple: everyone benefits from physical activity – and that really is everyone. What we do, for how long, to what intensity and how often can be adjusted for all ages and abilities. The point is to swap out sedentary activity for something active whenever we can. For the young, being active is critical to bone and neurological development, as well as academic and cognitive performance. For the elderly, it can protect against decline in cognitive and bone health, prevent falls and maintain functional ability.

As fast paced as cities are, they are also the hub of sitting still. JustStand rallies against this. While they promote stand-up workstations, their broader message is to raise awareness of the issues attached to our sit-down lifestyles; as far as their team is concerned, there are simple remedies we can start with to counter the impacts of all our sitting down (which amounts to at least twelve hours a day for most of us): stand up, sit less and move more. Considering it's so simple, the health benefits of standing over sitting are staggering. Our bodies benefit from better bone health and a boosted metabolism, and burn more calories, while our minds appreciate the extra brain power that comes from increased blood flow, the fresh oxygen and nutrients that release mood-enhancing chemicals, and sharper concentration and productivity that comes from having to actively keep ourselves on our feet.

One of the most common effects of too much sitting, particularly at a desk, is the weakening of postural muscles, tightening of the hips and weakening of the gluteals. This is the reason that fitness trainers spend so much time yelling maddeningly about that obscure thing called the 'core' (the band of muscles around our midsection that we need for balance and functional fitness) or, like me, have taken up the mantle of tackling lazy glutes (our butts, essentially), the biggest muscle group in our bodies and the one that is responsible for keeping us upright and helping us climb stairs. All our sitting down has even created a thing called 'dormant butt syndrome' which means – simply – that our glutes are not firing up because they just do not know how. All too often, our cities limit movement; parts are simply inaccessible to those in wheelchairs and others are not conducive to exercise, either because the terrain isn't navigable or because it doesn't actually work the muscles. In terms of getting our muscles moving, unless we're spinning or squatting or diligently taking the stairs, our body's posterior chain may be struggling to activate on its own. The less it fires up, the more we compensate with our anterior muscles (the front of our body), the more our quadriceps dominate, our spine rounds, shoulders hunch and hip flexors tighten, leading to creaky bodies and higher risk of injury, especially as we age.

For urbanites in the global north, where fitness makes its presence felt through the media, retail and recreation, inactivity seems impossible to conceive. According to research conducted by the Global Wellness Institute, the booming physical activity economy (including sports and active recreation, fitness, mindful movement, equipment and supplies, apparel and footwear, and technology) is worth US$828.2 billion and is predicted to exceed US$1.1 trillion by 2023. But in truth, fitness is a luxury and access to it is deeply unequal. Being able to pay top dollar for glossy, boutique fitness clubs in Los Angeles or Sydney is a far cry from reality for most people.

The *American Journal of Preventative Medicine* has observed that when it comes to our public recreational spaces, accessibility is a major barrier to participation by people with disabilities.

Movement should be encouraged for all city dwellers, and we need to be particularly mindful of making our spaces welcoming to those with disabilities or reduced mobility. As well as adapting our spaces, we need to offer movement, sport and recreational activities that are inclusive and adaptive. In some ways, the migration of physical activity advice online over the Covid-19 pandemic has enabled wider sharing of inclusive physical activity programmes, which we can only hope continues as we emerge from the pandemic's clutches. Cork Sports Partnership (part of Sports Ireland), for instance, has a comprehensive online offering for children, adults, older people and people with disabilities. Winchester in the UK has partnered with the Active Ability programme of Active Nation to make sport and exercise accessible to disabled residents of all ages. These moves are heading in the right direction but, until they are mainstream, the price we pay for unequal access to movement will be felt collectively.

In dollar terms, the healthcare costs of global inactivity are sobering – estimated to exceed internationally US$53 billion annually according to the worldwide study 'The Economic Burden of Physical

Inactivity'. In life terms, WHO has calculated that approximately 3.2 million deaths can be put down to insufficient physical activity. Oddly enough, we still seem to be getting worse, which suggests that, quite apart from all the knowledge and awareness raising, there are major gulfs to overcome to make physical activity equal and mainstream. The estimate is that 27.5 per cent of all adults and 81 per cent of adolescents do not meet WHO recommendations for physical activity (which are, to a fitness professional, quite modest) and that statistic has sat almost static for the last decade. So, we need to look closely at the barriers, which include gender (girls and women are less active than boys and men), ethnicity and faith, sexual orientation, disability and socio-economic status, the latter of which links to how much free time we have and what we do with it, as well as our disposable income.

THE MOVEMENT MIX

Physical activity is one of the most popular triggers for feeling joyful, happy and high on life, giving us that sense of play that comes naturally in our early childhood. When we push ourselves physically, we trigger the reward response in our brain – that chemical rush of endorphins and dopamine that make us feel happy and accomplished. Physical activity also tends to stimulate social activity; whole communities find themselves anchored around football, yoga, CrossFit and boxing, for instance. In 2020, the reality that our cities are a lifeline for play settled in, so this could be our chance to carry on new habits and keep opening the doors so everyone can get involved. The more we move, the more we can shape our cities to meet our physical and social needs.

Cities on Legs

Running is one of the most popular forms of exercise (and this was true even prior to the surge in runners during the pandemic) and has helped to make movement a customary sight in cities. In 2017, there were almost 60 million runners in the US; in Africa that number has been put at over 113 million and in Europe over 58 million. In 2020 a UK government survey revealed that approximately 6.8 million Britons went running at least twice in a twenty-eight-day period. Running is cheap and accessible, requiring little in the way of kit, and it can be moulded to even the most demanding of schedules. The physical benefits are clear: we raise our heart rate which is good for our heart and lungs, we build strength, stamina and speed, and we improve our mental health.

Beyond this, running has also proved its worth as a social activity, changing the way we experience and understand our cities. The fun runs and marathons that take place in cities across the world offer us the chance to get to know our streets in a slightly different way as they are cleared of traffic and other obstacles, and we connect with a community all sharing in the same experience – whether we are elites, amateurs or first timers, cheer squads, curious residents or volunteers.

Running is now so ingrained in the urban psyche that runners are a customary sight, inhabiting and exploring most of our shared spaces. Around the world, runners have embraced the city as an endlessly adaptable track; in Amsterdam the canals are as friendly to runners as they are to cyclists; Boston, home to the world's oldest marathon, offers well-established running infrastructure; Cape Town's landmarks and wildlife in Table Bay are a feast for the eyes en route; Munich's Olympia park offers the elite experience; in New York's Central Park health-conscious urbanites jog amid the chaos of one of the most frenzied cities in the world; San Francisco's cooler climes and stunning views of the bay lend themselves to the longer run; and Stockholm offers a real sense of exploration as runners island hop their way around the city. Meanwhile, Rio de Janeiro, Sydney, Perth, Miami, Los Angeles and Nice offer something at the other end of the spectrum – the beach run. For those who take their running seriously, there are numerous studies about what makes the ultimate running city, using measures of safety, air quality, access to greenspace, traffic and the strength of the running community. In the UK, *Runner's Need* published the findings of their November 2020 study to reveal that Wokingham, Slough and Reading are the best three cities for runners.

Beyond the competitive possibilities, running for fun has captured hearts and minds of all ages. From humble beginnings in Bushy Park, west London, the phenomenon of parkrun has expanded to twenty countries, including many capital cities such as Zelenograd in Moscow, Coronation Park in Mbabane, Estawani, and Poolbeg in Dublin. Its simple idea is powerful – walk, jog or run for 5km, at no cost, at the same time every week. Now, parkrun offers some 3 million people the chance to hit the ground running each weekend. Although the runs are timed, the emphasis is squarely on the social nature and the value of participation. All are welcome: running lovers and haters, the running-curious and -ambivalent, old and young, able-bodied and less able-bodied, and those with strollers and dogs in tow. Anyone who has turned up to a thronging local park on a Saturday morning can attest to the warm glow of community that surrounds a parkrun, and it is this that is thought to drive its appeal to groups who are traditionally under-represented in physical activity. It also seems to show that the positive effects are greatest for those who started out less active – the more frequently someone participates, the bigger the positive impact on their quality of life. The success of parkrun can be put down to its inclusive approach and the fact that people who may not identify as 'runners' feel welcomed into a community that is based around being active.

Of course, it's not all about speed. Slowing down and walking can be just the tonic to our weary minds and bodies. As Claudia Hammond says in her book *The Art of Rest*, walking 'pace is slow enough not to overwhelm the senses, allowing our minds to wander. It's the perfect balance between nothing and novelty.' Walking is also a versatile, affordable, low-intensity way to move that is friendly to people of all ages. There's no greater champion of a good, long walk than The Prince of Wales. Now in his seventies and as sprightly as ever, His Royal Highness is known for his lengthy marches across the hills in Wales and Scotland, often with a panting police officer in tow. Dubbed 'a mountain goat' by his wife, the Duchess of Cornwall, I can recall having to practically jog to keep up with his purposeful stride as he took off up the steep, stone steps of the Minack Theatre in Porthcurno, for example, or as he bolted up sixteen flights of stairs to return to street level from the London power tunnel, 104m below ground. His advocacy for walking as a key enabler of fitness reminds us that it is a form of exercise that often gets forgotten. Yet its effects can reach beyond the physical and offer up enormous mental-health benefits, regardless of age or background.

Again, walking has flourished in lockdown scenarios both as a form of exercise and for keeping us calm. In a bid to maintain if not increase the numbers of walkers in the UK, Dan Raven Ellison of National Park City is in the process of mapping 'Slow Ways' – a network of walking routes between all the towns and cities in Britain, with a mission to encourage people to walk part or all of the journeys they would normally use a car for. Dan reflects on walking as a way to improve 'health and wellbeing, tackle the climate and ecological emergencies, save people money, improve our environment and bring joy to people's lives'.

Behind Closed Doors

In studios, city basements, high-rises and even railway arches, another set of city playgrounds can be found. Indoor training spaces are their own world, sheltering us temporarily from the din and the crowds. As I chatted with Maria Eleftheriou, Lululemon ambassador and head of barre at Psycle, London, we discussed how, in this indoor domain, we get a taste of our raw strength and part of the appeal is that for an hour we can disappear to a place where we put ourselves first. We emerge feeling focused, re-energised and on top of the world. It is the modern-day equivalent of a rave without the hangover and makes us feel like we can conquer anything. The experience of training in a studio is unique and immersive, thanks to lighting, heating, air conditioning, equipment and music. To top it off, we have that wonderful euphoria that comes from working out in the company of others, united in sweat and commitment, and possibly a touch of momentary misery.

Speaking about small, local studios, Sapan Sehgal observes that there is a difference between these and the traditional 'community gym', with the latter often being run on a shoestring. Sapan's model is the former. His business plan for London Fields Fitness studio was to make the gym accessible for all. It's a one-off, without any membership contracts or franchising, and classes cost about the same as a drink at the local pub. Sapan reflects that 'group classes can help us meet others, which is important when we think about how transient our cities can be. Plus, physical activity bonds people – some of my best friends are the people I play football or rugby with because we've gone through something together.'

The studio is a Hackney gem – one of the most genuine examples of inclusivity around. As well as welcoming residents, Sapan recognises that newcomers aren't necessarily from the local area, and often not from the UK, so creating a sense of place is a priority. To find it, Sapan says, we're 'looking out for other spaces – not home, not work, but a "third space" to socialise'. London Fields was that space for me when I first arrived in Hackney and, as I've learned, it's a destination in its own right, with locals 'coming for the vibe, the humour and a good time'. Even its haphazard admin system adds to its warmth. As soon as you walk through the door, Sapan reflects, it's clear that this is a place that doesn't take itself too seriously, so it immediately removes the potential for intimidation. Everyone is known by name and there's a sense of fun about the place. So how do we make a model like this work? 'We survive on community love,' Sapan says. 'If you create something from the heart, you will get rewards.'

There is power in being with others, sharing and fuelling each other's energy, which is why studios tend to build up close-knit communities that often feel like family. While work, life and holiday might get in the way, and at times our routines fall out of sync, studios are there to welcome us when we are ready to return to routine, and we can walk back into our local knowing pretty much what we are going to get, who we are going to see and how we are going to feel after when we leave.

During 2020, gyms and other venues closed their doors for months at a time and it was only then that many of us, even as fitness instructors, fully appreciated the value of the physical communities we had built. While boutique studios are costly, they ensure that we are accountable to someone and keep track of our progress against goals. For those of us who are not travelling outside the city very often, they can also simulate the conditions of training in different environments and for different goals.

In July 2020, having not trained at a studio in months, I returned to Rod Buchanan's thigh-shattering barre class in central London after four solid months of training solo or with the aid of Zoom. But when I walked through the doors of the building, my own solitary regime melted into oblivion. Everybody in the class had chosen to be there on that day with Rod and, nearly fifteen minutes into the session, the room was sinking into a collective sweat puddle on the floor, and I realised that, however hard I had been training in lockdown, I had never got to this level of intensity under my own steam. Between the face-to-face exchanges, face-to-mirror grimaces, cheesy tunes, Rod's cheeky quips and the novelty of being surrounded by others after lockdown, the whole experience was almost overwhelming. I'd never felt teary in a barre class before, and thankfully it mainly came out as sweat, but it's a workout I won't soon forget. It was a euphoric, gratifying and immensely relieving feeling to be plugged back into this snippet of city life – the essence of why so many of us choose to be here.

In the absence of big, varied, natural landscapes in most downtown areas, gyms also offer us a ton of kit that helps keep things interesting. Functional fitness, which has been enjoying wild popularity, is basically just training in a way that humans were designed to move. Through it, we mimic the kinds of actions we do in everyday life, often without thinking and generally across multiple planes of movement (front to back, side to side and twisting). These are your average lifting-, carrying-, reaching-, bending-type movements, and if we don't have a strong foundation, we leave ourselves open to injury. The beauty of studios is that they allow us to focus on our technique and they can feel like safe spaces to push ourselves away from the gaze of others. For women or groups who feel less comfortable training outside, are put off by running or nervous about outdoor gyms, studios give us access to a community tailored for our needs.

They also open up a world of fitness styles, from indoor cycling to barre and bootcamp fitness to cross training. We can take a cardio session like high-intensity interval training (HIIT) to boost endorphin levels and increase serotonin, which we particularly need if we are feeling low or lacking in vitamin D. Or, if we want to build strength, barre will give us mental power and stamina, and enhance our mind-to-body connection. Indoor cycling meets the brief for a party atmosphere without the hangover. These hours spent training indoors offer their own perks – it's comfortable and we get to be in the company of others in a location that is convenient to our workplaces or homes.

Of course, if we want to open our intuition, improve flexibility and tune into our inner self, we find a yoga practice down on the mat. When we spoke, Maria Eleftheriou emphasised that we 'need to be more permissive and flexible' when it comes to our exercise mix. She recommends doing the things we are not necessarily great at or do not know how to do because, through this, we meet new people and shake up our routine. As a relative newcomer to barre, I spent 2020 wryly observing my own transformation from loathing to loving it as I realised it could fulfil my passion for strength training without adding to my soaring cortisol and also found that it could be a tonic for back-to-back spin classes, forcing me to slow down. Among all these possibilities for activity and expending energy in the city, it is just as important for us to incorporate time to rest and recover.

Recognising the different pockets of time for movement in the day is part of getting the right mix, says Maria. She uses her cycle to work as time to think about teaching and prepare mentally for what lies ahead in the day. Before and after work she walks her dog, Benji, leaving her phone at home. There is no fixed prescription but what seems to be shared among most city dwellers, including fitness professionals, is that we tend to put our emotional needs far down the list of priorities. While all movement is beneficial, we also need to make sure we are moving in a way that will nourish us most that day. Boutique fitness can breed a negative ride-or-die style approach to physical activity; taken too seriously, cautions Maria, it can also create more anxiety than enjoyment, so we need to make sure we still have love for what we're doing.

Even if we think we have all the social, emotional, physical and financial tools at our disposal, nobody is immune to life's pervasive stressors. Coming to the end of 2020, the collective fatigue, stress and anxiety was palpable. After months of being confined, dealing with financial stress, caring for and worrying about others, stress had taken root in cities across the world. While there was no precedent for the circumstances of 2020, there is anecdotal evidence I uncovered while researching this book that a softer, kinder, more gentle approach to working tension out of the body and mind has surfaced. When the initial novelty of home workouts wore off, friends and colleagues reflected on their decisions to take time out to rest. To see this resurgence of permission, acceptance and self-listening amongst a network of people whose lives are normally characterised by rigid timetables was a relief and something worth celebrating.

Maria also reflected that being flexible and feeding our cognitive cravings for variety are key. It might be about tweaking the time, for example; big chunks of time might not always be possible so setting small but realistic goals is one way of doing this (twenty to thirty minutes is all we need for the physical body to connect to our mental and emotional energy). Or perhaps it might be adjusting an intensity variable like music – running with music might help if we need to disassociate from the world, and at other times we might prefer to tune into the energy, sights and sounds around us to calm us down. Irrespective of type or intensity, training outdoors sits in a league of its own (even for the most dedicated indoor trainers). Our bodies feel different outdoors. We can quite literally connect with the ground beneath our feet and the sky above us, moving over different terrain and through rain, hail or shine. As attractive an option as it is, we need to work harder to promote inclusion in movement, both outdoors and in.

MOVING FOR CHANGE

Believe it or not, writing in 2021 women are still an 'at risk' or 'vulnerable' population group when it comes to movement. As it stands in the UK, 51 per cent of the population is female and yet 39 per cent do not move enough to meet the national guidelines (150 minutes of moderate intensity or 75 minutes of vigorous, weekly). The picture in America is bleaker. According to the Center for Disease Control and Prevention, 60 per cent of women fall below the recommendations and more than 25 per cent aren't active at all.

When we look specifically at women from under-represented groups, ethnic minorities or pregnant women, the situation gets a whole lot worse. For the latter group, one powerhouse woman, Sally Kettle, set out to change all this for women in the UK, founding the Active Pregnancy Foundation in 2020. The first woman to row across the Atlantic Ocean east to west, twice, Sally takes a gutsy, evidence-based approach to disrupting the myths that have led to inconsistent advice, fear and judgement behind physical activity during or after pregnancy. The exclusion of our mothers and mothers-to-be from many of the communities built around physical activity means they lose out on the long-term physical- and mental-health benefits of an active lifestyle. To move this population, the foundation trains fitness professionals, particularly those from under-represented communities, to increase their influence and role-model potential and has created a national support network for pre- and postnatal fitness.

However, the outdoors is still a sticking point for many women. The Australian Bureau of Statistics looked at the issue in 2012 and found that the participation rate in physical activity was at 70 per cent for boys compared to 56 per cent for girls. In Europe, 2016 data revealed that 45 per cent of men exercise or play sport at least once a week, compared to 37 per cent of women. The least active group is often the younger demographic; for example, in the UK it is 13–15-year-old girls, and Sport England's 2018 data shows that young girls still feel unwelcome in outdoor play spaces, and families are concerned for their personal safety when allowing girls to play and explore outside.

Some of the main hurdles to outdoor activities are language, awareness, safety, culture, confidence and perception of middle-class stigma. There are also practical barriers around access to greenspaces and inability to travel to them due to cost or logistics. Challenges to the stereotypes of the great outdoors are gaining traction, though. In Kenya's Amboseli National Park, Team Lioness, one of Kenya's first all-female ranger units have smashed gender and cultural norms as the first line of defence for protecting wildlife in the community lands of the Olgulului-Ololarashi Group Ranch. Black Girls Hike, founded in Manchester, England, by Rhiane Fatinikun, encourages the uptake of hiking in the Black female community. In Boulder, Colorado, Jaylyn Gough's platform Native Women's Wilderness, has increased representation of Native women outdoors and educated both Native and non-Native outdoorspeople about the land they choose to explore. Other examples are tackling representation in surfing, climbing, swimming and cycling. However, until everyone feels comfortable and welcome, activity stats will remain low.

The outdoors, then, where physical activity is at its cheapest and most fun, remains the province of white, middle-class men. Outdoors Queensland, in their 2020 *Inactive Young Australians* report, points to a lack of female role models when outdoor activities are promoted, and the fact remains that women's participation in movement is typically more passive rather than active, with some young girls saying that increasing gender difference as they progress through their teenage years can make it more uncomfortable for them to take part.

I hadn't really thought about my own experience of movement as a girl until I began writing this chapter. Although I'm in the fitness industry now, it's not something that would have ever entered my mind twenty years ago. As a South African girl, sport wasn't a big part of my upbringing despite an otherwise active childhood. In fact, it was only while rummaging through photos in 2020 – as my parents packed up and prepared to leave yet another country – that I found some evidence of a very early inclination towards sport (and competition!). I was about 5 years old, racing in the bush against a bunch of boys, barefoot and wearing a rara skirt and an expression of pure joy. I was pretty chuffed when I saw that photo, but even more so when I flipped the page over to find another of me, standing defiantly on the winner's podium. I don't know where that sporty little girl went but, as I got older, team sports – especially mixed – really put me off and as a teen I had a deeply unenthusiastic relationship with sport. It wasn't until I ended up climbing mountains later in life – more often than not the only woman in the group – that I realised and accepted I wasn't just part of the team, but generally leading it! Reflecting on the various expeditions, I've often had to break trail through snow drifts almost as tall as me and lead on the summit days, sometimes dragging 90–100kg men up the mountains. I've been a de facto altitude-sickness and relationship-issues counsellor, chief snack provider and cheerleader. This type of movement changed my life, and it was only after this that I trained as a fitness professional and began participating in sport more confidently.

We desperately need to find ways to bring these opportunities for team leadership in the sports arena to women at a much earlier age, so that they can see difference not as barrier but as a strength. In Brazil, the Guerreiras Project leverages the voices of female professional footballers as community ambassadors to do just this. As an article by founder Caitlin Fisher on the World Justice Project notes, by running capacity-building workshops and co-creating safe places to play football in underserved communities, the project brings to light 'strong empowered, talented [women] acting in a space that has been traditionally reserved for men' to challenge harmful gender norms. The project's pilot in Recife has led to greater participation of young girls in football, so much so that the city now has a dedicated all-girls team.

Even indoors, inclusion has never been the fitness industry's strong point, and many of our boutique studios have a serious diversity problem. Writing in the *Washington Post* in 2018, Lavanya Ramanathan said, 'Sweat through a class in one of these studios and it's very possible that you'll see it, too: many, many lithe young white bodies and very few people of color. Or older or heavier exercisers.' Some trainers are taking matters into their own hands. As ABC News has reported, Linda Berjaoui, founder of Sista PT in Canberra, Australia, is one such trainer, who now runs 'the city's only dedicated fitness training service for Muslim women and children'.

I spoke to my friend, Ahmed Jaffer, coach and Nike ambassador, who works both in studios and local parks. He reflected that, in cities, unequal access to exercise and education about active lifestyles is exacerbated by huge disparity in wealth. He says, 'If we're able to educate with best intentions and create equal opportunities to join a movement community, physical activity may become more inclusive, popular and diverse.' We chatted about how city dwellers can help to diversify the picture and he emphasises the power of supporting our local fitness offerings, whether gyms or park workouts. If we enjoy doing this, he says, we're more than likely to bring along our friends and family to the sessions. Ahmed is right, of course, and I recall watching a little community form around my weekly sessions in London Fields, as clients brought (and sometimes dragged) their teenage sons, colleagues, partners and out-of-towners along. Then their plus-ones would come back and bring another plus-one – this is a gentle, organic way of making movement more visible and attractive to different bodies, ages, cultures, languages and abilities.

SURVIVAL OF THE FITTEST

One of the biggest changes we need to make is instilling a love of movement from the earliest ages. Setting aside the immediate health benefits for a moment, the loss of physical awareness in children excludes them from essential skills like problem-solving, leadership, sportsmanship and negotiation. What often gets overlooked in the conversation around young people and exercise is how sport can help people achieve a sense of fulfilment and nurture a sense of aspiration that they might not find in the classroom. Sport can give us the chance to fulfil unspoken potential and the ultimate struggle is often not the run, the weight lifted or the pose perfected, but the process of setting and achieving goals.

In researching this chapter, time and again, the conversations came back to the number of young people growing up with limited resources and opportunities. Movement can have an immediate and profound impact on our quality of life. A day we are active is almost invariably better than one where we do nothing. When we move, we kick-start our happy hormones and connect with nature or other people in our community, or maybe even both. We might get muddy or sweaty or tired, and in those moments we can suspend our troubles and give in to the more innate pleasure of play. Understanding how people are feeling is important if we are to find the right solutions. In the Prince's Trust Youth Index, a UK-wide survey to gauge the happiness and confidence of young people, 2019 results (before the Covid-19 pandemic) showed that the wellbeing of our young people had dropped to an all-time low, with 28 per cent of young people reporting that they felt like they were going to fail in life. Among those not in education, employment or training, the figure increased to 40 per cent.

It was in response to youth disempowerment, increasing urban violence and a deficit in affordable physical fitness amenities that Steel Warriors was born. Operating across London, the charity melts down knives confiscated from the city's streets and reforms the steel into outdoor street gyms. I spoke to Juan Lopez, community manager for Steel Warriors. Juan was born and raised in Tottenham, and has used his own time on the streets and a career in the military to get under the skin of the urban experience of inner-city kids in the UK. Having dropped out of school at 14, he went back at 20, before joining the army for almost a decade. Juan argues that the most successful, practical solutions to address quality of life for disadvantaged groups in cities are those that understand the need for role models to help rewire the system.

Juan cautions against the misunderstandings that sit behind 'hard to reach' groups, explaining that this can be remedied by bringing on board the young people's perspective through focus groups, youth board members and so on. Listening is everything, he says. It is not often that you have someone from deep within the community that gets into the position to do something for the community, but when it happens it can be truly transformational and the success of initiatives like Steel Warriors can be pegged to a local, trusted member of the community like Juan.

Everybody wants to have quality of life. Or, as Juan counters, if we do not call it that, we want to be happy. Children and young people trying to find a way out of their financial, psychological, social, or emotional struggles are often looking for references of success. Around the ages of 9 to 14 years old, role models are a critical factor in shaping beliefs and aspirations. The influences that young people of this age are bombarded with daily are often overwhelming and embody a level of success that feels completely removed from their reality, which can make it easier for them to follow the crowd nearest to them. Juan, reflecting on his own experience as a youth on the streets in north London explained it like this: for those who try to reason their way out of the well-travelled path, they often look to education but in its current form schooling is often very limited in its reference to real-life skills. 'Disenfranchised young people don't have access to a directly relevant pathway through education to change their immediate future; siloed study of maths and history, for example, makes little sense to young people who are facing real-time risks of hunger, poor mental health, care obligations, street violence or domestic abuse,' he said. They want to be doing something more productive that will give them immediate, tangible results. So, they drop out of school and look for the most realistic and viable way of improving their quality of life.

Often, the models of success are hard to relate to. Juan observed the unhelpfulness of the 'urban fairy tale of rappers and footballers getting up and out'. He says, 'If kids want to succeed, they feel that they need to have super-human talents, which deepens the unrealistic expectations about future success.' Instead, often the most realistic references of success in the immediate environment are those living life on the fringes and making a living from illicit activities – drug dealers, gang members, sex workers – who have direct access to material wealth like designer clothes, fast cars and disposable income. Against the backdrop of a society that places material wealth above internal values, Juan observes that young people believe that this is what is realistic for them. Once started, it is easy to become trapped in this lifestyle and it is only after a while that the consequences become apparent: the associated violence, threat to freedom and life, deteriorating mental health, drug use and exploitation. Educated adults, who have either avoided or escaped this pathway, know this to be true but the young and impressionable often refuse to admit that this will become a part of their lives. In such instances community-led efforts, from people who understand the day-to-day realities, make a real impact and often it is physical activity that provides the entry point.

When putting together the programme for Steel Warriors, Juan was looking to create a fitness and health service that broke through financial barriers and would teach participants the kinds of life skills that are not taught in schools and may not be passed on through families. Steel Warriors offers a street-fitness programme, focusing on mobility, strength and performance, and a mentality programme, which applies the principles of combat missions to overcome psy-chological barriers to goal setting. The work is now to take the gyms to as many urban communities as possible to scale up a model for movement that truly empowers everyone.

The practice of applying military principles of discipline, respect and loyalty to goal setting in other walks of life is not new, but I was curious about its application in a city context. Juan's take on this is that 'the aggression of inner-city life makes it a natural fit with combat principles. When I took a step back and observed the city as an ecosystem, I saw that everyone is out of sync. The city is a place of chaos and can be likened to a warzone.' Drawing upon his experience from his time in the British Army, where the imperative to perform is based on life-or-death stakes and the pressure and stress are elevated, he realised that there is a similarly small margin for error in the city, so we have to operate with discipline and precision. Perhaps there are parallels that may be drawn here with how we can sharpen our approach to urban interventions, so that instead of being passive we draw communities together in a more cohesive and disciplined way in line with the goals that they are setting for themselves. The lessons from Steel Warriors are clear: if we want to create cities that harness movement and self-actualisation, we need to listen to the lived experience of the barriers, elevate the importance of role models and encourage relatable, achievable aspirations for all groups of city dwellers.

Sport proves its power even in cities where being in a warzone really is the way of life. In Mogadishu, Somalia, Ilwad Elman is making use of the spectacular city coastline in her surf-therapy programme for city children. Ilwad, shortlisted for the 2019 Nobel Peace Prize, uses the cathartic powers of the ocean to support the psychological and social recovery of young survivors of violence and trauma. Surfing, practising yoga, water games and waterside meditation celebrates and reclaims Mogadishu's coastal assets for its citizens, which were off limits for some fifty years, and promotes healing and rebuilding of social capital through physical activity.

The universal ability of sport to capture the imagination means that physical activity has an important role to play in improving the quality of life in cities. Inner-city neighbourhoods typically have less access to the physical activities that are so crucial to educational development, wellness and socio-economic advancement. Boxing often features here, as a sport that was born and thrives in the inner city. Boxgirls, which provides boxing training to girls in the urban slums of Nairobi, Kenya, harnesses the link between sport and security, dignity and leadership. Ironbound Boxing, in the Ironbound neighbourhood of Newark, was set up by US veteran Mike Steadman, and is founded on the transformative power of boxing. Mike insists on the company's website that training like a boxer builds the 'grit, confidence, and discipline that will enhance and improve every aspect of your well-being, personal development, and job performance'. Ironbound, Steel Warriors, Boxgirls and their kin are evidence of the power of community-led interventions rooted in movement and deep understanding of neighbourhood. They also show that small, incremental improvements over time lead to large successes. There is no reason we can't scale up movement opportunities in cities. After all, the request of our young people, minorities and other under-represented groups is simple – as the kids involved in Ironbound Boxing voice them, their aspirations are 'I just want to be great' or 'I just want to be remembered for something good'.

As we've seen, role models are important for all of us, across all fields, to point to success. The emphasis in cities is often not on quality of life and success tends to be defined by conventional measures of how much we earn, how good the buildings are and how well the infrastructure is run rather than the values underpinning them. In considering our measures of success in future cities, we could instead begin with how we would like to feel. When we think about what it is we really want, the feelings we tend to identify with are those of excitement, gratitude, happiness and so on. Steel Warriors' Juan Lopez suggests that we ask what kind of person we must be to achieve these positive feelings and then the way we conduct our lives becomes more about our values. The same is true of the city: if we think of it as a sentient being, perhaps we need to ask its collective consciousness (those who dwell within it) what kind of city it wants to be, what values it holds dear and what kind of activities bring these values to life. And the answer may well help us move forward in every way.

MOVING TOGETHER

It's clear that the thread that runs through all of this activity is a sense of community that comes from engaging in a shared activity, even if it is sometimes actually done solo. Thankfully, innovation in our cities has led to some heartening alternatives to conventional fitness activities, including many examples of combining physical activity with social care and nature conservation. The Good Gym is an example of how we can strengthen our local neighbourhoods through movement, and it's simple – you need nothing but a pair of running shoes and a kind heart. When runners sign up, they are paired with a person who could use a hand locally: they might be elderly, at risk of loneliness or mobility impaired, and the tasks vary from dog walking and prescription deliveries to changing light bulbs and calling by to say hello.

In a similar vein, Green Gyms (run by The Conservation Volunteers charity) have sprung up in urban centres across the UK, such as in Glasgow and Belfast. Joining in with a Green Gym programme comes with a network of benefits, alleviating loneliness and social isolation, improving mental and physical health, re-establishing a connection with nature and creating high-quality greenspaces for the community. It is conservation married with fitness; volunteers warm up and cool down before they start their activities, and they build functional fitness through planting trees or wildflower meadows or creating wildlife ponds, for instance.

There are similar examples all over the world; Chicago's Pull Up the City project is tackling health inequities in the west side of the city by creating community fitness gardens that combine neighbourhood clean-ups with fitness workouts. In a promising move in the UK, Green Gyms also have GPs and the mental-health charity Mind onside, with GPs now prescribing sessions to encourage patients to build movement into their lifestyle. The growth in Green Gyms speaks volumes; in London, the number of gyms has grown by 500 per cent since 2011. This is testament to how getting active reaches far beyond the individual good and creates a virtuous circle within the city that can lead to real community change.

Virtual Movement

What happens, then, when our usual way of interacting with our sports or fitness communities gets turned on its head? As the world grappled with Covid-19 and many of our activities turned online, the success of movement-based communities, which are so deeply founded on physicality, proved that they could be relocated or dislocated for a time.

While we can lament our digital lifestyles and the ubiquitousness of screens – and even blame them for discouraging movement – virtual fitness communities that let us train on demand, in any style, have blossomed. In the absence of the chance to train together physically, screen time can give us real-time access not only to our usual community but also to role models who might previously have been too far away from us. In the first few weeks of lockdown, I was recovering from my latest climbing trip and should have been resting, but I was so intrigued by the novelty of working out virtually that I couldn't help getting involved in everything. Suddenly having world-class athletes and trainers available on demand to show us the way they move, at no cost, at the tap of a screen, was too exciting to pass up. With the closure of gyms and indoor recreation spaces, trainers, athletes and fitness professionals helped to rewire some of our active habits. Some, like Joe Wicks (the Body Coach), offered free content that encouraged people of all ages and abilities to join in with short bursts of physical activity. In July 2020, Joe said that his workouts had received 80 million views worldwide, while yoga influencer Adriene Mishler has amassed a devoted following of 9.77 million subscribers.

At the time of writing, it is too soon to draw conclusions on the impact of Covid-19 on our physical activity. But the *British Journal of Sports Medicine* has already observed a relative increase in interest in exercise, which they have put down to a few reasons:

we might be compensating for activity that we no longer do (for example, our walk or cycle to work); we may have more 'discretionary time' (time not spent commuting or taking kids to school, for example); and there is also no shortage of health-awareness messaging coming from national and multilateral authorities across the world.

In France, the UK and Australia, even during lockdowns, exercise was still deemed essential and led to a boom in many activities. The fitness app Strava, which has 73 million users, gained 2 million new members per month during 2020. During springtime 2020, the UK's Strava members logged 82 per cent more outdoor activities than normal for that time of year, and user data from the US and Germany told a similar tale. Data from apps like Strava also shows us the variety of activities that we're taking part in; aside from running and cycling, members also reported more walking, hiking, indoor cross-training and outdoor board sports like paddle boarding.

While virtual training has become an essential tool in our back pocket, and an important supplement to our movement patterns, it cannot, in the long term, replace the energy of having others in the studio, field or surf around us. There are the inevitable days when city life gets us down and these are the times when, feeling low in reserves or self-belief, having a physical, open-armed community anchored in movement can lift our spirits.

The fundamental place of movement in our cities is clear. Our environment, health practitioners, bodies and minds are asking us to move more. One of the hardest parts of weaving movement into our day is that the non-stop rush of city life can be both addictive and deafening, so a balanced mix of movement for fitness, social connection, rest and joy has become elusive.

We may still not be moving enough globally, but there are certainly more people than ever before making room for movement in their lives. Examples like Steel Warriors and the Green Gyms show us that the momentum is out there to make movement inclusive of more than just those who can afford studio memberships. To scale up these initiatives, green and social prescribing from healthcare professionals and social-care services needs to become mainstream rather than fringe. When we talk about fitness, we can do so in ways that are inclusive and recognise the diverse needs, abilities and resources of the groups inhabiting our cities. Considering the lucrative fitness market, boutique studios and gyms might also consider how to become more involved in their communities, perhaps by increasing their community classes or running more outdoor programmes that are cheaper and accessible to a broader audience. This is vital to city-wide life satisfaction, as the Wellbeing Institute has observed a correlation between physically active nations and happiness. In 2019, fourteen countries made both top-twenty lists and Norway, Iceland, Sweden, Finland and Denmark all ranked in the top-ten spots for 'happiest' and most physically active.

Movement is intrinsic to our quality of life. It brings us energy and is a critical tool in helping us navigate the pressures of city life, but better than treating it as a tonic for the inevitable stress, our cities can help change our relationship with movement by blending it into the urban lifestyle. Making movement around the city more intuitive means supporting deliberate and incidental activity, as well as rest and recovery, depending on what our needs and sensibilities are at any given time. To make it inclusive, we need to look after the interests of the most vulnerable or underserved residents first. If we start with this as the baseline, our cities will become infinitely more inhabitable, enjoyable and appealing for all of us.

Active cities are our future; movement is what will keep the wheels of creativity turning, while sharpening minds, strengthening bodies and powering dreams. When we stop moving, everything else stops too.

4

CONNECTION

You could live your life here, working, shopping, eating, socializing and falling in love, all on foot.

Charles Montgomery, *Happy City*

HUMANS ARE SOCIAL creatures – we are better together – and cities that help us live lives connected to the bigger picture are the ones we need for the future. The Covid-19 lockdowns made many of us realise that we didn't really know our neighbours. This was a sad thing, but it resulted in something very promising – it made us realise that we wanted to! I've been extremely lucky with my building in London – a pint-sized converted factory in one of the city's artsy districts. Being a newly flipped building, we all moved in at the same time, and within the first few weeks one of our more gregarious neighbours had taken the bull by the horns and hosted a party. It was the start of a wonderful friendship, but it was more than that: we have barbecues on the shared terrace and drinks on the roof; we swap tools and spices and books; we help each other with bike repair, relationship breakdowns and DIY; we grow vegetables, exchange pho for tacos and go on holiday together. In the building, we have a photographer, stylist, graphic designer, actuary, chef, furniture designer, banker, gemologist and an environmentalist; a combination of freelancers, business owners and employees of organisations ranging from micro independents to publicly listed; and almost everyone has a side hustle – journalism, bike touring, illustration and so on. We're acutely aware that this isn't ordinary – we've all lived in enough other cities in the world to know this is a special case of aligning stars. But it needn't be! We could have a building like this on every street, and neighbourhoods full of buildings like this. We can walk, bike or take the train to work; we live between two massive public parks and a canal, and we encourage each other to use our local shops and businesses by constantly comparing new finds. Unofficially, we have created for ourselves a connected city, helped along by a few very important ingredients: infrastructure, the right enabling conditions and a willingness to roll up our sleeves and get involved.

To me, this is what makes city life special – a deep sense of connection and neighbourhood. However, all too often the way our cities are designed doesn't facilitate this on an everyday basis. Oddly, we've managed to make one of our most important physical determinants of the city experience – the very infrastructure that enables us to connect to the city fabric as a whole – abstract and removed. Personally, I find 'infrastructure' one of the least sexy words in the English language – the kind of word that causes an instant glazed look in the eye; put simply, it's the foundational structures that keep the city functioning. When we unpack what it means for cities, it's what powers our lives: electricity, water, internet, transport, waste services and so on. Critical to a civilised, healthy society, it's front and centre of our daily experience yet so often invisible. But our lives without it would quickly become untenable – we immediately notice when train lines go down in Sydney, energy load shedding in Johannesburg or the water supply gets cut in Cape Town – or a whole lot more difficult, as is the experience of those city dwellers who don't have the means or ability to heat or cool their homes, connect to the internet, or access toilets and water indoors. As this book went to print, it was all too obvious in cities across South Africa that damage to infrastructure like telecoms, power networks and retail outlets can quickly bring urban areas to their knees, leaving them without a secure food supply, healthcare and other critical services.

To get around the prosaic, abstract nature of infrastructure, it can help to ascribe a slightly more romantic or metaphorical meaning to it. I suggest thinking of it as akin to our body's circulatory system, which we know is mission-critical as it carries oxygen, hormones and nutrients around the body and removes the by-products we don't need, like carbon dioxide.

To feel at home in our cities depends on connection: connection to self, to others, to the 'grid' and to place. Thankfully, there are plenty of examples of creatives bringing this to life, which helps to bridge the knowledge gap between infrastructure and people. We can turn to infrastructure as a means of enabling inclusive and integrated cities. To do this, we/communities need to participate in its design and implementation so that it makes sense for the real lived experience.

Taking a glass-half-full view of the turmoil of the Covid-19 pandemic, this is an exciting time to be spreading our urban roots. The pace of urban responses to the climate emergency shows how momentum can coalesce around one overarching challenge and build out to create happier, healthier lives for city dwellers both now and in the future. The response to the pandemic will, we hope, be another, and the early signs are promising. Our cities need to adapt if we are to survive; their carbon intensity needs to be drastically reduced and their resilience to extreme weather must be ready for at least an annual test. This plays out whether we deliberately design and scale urban centres, or they emerge from unplanned settlements.

The great challenges of our time demonstrate that a viable plan to pursue a resilient future isn't always waiting in the proverbial wings, nor is it always evident or prioritised by the institutions we depend on. But if, as communities, we become more connected to, and invested in, our neighbourhoods because of their impact on our health and happiness, then this is a prime time to deploy democracy in local decision-making. Examples of successful participatory planning, supported by bold, forward-thinking authorities at a city level, are coming thick and fast. Sadly, they don't always make headlines as they are competing for space with the bigger scandals and sensations of international and national politicking so we need to sharpen our antennae to keep them surfacing.

According to the Royal Institution of Chartered Surveyors' (RICS) *Cities, Health and Well-Being* report, priorities that are universally shared (that's among low-, middle- and high-income countries) include: lack of opportunities for physical activity in daily life (how we commute to work or school; working locations or patterns), noise and air pollution, access to affordable housing, climate resilience, building quality, access to greenspace, and child- and disability-friendly design. Historically, our institutions have supported a fantastic ability to design siloed solutions to networked problems. But creating connected places requires connected thinking, and the key to this is understanding the deep grounding factors at play in feeling at home in our cities: proximity to things we love, safe passage and connection to each other via infrastructure.

These are the things that connect us to where we live at a deep level. However, often we forget that these things are intertwined, so we separate out our responses and try to tackle each issue as an individual concern rather than a part of the urban infrastructure and how we experience our cities as a whole. Ultimately, if we start to make connections between our infrastructure and vision for our future cities, and seek out community voices, then we can design places that allow us to get into the roots of our neighbourhoods for a life well lived.

THE DONUT CITY

Cities that confine us to our four walls would be very dull indeed, as Covid-19 restrictions gave us a flavour of. Although we tend to spend a portion of every day complaining about other city dwellers we have to share our spaces with, when the chickens came home to roost, it turned out that we quite like sharing our urban centres with other humans after all. The pandemic seemed to have two extreme effects on our opinions on life in the city: either we hated it more and plotted to leave, or our urban roots became rock solid. Angela Clutton of the Borough Market Cookbook Club is certainly in the latter camp, remaining committed and ready for the buzz to resume. When Angela and I spoke, she commented drily that 'if I'd wanted to live in a place where I had one outing a day, ordered shopping and food online and couldn't go to a restaurant and order from a menu, I definitely wouldn't be living in London'. But with eyes firmly on the horizon, we are cautiously approaching a return to city life with more of a pulse and, to find it, we'll have to venture back outside.

With so much of our daily activity dependent on life outside the home (paid work, unpaid care labour, shopping, sport, eating and drinking out, school runs, and so on), it's no surprise that the pressure on cities to enable safe passage and depth of connection to others is growing. While our recreational and household-based movement tends to happen organically in easy reach of the home, accessing services, shops and healthcare tend to be more demanding on our time and patience. Moving about the city needs to keep pace with the public mood, and after so many months of contracted roaming distances, there is a hefty appetite for keeping things local.

City dwellers have all felt the frustration of travelling across the city; it's an ordeal. Fran Lebowitz commented on this in Netflix's series *Pretend it's a City*, quipping, 'No one in the subway system has any spirit left. They've beaten it out of us. It would take one subway ride for the Dalai Lama to turn into a lunatic.' The pandemic may have helped us out a little here as the lull in the usual pattern has prompted a constellation of initiatives across cities worldwide, taking the cue that our urban centres need to be both more welcoming and efficient. The rise of green and multimodal transport (multimodal referring to the mix of options available) systems can help us to get a better mix of exercise, social interaction, time outdoors and convenience as we travel from one place to another.

It's already the case that few of us depend on only one mode of transport – we walk, cycle, scoot, skate, take the bus, tram or train, and often a blend of several. These are all terrific options and, at the moment, the only remaining thorn in our side is the car. This isn't to say that the car will be extinct from urban centres any time soon, but as we're dealing with declining air quality and compressing space, the health and quality of our lives is being materially impacted by its ubiquitousness on our streets. Cities have addressed this in different ways: introducing low emission zones, levying congestion charges, pedestrianising centres and converting roads to cycle-only ways.

As we well know, physical activity is one of the dealbreakers when it comes to surviving and thriving in this era of latent lifestyle diseases and poor mental health. Leaving aside the hard core of fitness enthusiasts, the best – and most equitable – way to scale up physical activity is if it gets packaged up effortlessly into our lives. Ideally, it becomes so ingrained in our daily routines that we barely notice it. Incidental exercise is hardly groundbreaking – the Parisians have been on to this for years with their *à pied* ethos (apparently the unofficial secret to keeping the pounds off without going to the gym or giving up cheese). But as walking becomes trendier, we have a whole suite of glossy ways to talk about it: active design, walkability, donut cities or fifteen-minute cities – take your pick, they are all shades of the same future, and it's a bright one.

RICS has defined walkability as 'a combination of factors which make a neighbourhood easier and more convenient for pedestrians: street connectivity, land-use mix and residential density. Getting city dwellers moving reaps dividends for more than just our hearts and lungs: higher footfall through civic spaces makes us happier and more sociable, and deters crime and antisocial activity; motorised traffic decreases, improving air pollution and releasing space that would have been taken up by parking; free space can be revegetated to provide shade, sports and recreation facilities, and small-scale agriculture, which in turn provide a home and food for wildlife, and improve soil, air and water quality. Active people, as we saw in the Movement chapter, are less prone to lifestyle diseases, and the longer-term behaviour change that comes from embedding move- ment at the core of daily life is also likely to result in us becoming less dependent on our sofas and screens and more insular activities (although there's a time and a place for these, too).

Imagine the alternative ... with everything we need within walk- ing distance, we are out in our neighbourhood more often, observing and creating community, spending our money and our time in local streets, shops, bars and restaurants. We are less stressed because we don't have to run the gauntlet of commuting great distances each day, and we are seeing more of our loved ones. Our local economy grows, with small-scale traders and artisans able to get their wares in front of people because there is more footfall on the high streets. The traffic that remains on the roads becomes conditioned to seeing pedestrians and cyclists, and this impacts driver behaviour resulting in fewer injuries.

The University of Melbourne actually conducted a ten-year study on the mental and physical-health impacts of living where all we need from life is just a stroll out of the front door. They concluded that, by creating a community that you could form a connection to just by walking there, health-promoting behaviours became embed- ded more easily. Walkable neighbourhoods also contribute to higher property value, which has been seen in Sydney, with one property expert stating in *The Sydney Morning Herald* as much as a 20 per cent increase in value being attributed to the walkability factor in 2012. In a walkable city, all the major elements of life – summarised by Charles Montgomery at the beginning of this chapter – are available to us just beyond the doorstep.

But walkability depends on there being something worth walking to! We come back to wildness here, because our natural areas often sit at the nucleus of neighbourhoods. They are as natural a convener for humans as they are for animals; I find there to be an irresistible comparison between the average waterhole in the African bush and the average urban public park. At the waterhole, wildebeest and zebra mooch between waterbuck. Young impala ruck and play. There might be a bit of sidestepping past a cantankerous buffalo or an apex predator but, generally, the atmosphere is one of peaceful co-existence (as long as no one is hungry) and makes for gentle mixing and mingling. Visiting a local city park, there is the same ease and comfort about the way people from all walks of life mix. Lycra-clad cyclists weave around kids on tricycles; slackliners wobble along-side yogis holding headstands; dogs tumble past group meditations in pursuit of frisbees; families meet for coffee by the playground; friends bring a sound system and beers to the picnic tables. There is a harmony and companionship that comes from sharing these places with others; this is where we remind ourselves of the city's vitality.

There are some heartening recent examples that the civic value of parks is being recognised. Mayor Anne Hidalgo of Paris, one of our city visionaries, has approved a €250 million makeover of the city's most iconic avenue, the Champs-Élyseés. The best thing of all? The plan was developed with local community leaders and businesses, who agreed that 1.2 miles of road would far better serve the population as a vein of garden, stretching up through the city from the Arc de Triomphe. By 2024, it will also be home to Europe's largest rooftop farm. The Champs-Élyseés has long been Paris' centre of promenading and pageantry but, so says the architect behind the plans, Philippe Chiambaretta, Parisians have fallen out of love with it. According to Chiambaretta's architecture practice website, there are four strategic priorities underpinning the project:

'reducing the impact of urban mobilities, rethinking nature as an ecosystem, seeking new uses, and the use of data for measurement and regulation.' Bringing nature back in is central to this. The plans for the renewed avenue include reducing space for vehicles by half (the avenue is currently choked by pollution from passing traffic and the city's ring road), turning roads into pedestrian and green areas, and creating tunnels of trees to improve air quality. The plans alone are a joyous sight, with several green arms reaching out from the Arc de Triomphe, looking every bit like nature is stretching and unfurling through the city, which embraces her long-awaited return.

THE CITY COMPACTED

At the 2020 launch of the World Green Building Council's Health and Wellbeing Framework, WHO's Director of Public Health, Environment and Social Determinants, Dr Maria Neira, commented that greener and more compact cities are a universal goal, as applicable in the global south as they are in the north. Fundamental to the pedestrian, cyclist and motor-reduced city is phasing out the ubiquity of the car. Ghent in Belgium, Helsinki in Finland, Tempe in the USA and Birmingham in the UK are, according to an article in *Fast Company*, some of the cities helping their neighbourhoods wrestle back the streets for humans. This is significant because, as *Fast Company* notes, we spend far too much time in unmoving traffic (119 hours per year in Los Angeles, 9 whole days in Moscow).

The implications of compact cities also re-open the doors to the concept of street play for children and adults alike. Street play has diminished significantly in cities across the world as roads have carved up our spaces. My road in east London (happily, soon to be closed to through traffic) can, at the wrong time of day, be treacherous; although it's a residential street, it also happens to be a convenient rat run for drug dealers driving at breakneck speed. Twice, cars have been implanted in the buildings, so fast were they travelling. The character of our street is worth protecting – our street community includes a marble works, art galleries, a beloved Italian restaurant, a guitar workshop, a hairstylist, a pub and a warehouse restaurant whose street parties and drag competitions are legendary.

Across the world, we noticed that when our car traffic fell to almost nothing, children and grown-ups returned to the street to play and chat. In my part of London, one of the more peculiar decisions made early on in the UK's pandemic response (quickly reversed) was to close the public parks. (We can hazard a guess that the people who thought that was a good solution to minimising the spread of Covid-19 had private gardens and weren't climbing the walls like everyone else.) So, even more than ever before, street play was vital for urban children, the majority of whom had no access to private gardens (in the UK the Office for National Statistics reports that 21 per cent of Londoners had no access to a private or shared garden during the Covid-19 lockdown).

Street play has been restating its claim on urban streets for a while and its benefits are obvious. Children learn to be creative and sociable, and their improvised games impart the soft skills of working as a team, handling competition and solving problems. Playing Out, which was started by a group of parents in Bristol, has had such success that its model for street play has become a global, community-led effort to bring residential streets to life. Ghent, Belgium, has linked this with car-free days in the city, and Toronto, Canada, has championed the return of street hockey. Play in our cities helps to reinstate the sense of adventure and fun, which we know can disappear from our lives if we're not careful. Child in the City, reporting on the UK government's Street Play study, highlighted that playing out had made for happier communities, pulling some mothers out of postnatal depression, replacing screen-based activity and making the city friendlier. One adult involved in the project in north Tyneside said, 'Playing out has made my street feel like home.'

Reclaiming our streets in this way goes further than play, too. Bringing different social groups together in kinder spaces can bring some unintended consequences, as the Transition Streets in Newcastle, Australia, have found. Students and elderly residents on the same street had fractious relations due to different opinions on socially acceptable noise and hours. When Transition Streets (linked to Transition Towns) invited them all around the table, they realised that the older residents felt vulnerable to crime when walking on the street at night and the students were able to take an active role in looking out for them because of the later hours they kept.

So, in this way, compacted communities are far from confined: they are liberated and more connected than ever before – able to walk to meet their needs for work, shopping and fun, and able to create space for those incidental but vitally important moments of joy in their daily existence.

REBOOT THE COMMUTE

In a pre-pandemic life-as-I-knew-it scenario, the daily commute would begin with the usual toss-up about route and mode of transport – would I prefer to be under someone's armpit on the Central Line or chance my luck with a delayed Overground, which might take longer but at least I could stop to smell the roses (literally) in one of the overground gardens. Or, if I was feeling brave and decided to cycle, I'd be accompanied all the way by caffeine-fuelled internal chatter: had I picked the least hair-raising path to the office; where could I park my bike so it wouldn't get stolen; had I brought my towel with me to shower? And on it went. One of the most commonly cited positive outcomes of the lockdowns has been the demise of the commute, which has simplified and elongated many people's days.

The approach to commuting is in a state of evolution and now, ushered in by Covid-19, possibly revolution. In most large cities, travel from home to work has been one of the most stressful parts of our day. As we left our homes in the morning, we reluctantly submitted to a period of time that promised a mix of irritation, confinement and possibly even danger. But travelling through our cities doesn't need to be tantamount to suffering; it is perfectly possible for future commutes to become pleasurable parts of our day, enhancing rather than squashing our moods. We need the infrastructure that helps us to feel safe, relaxed and inquisitive rather than frazzled, sweaty and defensive. Journeys that are, to use Charles Montgomery's language, 'self-propelled' leave us far more likely to feel cheery and energised rather than pissed off at life and all humanity. Getting to this point will depend on embracing an urban future where the car doesn't run rings around us. Multimodal means of transport need to be readily available in the first and last mile, and it needs to be safe, reliable and affordable. To move from tolerable to pleasurable, a smart city with green infrastructure and an active transport model should promote inclusion, social interaction and even give a platform to celebrate local businesses and community initiatives that improve quality of life. Some cities are experimenting with rewards for travellers who use green transport corridors, spend money with small local businesses along the way and contribute time or goods in kind to those who need it (such as older or disadvantaged members of the community).

Cities are the stage for regenerative ways of living because they are the site of 80 per cent of GDP, nearly two-thirds of the global population, more than 70 per cent of global carbon dioxide emissions and most new infrastructure development. Emerging or secondary cities going through rapid urbanisation can be spared the pain of first creating a 'take-make-waste' model that leads to severely degraded environments and stressed-out, unhealthy populations. Applying regenerative principles from the get-go can help cities leapfrog past this icky, transitional stage that cities like New York, Paris and London find themselves in now, and aim directly for a restorative model. We need to be looking towards emerging cities, as well as those that have been developed with innovation and holistic thinking in their DNA.

In this regard, the Ellen MacArthur Foundation points particularly to China. The challenge of air pollution in Chinese cities is well documented, and fewer than 1 per cent of China's 500 largest cities currently meet the air-quality standards recommended by WHO. The Ellen MacArthur Foundation estimates that scaling up the circular economy (in brief, an economy that is designed to be regenerative rather than linear, where economic growth doesn't come at the expense of the environment and scarce natural resources) in cities in China could reduce emissions of particulate matter by 50 per cent (particulates are the invisible particles we breathe in that collect in our lungs, disrupt our endocrine system (hormones) and contribute to respiratory illnesses, cancer and poor reproductive health). Circular economy approaches could also reduce carbon emissions by 23 per cent and cut traffic by 47 per cent. As home to some of the world's biggest cities, we can look to China's innovation and leadership when it comes to urban mobility.

Technological innovation is strong in China's cities and has encouraged the sharing economy to flourish. Where car-share and similar schemes may have struggled and waned in European cities, according to the Ellen MacArthur Foundation, China's sharing economy accounts for approximately 10 per cent of its GDP. Although consumer habits can take time to change, alternative models like car-share clubs show that the aspiration for private car ownership can quickly be dismantled if there are good alternatives to be found. Chinese urbanites mostly value safe, punctual, flexible and reliable mobility; they're not fussed that their journeys must be made by private car.

Yichang in China has been so successful in scaling up multimodal transport that journeys made in private cars dropped by 12 per cent within two years of its mobility schemes becoming operational, and use of public transport almost doubled. The steps seem simple, but they all need to fit together for it to work. The first mile and last mile will make all the difference in how we choose to make our journeys. Yichang's bus rapid transit forms a 'backbone' through the city, connecting all major transport modes (train, high-speed rail, long-distance buses and so on). Pedestrian and cycle routes and facilities have been prioritised for the last mile and there are enough bike points that people are not worried about where they need to dismount as there will always be a terminal within 400m. Those using the Vélib' in Paris, Citi Bike in New York or Santander Bikes in London might identify with the pain of cycling around in panic looking for a terminal only to realise the zone finished several blocks back, by which point we're frustrated, sweaty and late for whatever appointment we thought we would so virtuously cycle to. As well, the pedestrian routes in Yichang are not just walkable – they also integrate artwork, greenspace and soft landscaping along the way. Use of this kind of transport hinges on social acceptance and behavioural change, which depends on a welcoming, user-friendly experience as much as speed. As the Ellen MacArthur Foundation report on China points out, investment in a holistic transport system can be demanding in terms of up-front capital expenditure; local authorities alone can't achieve this and need financial support from public–private partnerships to make it happen. However, a global will is emerging, as can be evidenced in many parts of the world.

Ethiopia announced its Non-Motorised Transport strategy in 2020, which is working towards a more equal, sustainable and inclusive approach to all elements of city design. By 2030, Addis Ababa aims to make 80 per cent of all motorised trips available on public transport, and 60 per cent of all journeys to be non-motorised. It goes further: the plan aims to boost gender parity – as more public transport options can increase women's workforce participation – and recognises that increased uptake of non-motorised travel could reduce pedestrian and cyclist deaths by 80 per cent and bring city ambient air quality to 95 per cent of WHO's standards. In a similar vein, Kampala, Uganda, is also piloting a motor-free transport corridor. Although Kampala starts from a higher base as the most physically active country in the world, it still lacks safe and accessible public spaces within walking distance, and infrastructure to support walking and cycling has a long way to go, despite surges in cycling during the initial stages of the Covid-19 pandemic. The city hopes to remedy this by repurposing a 2km arterial road through the city centre as a pedestrian and bike zone.

The commute is central to connected cities, so if we can crack this then it can have a range of knock-on benefits that reach far beyond just how easily and quickly we get to work. It is clear that, whether we are looking at Asia or Africa, Britain or Belgium, offering city dwellers travel options that also promote health and vitality of urban connection can only be a good thing.

SAFE PASSAGE

Feeling welcome in the city depends on whether it assures safe passage for everyone, and personal safety is an issue for women in cities the world over. Nanjala Nyabola, author of *Travelling While Black*, asks whether she can show up in a city in her trainers and hit the ground running, and uses this as a personal benchmark of urban safety.

The murder of Sarah Everard while she walked home in London in early 2021 left cities in the UK and Europe reeling. I was in South Africa at the time, where I was already making daily decisions about when it was safe to go to the beach and which running route I should take to ensure maximum visibility, and when to alter it so my routine wasn't obvious. Friends in London and Paris were on edge; WhatsApp groups were pinging overtime with everybody asking their friends and family to confirm, from now on, when they'd reached the safety of home, and reminding them to take cabs instead of walking or public transport. From official channels, the usual precautionary advice began to circulate – don't go out alone, don't stay out late, don't wear headphones, don't, don't, don't ... As a woman, a city dweller and a tax payer, I find it maddening that the trade-off between safety and freedom is ingrained in our lives – and the costs (financial, psychological and quality of life) are borne by us. In an article in *The Conversation* in March 2021, Hannah Bows aptly refers to this as another 'gender-specific tax' that women pay. We need to recognise that our critical infrastructure doesn't have our backs and be prepared to hold our leaders to account for this. I bristled as the promises emanating from the British government pointed to knee-jerk attempts to triage symptoms (for instance, placing plain-clothed police officers in our nightclubs or lighting up our parks). These 'solutions' completely miss the point. Lighting won't stop women from being victims because it does nothing to remedy the underlying culture that leads to gender violence in the first place.

Interestingly, from a planning perspective, a web of unintended consequences sits beneath assertions that lighting is the answer. The Cities at Night project, which investigates urban light pollution as seen from space, cautions that we're often getting it wrong. They show that more lighting can be overpowering and disorientating for people as well as wildlife, making opportunities for crime worse rather than better. Their website compares different examples of street lighting aimed at improving public safety. Scarily, in the example solution that we'd most commonly leap to, the increase in light sets the footpath aglow but, in doing so, makes it impossible to see that there is a person lurking immediately under the lamp. We should be wary of the effect of these band-aid solutions on our wellbeing as well. Light pollution, alongside noise and air pollution, 'is damaging to our health and interferes with our ability to rest and sleep'.

If transit in cities was an issue before Covid-19 (and we know it was – sexual violence often goes hand in hand with our experience of travelling in urban centres), the picture has only been made worse in the months of the pandemic. A 2021 UN Women policy brief reflects on the deterioration in mobility options since the outbreak of the pandemic and its link to an increase in sexual violence against women. The document clarifies that sexual violence includes unwelcome sexual remarks, looks, gestures and touching, attempted rape, rape and femicide. A report by the All Party Parliamentary Group for UN Women in 2021 set out the overwhelming evidence of threats to women's safety in the UK's public spaces and particularly on public transport. In the UK, 71 per cent of women of all ages have experienced some form of sexual harassment in a public space. This number rises to 86 per cent among 18–24-year-olds. Beyond transport, wider urban infrastructure that fails women is still a real threat that plays out in cities everywhere. In Cape Town in 2016, for instance, 21-year-old Sinoxolo Mafevuka was raped and strangled when she visited her nearest communal latrine. These risks to life are commonplace in informal settlements, where indoor plumbing and other domestic utilities tend to be absent.

It's widely understood that women modify their behaviour as a matter of safety, but without a sharp nudge from innovators in our community, our infrastructure is often slow to modify in support of our lives. To address this, ElsaMarie D'Silva co-founded SafeCity, a tech platform that analyses crowdsourced, anonymous reports of violent crime in cities. The largest platform of its kind in the world, SafeCity covers India, Kenya and Nepal, among others, and was created in reaction to the gang rape of Jyoti Singh as she travelled through Delhi on a bus in 2012. By bridging the data gap in official gender violence reporting, SafeCity's data can translate directly to the democratisation of public spaces through far greater understanding of how our neighbourhoods are being used.

Reflecting on the power of data, Elsa notes that sharing the data with city authorities in Mumbai and Delhi has led to more police patrols, with the timings altered to coincide with the time of reported spikes in crime. One case in point:

> At Lal Kuan, an urban village in Delhi, our data identified a hotspot where there was a lack of access to public toilets and women were harassed while relieving themselves in the bushes. The public toilets in that locality were locked because local authorities were not willing to maintain and clean them. SafeCity's data and the media pressured authorities to re-open and maintain the public toilets.

The threats to women's safety in cities are pervasive, and they persist because of repeated institutional and social failure to take our needs seriously. The city – and in this I include its institutions, communities and individuals – needs to take collective ownership of the safety threats that women have long internalised.

We need to start by asking who is in power, who holds the institutional reins and who is making the decisions about the systems that dictate how our lives play out. A recent example of how ugly this can get is in Canberra, Australia, where gender violence (both acts of and sanctioning of) has been traced all the way to the federal parliamentary staff. Speaking to *The Sydney Morning Herald* in March 2021, Catherine Lumby, media professor at the University of Sydney said, 'To be a feminist you have to be an optimist.' And the optimist in me tells me we have reached a tipping point on the issue of sexual assault as the vast majority of Australians are outraged by what they see going on in the building that allegedly houses their leaders. Australia's parliament is not alone in this, and nor is this a new issue. Former Australian Prime Minister Julia Gillard's speech in 2012 went viral as a trenchant observation of the barriers facing women. Why is this relevant? If we want diversity in leadership, we need to understand the reality of the obstacles to embedding women at all levels of political, economic, social and community decision-making. The Canberra example shows us that there are still those in leadership who object to sharing this decision-making power with women.

WAVE, an Asia-Pacific-focused women's leadership programme, funded by the Dutch government, emphasises the link between gender-based violence and the statistics on women's leadership. Globally, women represent 24 per cent of participation in parliaments – astonishing when our international frameworks enshrine safe, free and full public participation as a human right. Until we rebalance this, we will continue to see decisions being made that fail to prioritise the needs of vulnerable communities in our cities – where the pressures and risks are at their most acute. In a November 2020 article for Soroptimist International, Berthe De Vos reflected on the ripple effect of women in leadership on society. Women 'have a different approach to leadership. By giving more attention to social welfare and legal protections, they will improve trust, yield the economy and add equal value alongside their male counterparts.' We've seen this in Rwanda, where, according to the UN, increasing the number of women in leadership has led to significant improvements in public health. Looking at how the world recovers from the destabilisation of Covid-19, Phumzile Mlambo-Ngcuka, executive director of UN Women, reminds us of the implications of this inequality in a statement in 2021: 'It is inconceivable that we can address the most discriminatory crisis we have ever experienced without full engagement of women ... At the moment, men have given themselves the impossible task of making the right decisions about women without the benefit of women's insights.'

We need to question the responses of the people in power who think that tweaks in the margins are sufficient to remedy the experience of being a woman and a city dweller.

DESIGNING THE COMPASSIONATE CITY

Moving beyond safety, we can't hold cities up as the paragons of an inclusive future if they are geared up as urban playgrounds for men. It seems unjustifiable that women, who make up near to 50 per cent of the world's population, and often bear the brunt of climate change and poor urban planning, can end up without a seat at the table when it comes to making the decisions that affect how they live their lives in the city. The novel idea (with tongue firmly in cheek) of creating a city that works for women as well as men began in Vienna in the 1990s. Long before the gendered impact of the built environment design was considered anywhere else, Vienna was trailblazing the way. To do so, they needed data, hence the City Women's Office was established. Caroline Criado Perez, in her incisive book *Invisible Women*, emphasises that data is at the heart of entrenched gender bias. Vienna's City Women's Office found that men favoured cars and bikes, while women preferred walking and public transport. This was not a matter of personal preference but rather because of the biases in the way work (paid and non-paid) was divided between men and women. Men typically had simple routines – they travelled to conventional workplaces from the home and back again – whereas women's routines had greater variability due to unpaid care labour, which includes looking after children, shopping, domestic work, visiting elderly relatives and so on.

Another Viennese example is the Frauen-Werk-Stadt (Women-Work-City) I and II housing complexes. Again, these were well ahead of the game and they offer lessons that most modern cities can learn from. These female-designed residential spaces (the largest example of female-friendly residential and urban development in Europe) have the everyday needs of women at their heart, including green-space for children to play within a moment's reach of their front door, essential services like doctor's surgeries, pharmacies and nurseries in the complex, provision for assisted living in old age and rapid access to public transport networks. Similarly, the planners behind

Berlin's gender mainstreaming city plan have noted that a compact city eases the issues around balancing careers and caring.

Intelligent city leaders are recognising the opportune moments, pauses or inflections in public sentiment, that they can harness to accelerate innovation and experiment with ways of reconfiguring how the city looks, feels and acts. In many ways, Covid-19 has helped to build a consensus that public space is central to public health. Cities such as Barcelona have moved swiftly to capitalise on this by launching a renewed plan to reclaim greenspace in the city and prioritise communities over cars. Barcelona, which has the highest density of cars in the EU (6,000 per square kilometre or 60 per cent of its total surface area), is already in the midst of an impressive transformation. Its streets have become prime candidates for 'tactical urbanism' through seizing opportunities to reclaim roads for pedestrians and bikes by using giant planters that close roads to through traffic. Using its superblock strategy – which groups city blocks in clusters of nine – the city is closing blocks to passing traffic, swapping parking space for greenspace, play areas and cycle ways. There are six superblocks already in action, with some promising results. The Sant Antoni *barrio* has seen an 80 per cent reduction in traffic, a 33 per cent reduction in nitrogen dioxide pollution and a 5-decibel drop in noise in its two-year history. Public support for the *barrios* continues to soar, with residents describing a kind of utopic paradise where neighbours of all ages gather daily to eat and play games, and help one another with homework, childcare and dog walking. Residents have commented on the profound impact that placing picnic tables and benches has had on the feeling of ownership, pride and social attachment to their outside space.

Responses can be mixed but, if town planners correctly read the room, the wins can be quick and meaningful, as seen in Addis Ababa, Barcelona and Paris. The situation can be very different depending on city tensions and, while the goals of compact cities are set with health and kindness in mind, the transition period can be triggering. Oaklands, California, was one of the early adopters of Slow Streets – essentially using blockades to cut off or minimise traffic – and closed about 10 per cent of the city's road network to cars in April 2020. Mayor Libby Schaaf, taking advantage of the lull in traffic during the initial Covid-19 lockdown, observed to *Bloomberg* that 'closing roads means opening up our city'. While this more forceful approach to compassionate living was grounded in empathy and a mandate for climate action, latent urban, social and racial tensions were not accounted for in the rapid roll-out. As Laura Bliss of CityLab and author of the *Bloomberg* piece observed, resistance to the Slow Streets emerged because the changes hit a sore spot in a uniquely sensitive moment. As Black Lives Matter ignited global outrage and ethnic minorities were being disproportionately affected by Covid-19, unilateral decisions that affected the lives of minority groups without including the voices of the community were bound to attract controversy. The importance of deep listening carries across any city, and Oakland's lessons are useful for us all. Since the early stage of the roll-out, the focus has shifted to co-ownership, and Oakland planners are working with local non-profits and community representatives to choose their own Slow Streets, and create signage that visually chimes with the identity of the neighbourhood (new signs feature a scraper bike and Black girls running, for example).

On the flip side, Jamie Lerner, former mayor of Curitiba, Brazil, has spoken candidly about having to work quickly to beat the resistance. His first project in 1972, which aimed at pedestrianising the Rua Quinze de Novembro and increasing public greenspace, attracted the wrath of shopkeepers, all of whom had been engaged in the plan. Their resistance was to culminate in a judicial injunction, which would have dissolved the project. Controversial as it seems, Lerner's planning philosophy is 'act now, adjust later'; beginning stealthily one Friday night when the courthouse closed, he and his team completed the project in seventy-two hours instead of four months. In a 2017 interview with Change Agents 'Building a Shared Dream', he commented that he would 'rather have graceful imperfection than graceless perfection'. Speaking of the paralysis that can come from bureaucracy and fear of innovation, he says, 'Planning is a process that can always be corrected if we pay attention to feedback from the people. We should imagine the ideal, but do what is possible today.' For this, we need leaders who can act decisively on strategic issues that create more equitable, liveable urban centres, but who are also committed to tweaking the granular detail with communities directly. Curitiba's somewhat technocratic story is a living example of the success of this strategy, and the city has been held as a model of sustainable urban planning ever since. Sometimes these bold moves need to seize their moment for the sake of the greater good, though this only works when we have honest, switched-on, empathetic leaders who are invested in the communities they are serving.

What many of these solutions have in common is their attempt to salvage our deteriorating urban air quality. Cleaning the air is about more than just burning less or burning better. Instead, it depends on us looking for solutions that deliver on multiple counts – the actions that address the root cause of the problem rather than triaging the symptoms. With the ambition of net zero carbon becoming louder, businesses and cities have some big decisions to make. Do we go big on the 'next' step in the process of decarbonising the car (making them driverless and electric) or do we skip this expensive staging post and accept that the future city is a coup in which the car has been dethroned? Do we redirect the capital that is currently flowing into research and development for these technological panaceas or do we make our goals bigger, hairier and more audacious, to borrow Jim Collins' and Jerry Porras' phrase?

Given its impact on our lives and how we understand and interact with it, energy is worth specific mention when it comes to our city homes. Speaking to Tortoise Media during a breakfast interview in 2021, Keith Anderson, the CEO of Scottish Power, quipped that 'utilities are the new black'. Getting closely acquainted with our critical infrastructure isn't just fascinating, it's one of the routes to levelling out the inequalities in the urban playing field. My conversation with the pioneering Aga Otero sparked a chat about community action networks and co-operatives of all kinds, from food all the way through to energy (we heard about his Energy Garden in the Wilderness chapter). Speaking from extensive experience in creating conscious, connected neighbourhoods he observed that co-operatives show what we are capable of as a population: 'While their scale may be small and localised, they help to guide behaviour change, build resilience, and shift residents towards community networking and awareness of their surrounding context because the infrastructure our daily lives depend on is embedded into the community.'

Taking renewable energy as an example, Aga reflected that the biggest per capita reduction in energy consumption will be achieved through behaviour change; yet, in the British context, with less than 1 per cent of energy infrastructure owned by the British population, our sense of public connection to the system is remote to say the least. If we feel that we have no say over our most vital infrastructure, he says, we tend to have limited interest in it. The reverse is also true: if we have a sense of ownership and participation in where our power is produced, by what means and by whom, we will have far greater interest in how it gets used. Through Aga's astute and sensitive stewardship, and willingness to invest in true community leaders, Energy Garden has brought the story of energy home, landing it in front of our noses in our overground stations and community gardens (he has planted more than 200,000 square metres of track-side land in London and will scale it out to other cities). 'The premise,' he concludes, 'is simple – if we have a relationship with our community, we will have a more profound experience of living.' This clear narrative can help to crystallise the type of change that is within our power.

It helps also to be reminded what is at stake here and we can help ourselves out by asking what we stand to gain, rather than what we stand to lose. A city that is walkable and liveable is one that offers children the chance to play and socialise safely from a young age; it is an attractive place to live in advancing age; it keeps essential care services within our neighbourhood; and it helps us to stay active, sociable and connected with the wilderness. At the heart of a compassionate city is the concept that everyone's needs have to be planned in.

PLANT-POWERED DEMOCRACY

The gritty truth is that urban environments can exacerbate health inequities, where residents may have little opportunity to escape unhealthy living and working conditions. City dwellers in low- and middle-income countries are particularly vulnerable because of limited access to clean water and sanitation, secure and permanent housing, and essential services. In Africa, where the world's youngest and most rapidly expanding population is flocking to the city, the World Bank estimates that there will be more than 1 billion urbanised Africans by 2042. The emerging megacities (cities with a population of 10 million plus) face a long list of challenges: from climate stress, spatial planning, land use and land conversion, to public-health crises like Ebola, mosquito-borne diseases and Covid-19, to land subsidence, air and water pollution, flooding and weak infrastructure. While African cities are not alone in their experience of disasters, exposure to the direct impacts of sea-level rise and severe storms associated with climate change is disproportionately felt by those in unplanned settlements – where, according to 2015 UN data, 40 per cent of the urban population lives. As migration towards urban centres increases, so too does competition for land, which leads to settlements springing up in unsuitable environments, such as flood-prone wetlands and low-lying coastal areas, or on steep slopes that are at risk from landslides and erosion – where the ground can fall out from beneath residents' feet.

In Dar es Salaam, Tanzania's fastest growing city, 2020 figures from the World Bank approximate that 70 per cent of urban development is unplanned and a quarter of Dar residents live in the Msimbazi river basin – an area that suffers from severe and frequent flooding. In 2018, the flooding was so bad that the government called a state of emergency and the city ground to a halt. In just three days, the flood was estimated to have caused economic losses of over US$100 million. While this used to be a once-in-a-generation event, Dar es Salaam flooded twelve more times between 2017 and 2020. In developing a response that recognised the disproportionate suffering of those living in the Msimbazi river basin, local insight and ecological knowledge were critical. As reported by the South African Institute of International Affairs, the Tanzania Urban Resilience Program that emerged in response to the disaster addressed this by launching the Msimbazi Charette. The Charette combined the local knowledge and insights of communities with scientific evidence to develop a flood mitigation plan, meaning that both planners and the community were informed of the risks. This type of process needs to become normalised in cities. Retrofitted solutions are necessary but, ideally, we need to ensure that climate resilience and urban health is addressed from the get-go. This is a challenge when we consider the lightning speed of urbanisation.

In my research for this book, I caught up with Ben Bolgar MVO, of the Prince's Foundation, who had designed a rapid planning exercise in Bo, Sierra Leone's second-largest city. The Foundation's work on rapid planning focuses on secondary cities because this is where the most significant growth will occur. In 2020, the Foundation launched the Rapid Urbanisation Planning (RUP) Toolkit to help town planners get ahead of the pace of informal settlements. When unplanned, settlements become an economic drain. This basic plan gives citizens a better chance of a higher quality of life, because with structured spaces they can safely travel across town and their food security is protected as their natural environments remain intact.

Population growth projections combined with migration towards urban centres could mean a near tripling in urban landmass from 2000 to 2030. When thinking about what our cities could and should look like, we also have to take on board the need for dramatic reduction in carbon emissions by 50–60 per cent. As Ben says, there is simply no way we can achieve this if we don't plan our urban spaces. As dry and abstract as town planning can seem to an average city dweller, 'it is not just bureaucratic nonsense. If we do not plan our cities, we are stuffed.' Without planning, we end up with informal settlements that are difficult to move and trigger issues of displacement, personal security, and quality of land and waterways. Right now, a lack of forward thinking prevents us from protecting our health and biosphere at the scale we need. Left unfettered, the rapid city-creep we are witnessing the world over threatens precious biodiversity and our ability to reduce greenhouse gas emissions, and with this comes knock-on impacts to our wellbeing. Often this is because urbanisation has a 'run before you can walk' feel about it, in that cities grow faster than those who are in charge of them can envision how they should look and feel.

As Ben commented when we chatted, the irony in all this is that our most rapidly growing places have the least professional resources in their arsenal. The likes of London and New York continue to grow slowly but they also have the highest concentration of built-environment professionals (engineers, architects and landscape architects, consultants and so on). As a result of this imbalance in the distribution of professional resources, we tend to focus on tweaks in the margins of our existing cities rather than looking at secondary cities in low- and middle-income countries where half the projected growth is occurring. Working with the Commonwealth Sustainability Cities Programme, the Prince's Foundation has a vision to empower local mayors and leaders in secondary cities to implement bare-bones plans. In Bo, the population is projected to triple in the next twenty years, taking it from 180,000 to 540,000 citizens. Having started the rapid planning process in late January 2020, within seven months the city had adopted and implemented a charter for growing the city.

Describing the process of an urban centre developing, Ben explained:

> As neighbourhoods emerge, they are structured around centres. The centre will tend to have a primary school, shop, market and so on, and will be bounded by watercourses and/or greenspace. The bare bones plan offers a plan to protect primary roads, public sites like markets and schools, and critical habitat.

The work in Bo began in the north-west of the city, where most deforestation was happening, with the first step being the creation of a locally agreed plan. Ben reflected that, in the initial workshops, community support for the programme was driven by the loss of one of their local children who was hit by a car in the settlement weeks before. Once agreed, 700 trees were planted to protect routes and boundaries. One of the biggest lessons our cities in the global north can learn from this is that infrastructure should not lead the process; emerging cities in the global south can begin with protecting routes, and infrastructure will flow from this. Marking out routes is a crucial way that we can get trees involved in our urban environments. Planting is softer, diplomatic and democratic because it appeals to bureaucrats, school children and communities. Trees, says Ben, are 'non-threatening, immediately deployable and non-egregious' – the antithesis of many of our planning processes. Once neighbourhoods have been marked out democratically in this way, they almost become self-policing because communities are invested and become the protectors.

In many cases of rapid urbanisation, Ben observed that planning tends to follow development, which means that planners are more typically mapping what is happening. Obviously, this is not the point of a planner! The RUP Toolkit is potentially a game-changer because its aim is to protect valuable routes, encourage adoption of a city charter to protect and shape neighbourhoods, and – most crucially – be implementable within a year. It helps planners to understand the local context and shape what comes next. The vision is to create a basic framework to allow any type of settlement to be structured around walkable neighbourhoods and to allow corridors and edges to be protected for future investment. By doing all of this, the toolkit allows for a prosperous city. Bo also shows that walkable neighbourhoods are a universal possibility and are even more important in low-income countries, where injury and death statistics of pedestrians due to road traffic are sobering. The city's neighbourhood strategy shows the charisma and democratic power of trees which become part of the foundation of the city. It also highlights how thoughtful planning can sow the seeds for compact and connected cities.

THE RACE TO REVEGETATE

Trees and other plants – the green infrastructure mix – are so important to how we think about infrastructure and connection in the city
that it is worth looking a little more closely at them. Restoring vegetation is especially critical in hotter, drier climates, which are also
facing rapid deforestation. Australia (aptly nicknamed 'the sunburnt
country') is one example, and stripping out forests is so rampant it's
now a global deforestation hotspot. The impacts of deforestation
are far-reaching but here are a few: it displaces Indigenous peoples,
extinguishing their connection to land and associated ecological
knowledge; it decimates habitat and wildlife populations; it causes
desertification and topsoil erosion; and it opens up new vectors for
disease and pathogens.

Our cities aren't immune to these impacts – many are also suffering from receding vegetation, sprawling suburbs and road networks,
and swelling urban population, all of which contribute to the 'urban
heat island effect'. As Australian summers get hotter, drier and
angrier, cities that fail to restore natural habitat face considerable
public-health risks. *Foreground*, a partnership publication with the
Australian Institute of Landscape Architects, explains the benefits of
green infrastructure succinctly:

> Planting moderates temperatures and lowers energy use and
> energy infrastructure loads. Pleasant, cooler environments
> change transport use with more walking and cycling which
> reduces pressure on road and rail infrastructure. Because [green
> infrastructure] lowers temperatures, improves soil moisture
> retention, and mitigates pollution and dust spread, it reduces
> piped water use for irrigation, cleaning and general home use.

In Sydney and Melbourne, the Cool Streets© initiative, founded by
architect Libby Gallagher, uses software to model streetscapes and
advise on the best planting options, including the types of trees and
the best layout to reduce carbon dioxide and increase shade. The

logic behind Cool Streets© is that streets comprise up to 50 per cent of urban areas, so they're a prime target to boost canopy cover. The projects under way in Sydney and Melbourne suburbs prove the point – they offer seven times more carbon dioxide reduction than standard street design and reduce household electricity bills by over A$400 per annum.

Trees are only one part of the 'green mix' – other plants are essential to deliver a network of benefits. The Max Planck Institute of Chemistry, suspecting that the slightly less sexy categories of algae, lichens and mosses might be underappreciated, looked into their role in the city and their findings are astonishing: algae, mosses and lichens (also called cryptogamic covers) are like sponges, soaking up approximately 14 billion tons of carbon dioxide and fix approximately 50 million tons of nitrogen per year. To put these numbers into perspective, they collectively capture and store as much carbon dioxide as is released annually from burning forests and other biomass. Using such plants, either by incorporating them into our new buildings or, where they already exist, leaving them alone, is an exciting opportunity in landscape architecture.

Planting is one of the most manifest demonstrations of local government and city leaders taking up the mantle of climate action while national governments dither on the side lines. The declaration of a climate emergency was led by cities, and local responses have leaned into the 'soft' assets of communities connected to nature. Many Australian cities are working to restore vegetation, again showing that they tend to be closer and more responsive to the lived experience of city dwellers. Canberra, Australia's 'bush capital', is managed as an urban forest, and Melbourne is aiming to green its iconic laneways and increase canopy cover in the city to 40 per cent by 2040.

As we saw in Bo, Sierra Leone, trees have become a vital tool for democratic and participatory decision-making about our spaces. In Palo Alto, California, urban forest stewardship is a matter of great civic pride. Beyond the beauty of Palo Alto's treescape and network of gardens, the town's managing arborist, Dave Docker, in an article for the Pacific Horticulture Society, has pointed to other less obvious benefits, like amiable neighbourly relationships; he says that 'lower levels of fear, meanness, and violence; and reduced symptoms of ADHD in children can be attributed to an abundance of trees'. These examples show how we can build on the wilderness that we explored earlier and make green planning integral to our urban infrastructure and at the heart of how people make practical and emotional connections in the city.

COOLING THE FLAMES

As *Foreground* notes, traditionally our cities have proliferated the planting of 'regularly spaced, non-native, single-species, street trees'. While this planting may look neat and inoffensive, its benefits in biodiversity and biomass terms are severely limited. Vastly increased planting, with a mix of greenery that moves beyond an outmoded human-centric aesthetic, is fundamental to this transition and, following the magnitude of Australia's Black Summer bushfires in 2019–20, greening the urban environment is mission critical for health, especially because 90 per cent of Australians live in cities. According to the *Medical Journal of Australia*, the smoke from the 2019–20 fires was responsible for 417 excess deaths, 1,124 hospitalisations for cardiovascular problems and 2,027 for respiratory problems, and 1,305 presentations to emergency departments with asthma.

Greening, though, goes far beyond reconnecting us to the wild or making our everyday connections of road, rail, bike or boot healthier. Designing green infrastructure is intrinsic to resilient cities – a resilience that is being called on ever more frequently worldwide, and one that is likely to be crucial in facing the challenges yet to come.

During 2020, fires raged across the world from the Aegean to the Amazon, Chernobyl to China, the Canary Islands to Kerala, Madrid to Mount Kilimanjaro – throughout provinces and into cities – and apocalyptic scenes were reported from fires in and around Athens, Greece, in 2021. Not all fires are natural disasters, but certainly the Centre for

Climate and Energy Solutions has concluded that climate change has played a key role in exacerbating wildfires in the western US.

Natural disasters intensified by our changing climate are tragic not only because of the cost to human life, but also because they shatter populations of vulnerable species of wildlife. Our fortunate position at the top of the food chain means that wildlife is at the mercy of how we humans choose to respond to climate change. We have to ask ourselves whether we have the empathy to take small actions that cost us very little but mean that our animals also have a home for generations to come. If cities have accelerated the loss of vegetation, either directly due to expansion or indirectly by being the seat of decision-making power, they need to take up the mantle of remedying these losses. Politicians may not be ready for this level of responsibility, but the public, multilateral agencies and philanthropic bodies certainly are, as are many businesses and investors.

The impacts of a changing climate are not bounded by species or city limits and, again, we can return to the example of Australia's bushfires to see this. Over 1 billion animals are estimated to have been killed in Australia's Black Summer fires, with 18,983,588 hectares of land burned. Following the fires, a research team, writing in the *Journal of Safety Science and Resilience*, pointed to the alarming ability of smoke to travel, highlighting that:

> a blanket of smoke from the Australian fires covered the whole South Island of New Zealand on 1 January 2020. People as far south as Dunedin reported smelling smoke in the air. The smoke moved over the North Island the following day and affected glaciers in the country, giving a brown tint to the snow. By 7 January 2020, the smoke was carried approximately 11,000 kms across the South Pacific Ocean to Chile, Argentina, Brazil, and Uruguay.

When it comes to poor air quality, pregnant women and children are particularly vulnerable to its impacts. Studies conducted in China and Salt Lake City, USA, now show a link between air pollution and rates of miscarriage, and WHO has declared that poor air quality can affect children's lung growth and brain development, and increase risk of asthma. Air quality in cities is, for many, an everyday concern, but it is also one that can be exacerbated by climate shocks, such as those seen during recent fires in California and Australia, and the less-discussed moorland fires in Manchester, UK, in 2018 – the pollution from which researchers, in a study published by Environmental Research Communications, found had reached 5 million people.

COLLECTIVE DREAMS

One of the routes to connecting people to where they live and giving them a sense of autonomy over their environment is through the neighbourhood-planning movement. Lobbying local governments and planners can be ineffective because most of our local authorities are too overstretched and under-resourced. This is why we might feel disempowered. Ben Bolgar highlights the role of minor, practical interventions that can make marked improvements to quality of life. Community-based action is a powerful tool here because it is propelled by local residents who understand, and have a living interest in, their local environment. It might be as simple as opening up new routes to cyclists or introducing a pedestrian crossing. Ben observed that these simple, implementable solutions 'sit somewhere between guerrilla tactics and bureaucratic processes'.

In the Project for Lean Urbanism, the late Hank Dittmar, former CEO of the Prince's Foundation, spoke of the Pink Zone ('where small is possible') which sought to concentrate resources on 'enabling small-scale, community-centred development and revitalization' – solutions that have a major positive impact on communities but are below the threshold of bureaucracy because they are not big enough to be invested in (like benches and street planters).

Because planning tends to be complex, multi-disciplinary and long term, single issues tend to do well. For example, bike-share schemes in cities have taken off primarily because they are simple and achievable in the short term. The beauty of neighbourhood planning is in their focus: take three or four good ideas, Ben advises, agree the priority list, commit to practical, simple solutions and make it happen quickly. He continues, 'This instils more faith in the process. We need to flip the trend of planners being bureaucratic form fillers towards doing and implementing. Successful neighbourhood plans in Kentish Town and Highgate, London, for example, won favour because they focused on a handful of important sites and issues. Community-level planning workshops identified simple solutions like bike lanes to increase local mobility and placing benches on the high street ... to create shared public spaces. The key was the simplicity.'

To borrow phraseology from Ben and his colleagues, who I'm told developed this over a beer near their Shoreditch studios, when it comes to planning, 'abstraction is the enemy'. Planning processes need to be relatable, but they also occur at two levels: local government or landowner level, and community level. To explain it, Ben suggests we think of it in terms of applying universal principles and local solutions. At the top-down level, planners should understand the strategic issues and be able to make the planning idea popular with the local population. Returning to the example in Bo, Sierra Leone, the idea to be popularised was the importance of protecting thoroughfares for basic services. Ben recounted that, during his time in Bo, the community understood the importance of protecting vital routes and services with reference to a local child dying the week before and the ambulance not being able to get to him in time. In Bo, the local radio station provided a regular spot to talk about the opportunities to create the plan. This meant that, by the time the planners went into the neighbourhoods, the community understood the reasons behind the plan, so they were not challenging the strategic detail.

This idea of growing a 'collective dream' rings true in Curitiba, Brazil, where pedestrianisation and rewilding of the town's amenities from 2016 was used to reduce knife crime and drastically improve quality of life for the local population. Jamie Lerner, former mayor of Curitiba, pointed out in a 2016 *Guardian* article that everyone needs to understand and see the desirability of a plan 'then they will help you make it happen'. Jonas Rabinovitch, a former planner at the Curitiba Research and Planning Institute, observed in the same piece that 'administrations change: people change, leaders change. But there is still ownership by the population. The city centre is already preserved. No one would be so crazy as to eliminate the pedestrian streets now ...'

As our communities become more engaged with climate action, social inequality and other urban challenges like energy and food security, the drive to empower local planning is increasing. Ben suggests that once the strategic plan has been set up, the sweet spot for grassroots planning kicks in when it comes to looking at how it will all work in practice.

In an article by Maisha Fisher on poets and writers in the urban context, she writes that 'every city has soldiers'. The qualities we need for leadership aren't always the ones our authorities lean on; at a grassroots level, where most of us live, our real leaders are those with skin in the game. Aga Otero has been at the forefront of some of the most innovative projects in London, and when connecting communities to power (both the renewable electric and the human kind), he has observed that our greatest and most inspirational community leaders can often be found in our urban matriarchs, who have raised children and grandchildren in the community. Their longevity creates trust and builds intergenerational relationships. Aga likens them to ancient trees whose root systems have grown together over time and are able to draw nutrients to where they are needed most; urban matriarchs are resilient, hold deep knowledge about their community and can pull resources from different pools. This kind of knowledge can't be replaced and yet our traditional, formal leaders tend to bring in external consultants or arm's-length bodies to 'assess need', whose understanding of the people, place, history and heritage can't possibly match that depth.

However, we should be energised by the emergence of a network of everyday leaders who are rooted in their communities and whose solutions reflect the lived realities of those they serve.

Not all cities need to pursue every opportunity, and intelligent, empathetic leadership will embrace diverse community voices and recognise the nuances and strengths of individual cities. As the Ellen MacArthur Foundation observed when looking at 'The circular economy opportunity for urban industrial innovation in China', well-established cities with a large portion of middle-class consumers can go big on regenerative urban agriculture and rewire the food system; a city that excels in the service industry can focus on stimulating innovation to use data to inform supply-chain transparency or shared mobility schemes, while a city with a strong manufacturing industry can emphasise product redesign to allow for reuse and repurposing.

If we don't think about the systems as a whole, we run the risk of creating yet more siloed solutions. Returning briefly to the example of increasing lighting, on the surface this feels like a simple solution: no dark shadows, no problem. It certainly would have made my walks through urban parks and streets more reassuring after late nights at work. But do we want to live in cities that are lit up like football pitches 24/7? And this is before we get to the implications for species other than us, such as the ecologically vital insect life. Lighting is a death sentence for vast swathes of the insect population which is already in catastrophic decline.

Ultimately, if we are to feel truly connected to our city homes, then we have to look further than our smartphones, trams, trains and cycle lanes, and delve into what makes the city experience good for us. Then we need to get involved with how we can amplify that and share it with others – not just those in our immediate neighbourhood, but with our fellow city dwellers across the globe.

We need to engage with our less sexy systems like infrastructure and planning because these are at the root of how we connect to people and place. Green, socially sensitive infrastructure that we help to design, shape and make can translate into urban centres that have safety, public health, social bonds and the lives of others (including other species) at heart.

5

DWELLING

I don't think that architecture is only about shelter, is only about a very simple enclosure. It should be able to excite you, to calm you, to make you think.

Dame Zaha Hadid

MOVING HOUSE HAS been a Bradbury family pastime. I've had too many homes to count, so I'm selective in my recollections of them. As a child, the first family home I can recall was in a mining town on the Highveld. I remember it because it was the one I left to move to England. I distinctly remember the confusion of leaving and feeling irate – we'd just had automatic garage doors installed and I wanted to take them with us. Another more recent example was in the UK, where for the first time in many years my parents and I lived on the same soil. For a few years there was a nest to return to and in many ways the house symbolised certainty and comfort. The decision to leave this home was baffling and I was probably as rattled by this as I had been by the South African exit several decades earlier. But it left me with the lived lesson that homes might be grounded in bricks and mortar, but they are as much about the intangible.

The prolonged and involuntary grounding of so many of us during the Covid-19 pandemic has caused us to think about what it truly means to dwell in our cities. Being consigned to our homes and immediate neighbourhoods has helped us to see them through new eyes. For me, this book came into being at a time of non-stop travel, which was swiftly replaced by successive lockdowns. Being forced to bridle my nomadic spirit and bed into home in London, I thought about both dwellings and dwelling. It's interesting to think about what makes our homes, whether they nurture us and whether we feel able to return to them as sanctuaries of comfort and calm.

As it turns out, even pre-pandemic we spent a great deal of time in our homes. In fact, the stats on this are pretty arresting: the US National Human Activity Pattern Survey conducted during the early 1990s found that the 'average' American citizen spent 93 per cent of their life indoors and, decades later, a 2014 report from WHO put the figure at much the same level, estimating that Europeans spend 90 per cent of their time indoors, with it being likely that two-thirds of that is spent within the home itself.

Following the pandemic, this figure has risen, either temporarily or permanently, as we've shifted to home working or been forced to stay at home because our jobs have been lost or put on hold. This means that we are asking a lot of our homes; as our most vital and personal space, they are where we rest, socialise, work, love and play. Now more than ever, homes also need to be able to withstand relationship pressures, childcare, a blended work–home life and general uncertainty. The permeability of our walls has increased, as digital technology, working patterns and routines have changed, so we need to be attuned to when the city strays too far into our homes. Embracing the concept of dwelling seems to be one of the keys to creating more permissive, enjoyable urban lives.

DWELLING TIME

When I first discussed the concept of this book with my friend Grahame, a Welsh poet and master of words, we talked about how old-fashioned the word 'dwelling' was. Indeed, according to the *Oxford English Dictionary*, common usage of the word 'dwell' is at an all-time low, having last peaked around the mid 1800s. The word itself is of Germanic origin and its current English form can be traced back to the Old English *dwellan* 'lead astray, hinder, delay' (in Middle English 'tarry, remain in a place'), which is also related to the Middle Dutch *dwellen* 'stun, perplex' and the Old Norse *dvelja* 'delay, tarry, stay'.

The language of dwelling harks back to a time when stillness, or at least slowness, was a necessary part of achieving daily tasks – when the ritual of the mundane had an in-built quietude. Tasks like writing letters and preparing food demanded more focused energy from us. In today's world, focus has become fragmented, multitasking is lauded and stillness has faded out of fashion. There is something rather extraordinary about the gravity of the circumstances that it took – a pandemic – to reconnect us with the value of having time and space to dwell.

To me, the term 'dwelling' also refers to time that is spent deliberately not rushing from one thing to the next and where focus isn't being split across many things at once (even this feels like the urban modus operandi). This runs counter to the life of an urban- ite where busyness has cache. Dwelling, even momentarily, gives us the chance to notice the quiet moments of peace that settle when we walk in the door of our home, when we pause in a welcoming nook on the street or on a park bench to watch life go by for a moment, or even when we are halted by the sight of a particularly beautiful building. Our cities can offer us all of this – our challenge is noticing that we need it.

City life, as we know it, can be frenetic. In running from one com- mitment to the next, the time we have with ourselves is often fleeting and undervalued. Interestingly, urban designers and developers are on to the fact that these pauses in the rush are as good for places as they are for people. This is why the concept of 'place-making' has become popular. The aim, as articulated to me by a group of col- leagues at the Royal Institute for British Architects, is to 'lift our gaze' because, when we see things worth noticing, we naturally slow down. Whether we are aware of it, much of our urban day can be spent with our eyes down; we tend to avoid eye contact with others, focusing instead on scrolling through news, emails, social media or dating matches. It isn't any wonder that we use our commuting time to do this when we are so short on time overall during the day. But, as a growing appetite for time in nature and changes in urban plan- ning begin prioritising compact, walkable cities, we may also have the chance to rethink the pace that we move at through them. With less pressure to cross cities at peak time every day, and with better supporting transport, our habits around our homes are changing. The Covid-19 pandemic produced a net increase of approximately one to one and a half hours of time per day (seemingly applicable across many parts of the globe, from the UK to the US to Australia), which has given us the option to exercise and play differently, explore neighbourhoods, holiday locally and increase time spent with family and loved ones. Essentially, the currency of home life has gone up. Unhooked Communications, a home interiors PR agency, has found that spending on home improvements has increased, with some 75 per cent of Britons focusing on redecorating, DIY, landscaping, and kitchen and home office investments. The same is true in the US, where 80 per cent of homeowners had begun DIY projects by June 2020 according to surveys by The Farnsworth Group and the Home Improvement Research Institute. As well as having spent less on recreation, people are also seeing the value of channelling effort and thought into the sanctuaries we have come to depend on.

DWELLING PLACES

Having places to dwell in our cities has real synergy with the rewilding conversation. The city is very much its own ecosystem, though one that we intensely overengineer. Much like in nature, its true quality and value depends on variety and a degree of freedom to create the most appropriate life-support systems and processes for the area. Some of the most successful rewilded landscapes have been given a little breathing room in order to get there, so we can learn from nature here. It's time for us to apply that same outlook to our urban homes – now, more than ever, we should give these places a little mental space so that we ensure they are truly nurturing environments. When talking about creating places to dwell in the city, I think it's useful to consider what our homes should offer us.

As a material concept, the home is simply where we live. Philosophically, it is much more than this. In the city, our homes provide us with a buffer from the outside world. They are often the first and last line of defence in protecting us against the hubbub and stress of city living and affording us some much-needed privacy.

If we are privileged enough to have a home, owned or rented without insecurity, the housing crisis can feel a little distant. But, in fact, it is almost always on our doorstep and often the way our neighbours experience the city is in a parallel world. Bridging this disconnect is vital because, as we've seen, our cities are only as valuable as their richness of diversity, tolerance and openness – all of which contribute to vibrant places, strong sense of identity and creativity. The world over, houses are disappearing and, with them, the opportunity for city dwellers to create homes.

The Case of the Vanishing Houses

When it comes to disappearing houses, George Clarke – architect, social-housing champion and presenter of the beloved *Amazing Spaces* programme – has the bit between his teeth, running the campaign 'The Council House Scandal' to urge the UK government to replenish social-housing stock. But why are houses disappearing and where are they going? The individual circumstances differ from city to city but broadly, over the past forty years, several issues have converged: stigma surrounding rented council housing has grown, earnings have shrunk, competition for land in cities has become ferocious, house prices have skyrocketed and suburbs have sprawled. The result is fragmentation of neighbourhoods, and this is a problem for all of us.

We talk about money a lot in our cities, because the costs of living in them can be prohibitive – as Fran Lebowitz commented in *Pretend It's a City*, 'No one can afford to live in New York. Yet, eight million people do. How do we do this? We don't know!' Housing, though, is one of our dealbreakers – something we cannot do without – and the clamour for affordable housing is becoming louder, without any silver-bullet solutions. To give a sense of the global affordability picture, the Ellen MacArthur Foundation has found that a third of the world's urban residents struggle to secure decent housing. A study by the Lincoln Institute of Land Policy also revealed that of 200 surveyed cities around the world, 90 per cent of them were simply unaffordable to live in, with the average house price being more than three times the median income!

The reality, according to the UN Habitat programme's 2020 *World Cities* report, is that those of us wanting to buy a house need to be prepared to save more than five times our annual income (and this is just to afford a standard, no-frills house). But this kind of saving seems completely unattainable when renters are often having to spend more than 25 per cent of their monthly income on rent. Indeed, in the UK, Trust for London has found that renters in the city need to pay 46.4 per cent of their pre-tax income per month for an average one-bedroom house or flat. According to the 2021 State of the Nation's Housing report from Harvard University's Joint Center for Housing Studies, in 2019 nearly 50 per cent of renter households and 20 per cent of homeowner households spent more than 30 per cent of their incomes on housing. The US Department of Housing and Urban Development considers that those paying more than 30 per cent of their income on housing are 'cost burdened', meaning that they may struggle to afford essentials like food and healthcare. It's no wonder, then, that many cities are populated by 'Generation Rent'. Young people entering or growing up in urban environments simply can't earn enough to afford to buy a property, no matter how hard they work.

Beyond the immediate implications of where we're able to live, it's also worth thinking about the psychological impacts that this uncertainty, lack of choice and pervasive financial strain has on us. For the younger generations coming up through urban environments, we have to wonder how this impacts choices about personal and professional lives; the Covid-19 pandemic shed light on the primacy of essential workers in our cities – in healthcare, childcare, education, logistics and food supply – but at the moment we simply aren't making the space for them. Cities are also increasingly celebrating their single citizens and without merging incomes in conventional ways, like marriage, home ownership becomes the stuff of history. When we consider what this means for anyone contemplating their future options in the city, the incentives to stay (or feel excited about staying) are way off.

When housing options don't match the income of city dwellers, a few things can happen. In the global south, unplanned settlements and informal housing expands and, as we saw in cities like Dar es Salaam in the Connection chapter, this can come at significant human and environmental cost. The global north isn't off the hook either, with a stark increase in homelessness and people forced to live in temporary accommodation in established cities. The fixes we need are complex and often at the mercy of institutions beyond our direct or immediate control, but I think it is worth breaking this down a little so that we, as residents, understand more about the problem, what solutions might look like and how we are already supporting changes to the system.

The things we need to fix come down to this: supply (the number of houses), the model (how they are made affordable) and design (how they look and feel). Housing, done right, creates community, enhances our health, sits in harmony with nature and is resilient to climate risk. But, above all, let's not forget that the housing issue is, at its heart, about the opportunity to make a home. Our bricks-and-mortar homes are the most physical manifestation of roots available to us, and if the value of our cities is based on their rich-ness of cultural and social exchange, we all have a say in making our neighbourhoods as open and inclusive as possible. If life in a pandemic has shown us nothing else, it is that we all need these places of solace and privacy, where we can live, love and decompress with-out judgement or interruption.

Chasing Utopia

When it comes to fighting for good housing, it should be no surprise that local governments, councils and city leaders are on the front line. They can help redress the imbalances in our systems by being more alive to community needs and neighbourhood dynamics. The agility of local governments to respond to the housing crisis at scale can be limited because in many cases they are stifled by their dependence on central government for funding. Globally, central governments often fall prey to the seduction of short-term investment horizons, when investing in things like housing actually requires a plan that lasts beyond the tenure of a single government. But the picture isn't all bleak. Cities around the world are showing that they can take bold action and offer nuanced, thoughtful solutions. We need this in the absence of leadership from central governments, who are often too slow, blinkered or dispassionate to act.

In the north of England, the city of Salford's council set up a new housing company using the money that had come in from private developments. If used properly – and I caution that scandals abound on this score – communities stand to benefit from this reinvestment. In the Salford example, the council bought properties off plan from the private Riverview development and rented them at social rates. The scale is still small, and the problem is that we need a lot of houses very quickly, but it's still a positive example of local leadership.

To speed things up, councils might be able to make the most of dips in the market. The Smith Institute think tank's Affordable Housing Commission estimates that in the UK another 42,000 council houses could become available if councils buy up excess new-builds, persuade developers to 'flip' commercial sites over to social housing (Toronto has had some success with this) and take advantage of unused office space, left languishing in the wake of the Covid-19 pandemic, and turn it into living space.

In the periods of lockdown that spanned writing this book, I spent many a sanctioned walk wandering through the vacant streets and shuttered units in the City of London and Canary Wharf. Without the throng of commuters, it felt eerily quiet and is still a shadow of its former self. We don't yet know the long-term implications of the pandemic on office life, but a grand return to the old days of rigid 9 to 5 faces some obstacles and will be the subject of some resistance for those who may have enjoyed a new sense of autonomy. Pre-pandemic, 60 per cent of office space in Europe was unused during working hours. Looking at London, the Ellen MacArthur Foundation suggests that a combination of 'peer-to-peer renting, better urban planning, office sharing, repurposed buildings, and multi-purposed buildings increases the value of new buildings and can double utilisation of 20% of London's buildings by 2036, saving over GBP 600 million annually'. As inner-city areas have seen considerable community displacement over the years because of extreme gentrification and private development, repurposing buildings offers a way to achieve affordable housing in the places that need it most.

In UK cities, at least, housing for all has had its moment of being more than a pipe dream. We 'solved' it in a fortnight back in March 2020, when the homeless were taken off the streets and housed in hotels in a rare, speedy reaction from central government. Since then, these threads unravelled and we've managed to 'unsolve' it, and we now have the added threat of Covid-19-related financial stress causing evictions and defaults on payments, resulting in more people becoming homeless. The homelessness charity Crisis pointed to a 23 per cent increase in the number of homeless people in the UK in one quarter alone in 2020. Across the world, cities with the highest numbers of homeless include Moscow, Los Angeles, Mumbai and the Philippines. To address this at a city level, the tools at the disposal of local leaders include not only buying up underutilised property, but also supporting co-operatives and tenant organisations. This is not to forget that the mandate for building and dreaming big here is important – George Clarke reminds us that we need 100,000 new homes every year.

The World Economic Forum, in a 2019 article, has pointed to cities like Bristol and Melbourne, who've shown intelligent local responses to housing demand by resisting privatisation of collective space and directing public resources towards social connectivity. In Bristol, 161 homes are being constructed on a former primary school site, with six different types of tenure on offer to residents. A housing association, community investment company and private investor have worked together to create this model, in which some houses will be sold at market price and others made available through tenure schemes, including shared ownership and rent to buy. The idea behind this model is to offer affordable housing alternatives to vital workers who are currently being priced out of the city. Similar outside-the-box thinking is being applied to the Melbourne Apartment Project: the Barnett Model Development in north Melbourne is a privately funded development supported by the University of Melbourne, Melbourne City Mission, Resilient Melbourne and the City of Melbourne. Six of the thirty-four apartments are being sold at market rate to subsidise the sale of the other twenty-eight to social-housing tenants through a 'deferred second mortgage' model that reduces the usual deposit and repayments. Meanwhile, as reported in *The Los Angeles Times* in 2018, Los Angeles passed a law permitting motels to be temporarily repurposed to house the city's homeless while they wait for permanent housing to be completed. These initiatives all show that, if a little creative thinking is applied to how we buy, sell, rent – ultimately – value our city dwellings, then we can open them up to those who really need them. It also shows that what is required is ambition, systems thinking and a refusal to capitulate to the dominant model.

Under One Roof

For most of us, housing is something we think about in isolation, but this misses the point that we are part of a much bigger eco-system. Neighbourhood approaches to uplifting the quality of our homes have been successful and the appetite for them is growing, especially in the aftermath of successive lockdowns where we have become even more intimately acquainted with the spaces behind and just beyond our front doors. To borrow again from Ben Bolgar's expression, getting housing right will require 'universal principles, applied locally'. City leaders are closest to their challenges and, if they are supported and empowered by central government, they can make bold decisions. We already know that private investors, phil-anthropic organisations, multilateral agencies and planners are part of the mix, but the value of direct community participation is one we need to amplify and celebrate. Participatory democracy, as it's called, will only work out in favour of city dwellers if we have a voice and agency. This is far beyond the mailbox drop we've all had from our local councils seeking 'consultation' on proposed developments that are a fait accompli; this is about actively co-creating solutions.

We've already explored the notion of superblock, fifteen-minute and donut cities, and now Stockholm, Sweden, through its Street Moves initiative, is taking this a step further with its 'one-minute city': a project that empowers residents to reclaim their street through 'street furniture' immediately outside their door. The premise of Street Moves, as explained by Fergus O'Sullivan in *Bloomberg CityLab*, is that 'the doorstep is a great place to start in engaging with people's daily lives'. Street Moves uses kits of street furniture that can be adjusted according to the use of the street. Endlessly adaptable, modular and fitting into the size of a traditional parking spot, Dan Hill of the Swedish Centre for Architecture and Design (ArkDes) likens the kit to Lego, IKEA or Minecraft blocks. They can offer parking for bikes, seating or planters, for instance. O'Sullivan summarises the value of street furniture thus: 'Piece by piece, these installations can transform streets into sites of sociability and mixing, joining up steadily into neighbourhoods where the space used daily by residents extends little by little out into the open air.'

Certainly eighteen months of lockdowns in cities throughout the world have spawned a reclamation of the street by our communities. 'Parklets' and 'streateries' are becoming more than just cute terms – they are emerging alternative models of street life that successive lockdowns have accelerated.

Participatory democracy also underpins community housing models, where communities purchase, design, build and manage the homes they live in. Dar es Salaam, Tanzania, has shown the power of this in Kurasini following the forced displacement of 36,000 people in 2006 when the government demolished houses on the fringes of the city's port. The community set up the Chamazi Community Based Housing Scheme and, working with local members, the Tanzanian Urban Poor Fund, Slum Dwellers International and Homeless International, the scheme raised enough money to buy 30 acres of land for resettlement. The construction materials for the houses are made on site and the community was trained in construction skills by the Centre for Community Initiatives. Other partners contributed expertise and professional advice on surveying and acquiring land, developing building plans and designing the houses. To date, seventy-five new homes have been provided. While the numbers seem low, this is a huge achievement for a small community with no prior construction or planning expertise. Transformative Cities notes that, by being in control of the allocation of funds in the immediate vicinity, the Chamazi Community has prioritised access to water and sanitation via a communal borehole, a solar-powered water pump and reedbed sewage treatment.

But scale isn't always a challenge. In Solapur, India, the Centre of Indian Trade Unions mobilised to remedy the unsafe informal settlements that were housing female cigarette workers. The scheme that emerged, the Comrade Godutai Parulekar Housing Scheme, was 10,000 houses strong within five years and is one of the biggest co-operative housing projects for workers in Asia. The project was designed and built by a local construction firm and women who would be the ultimate residents participated in designing the homes. The project has since expanded to include textile workers and other unorganised sector workers.

To accelerate affordable housing, we need real-estate investors onside. According to the European Association for Investors in Non-listed Real Estate Vehicles (INREV), real estate makes up 8.9 per cent of institutional investors' total assets globally and now those with money to spend are turning towards well-performing cities to diversify their portfolios. Interestingly, some of the factors that are now affecting their investment decisions include carbon neutrality, connectivity and quality of life. In the Netherlands, the Dutch government has committed to engaging city dwellers, academia, business leaders and cities in its Green Deal, demonstrating that communities, co-ops, local government and investors can, do and should work together.

However, our thoughtfulness needs to extend beyond just putting roofs over heads. Our homes are an extension of our neighbourhoods and often a reflection of our resilience. It's pretty clear that some of our most fundamental pillars of a joyous existence aren't yet made available to everyone.

A Just Home

Good housing can act as a guardian of our human rights. Our homes should provide us with safety, including insulation from noise, poor air quality and artificial light. But the aspiration goes further – we would like them to provide us with space to rest, socialise and be quiet at any given time. Though private greenspace isn't a given for many inner-city homes, at the very least we need access to quality outdoor space to promote social networks, physical activity and mental health. Joseph Chamie, Director of Research at the Center for Migration Studies in New York, puts forward the startling statistic in a *Yale Global* article that 20 per cent of the world's population lives in inadequate housing, and while this can seem remote from us if we have our own homes or secure rental agreements, there are times that we are reminded of the ruptures in the city landscape. The global signatories of Cities for Housing (a Municipalist Declaration of Local Governments for the Right to Housing and the Right to the City) points to how a 'lack of national and state funding, market deregulation, growing power of global corporations, and increasing competition for scarce real estate often become a burden on our neighbourhoods, causing serious distortions in their social fabric, and putting the goal of ensuring equitable, inclusive, and just cities at risk'.

In 2016, these interrelated crises converged when Grenfell Tower, a social-housing block, was engulfed in fire in one of London's most well-heeled boroughs. The fire, which killed seventy-two people, pointed to an injustice in the housing system that is common to cities in the global north and south: that it has become the norm for low-income residents' concerns to be drowned out or ignored. The fire was an example of the type of catastrophic systems failure that results when equity and empathy are designed out of our cities. Not only was the local community fractured and hurt, but the reverberations were felt far beyond London. In many ways, Grenfell Tower as a building reflected the experience of many contemporary urban residents – inner city, high density, occupied by a mix of residents with many lower-income and vulnerable groups. But it also represented a cross-section of a vibrant, creative, diverse and tolerant community.

The latent inequities in our housing system were present long before the fire broke out, and we know that the cumulation of ruptures in the system led to such a disastrous and wholly avoidable loss of life. Since Grenfell, the estimate in the UK is that some 700,000 people are trapped in dangerous houses or flats that they cannot sell because they contain unsafe materials and structures or lack safety controls. Setting aside the enormous financial cost to the individuals and families in this position, the human cost is significant and has contributed to rising cases of anxiety and depression. A parliamentary debate on 1 February 2021 raised cases of first-time homeowners on the verge of bankruptcy, parents frightened to bring up their children in unsafe homes and leaseholders trapped in a situation that is not of their own making. Remedying the need for equity and empathy within our housing system will need the support of a central government that recognises the links between secure housing, health and wellbeing, and the fact that many of our current systems allow urban citizens to fall through the cracks.

As we have seen through the numerous examples in these pages, reserves of social capital can be created when marginalised or vulnerable groups are empowered. Participatory democracy is critical to tapping into the social value of cities. It is only when we actively empower groups like low-income residents, the homeless, slum dwellers, ethnic minorities, young people, the elderly, the disabled and those routinely marginalised to steward existing places and co-create new ones that we can make cities places where everyone gets to dwell safely and contentedly.

Contrary to popular belief, building and maintaining houses that are inclusive for all doesn't need to be quite so painful. The complexity of sub-contracting often muddies the waters of public accountability and we, as city dwellers, are left frustrated and disillusioned by the abstract and unfathomably lengthy planning processes. But the good news is that there are lots of ways to make this quicker, and we should particularly turn our attention towards emerging cities in the global south that might have another opportunity to leapfrog over the unwieldy public planning processes that paralyse the global north. UN Habitat's 2020 *World Cities* report estimates that 96 per cent of urban growth will take place in East Asia, South Asia and Africa. Specifically, India, China and Nigeria will account for 35 per cent of the total increase in global urban population from 2018 to 2050. Cities like these know that they need to get ahead of a boom in housing demand and build houses that are fully equipped for the climate challenge. To do this, designers and housebuilders need to step up.

Design matters far beyond aesthetics; it matters because our buildings stick around. In Europe, for example, 90 per cent of the buildings that already exist will still be in use in 2050. So, anything we build now needs to be able to withstand the changing climate we expect to see in the coming decades. We need to pivot urgently on housing design, materials and construction methods because, at the moment, more than a third of total global resources are hoovered up by construction materials and the building sector. The circular, or regenerative, economy comes into play again here. Not only can we use design to limit the average global temperature increase, but in doing so we can unlock new potential for jobs and growth in the construction industry – one of our slowest-moving sectors. Good design tends to open up more jobs, because building becomes more about craft and specialised skills at each stage of the process, including manufacturing the materials that go into our buildings. The Ellen MacArthur Foundation used Amsterdam as an example of this, as it is estimated that, using circular economy principles in the construction of 70,000 new homes here before 2040, 700 additional jobs could be generated – this would result in a 10 per cent drop in unemployment in the country's construction sector.

Joseph Daniels is a beacon of hope in this regard and his challenge to completely rewrite the rulebook on housing is one of the most energising signs of a more hospitable city-housing landscape emerging. Joseph is irrepressible, speaking at a million miles an hour. In one breath he mentions that he comes from a broken home, was homeless at 15 (the first of four times), has no formal qualifications as he dropped out of school, founded Project Etopia at 23 and can train six people to build a hurricane- and flood-proof climate-positive home in six hours. Project Etopia isn't just a housebuilder, Joseph is keen to point out: 'We want to create community.'

Project Etopia mobilises empathy and innovation to address the housing crisis for what it is: 'an environmental and human one.' Joseph proves that there are ways of building houses rapidly, which means that alleviating the housing crisis suddenly feels closer to the here and now. Project Etopia's modular housing can be put up in a matter of hours, making use of off-site construction. Simply put, off-site construction refers to buildings, or parts of buildings, that are made in another location (like a factory) and then brought to their final location, where they are assembled. This means that buildings can be constructed more quickly and efficiently, and it reduces dust, noise and disruption in the area around the build. It's like high-quality flat-packed housing, but hurricane-proof and with such high energy efficiency it actually takes carbon out of the atmosphere. From the UK to Namibia, 'each house Project Etopia builds', he says, 'is the equivalent of planting 2.3 hardwood trees per square metre or taking a Boeing 747 out of the sky for 1,861 hours'. Joseph's tenacity and fearlessness behind his vision is clear. Solving the housing crisis will require rapid growth in solutions like his ('hyper-scaling', as he calls it). Above all, Joseph is passionate about telling people the story behind the housing crisis – what it's like to worry about having a home, and why we should be chasing an 'economic and environmental utopia for future generations'. For housing to work, he says, 'it has to be socially acceptable and versatile'. To change the model, we need to chase three ideals: 'sustainability, affordability and scaleability'.

When we spoke, he talked about the dream of building a million homes by the time he's 40 (he's 27 now). 'We have to fight the good fight,' he says. Reflecting on where we are in the fight for human and planetary health, he agreed that the picture is bright. Of our generation, he says, 'We give a fuck. Them's the rules.'

Designs for Dwelling

The housing conversation brings us full circle to compact, connected cities, and we know that flexible, human housing will depend on mixed-use public spaces, access to nature and social connection. The Urban Land Institute calls this 'good density'. By being thoughtful about housing, we can attract and keep urban residents in their cities because they are liveable for the long term rather than for a narrow period in life. Vibrant, compact and connected neighbourhoods with resilient housing can reduce city energy consumption, carbon emissions and infrastructure costs. In health terms, again the business case goes a step further, with the Royal Institution of Chartered Surveyors' *Cities, Health and Wellbeing* 2018 report revealing that 'for every £1 spent on the planning process to promote walking, cycling and insulating homes, the health service could save £50, £168 and £50 respectively'. The conventional brief of high-volume housebuilders is being challenged and we are in a race to escape 'pathway lock-in' – to ensure that developments being planned now provide high-quality, natural spaces in which neighbourhoods can come together.

Much of the conversation still turns on the appearance of houses rather than what they are made of and, rather shockingly, we don't know nearly enough about the materials we invite into our most intimate spaces. When we spoke, Ben Bolgar cautioned that indoor air quality is often four to five times as bad as outdoor air quality, and less than half of our materials are tested for toxicity in the UK. The Royal College of Physicians in London attributes toxic indoor air as contributing to approximately 99,000 deaths per year in Europe, and WHO attributes 3.8 million deaths every year to household exposure to pollutants from cooking and heating in our homes.

In retreating to the home, Ben says, 'we are often sealing ourselves up in toxic boxes, made worse by poor ventilation'. Housing design for tomorrow's cities should focus on the use of non-toxic materials that tend to be more natural and use passive means of ventilation. We need to understand our climate (for ventilation, heating and cooling) and our supply chain (for materials). The Naturhus (Nature House) brief, developed in Sweden by the late Swedish eco-architect Bengt Warne, integrates nature into the home by building it within a greenhouse structure. With this comes the space and climate to produce food and energy, and to contain sewage and grey water in a closed-loop system that retains nutrients. Contrary to what we might first think, the lived experience of this is overwhelmingly positive (as portrayed in the Netflix documentary *Home*) and we also stand to save money from living in such a symbiotic environment, according to the *Financial Times* article 'Why Some People Are Enclosing Their Entire Home Within Glass': 'In 2010, research by Lester van Ree, of Eindhoven University of Technology in the Netherlands, showed that a greenhouse residence is less likely to overheat than a super-insulated, airtight house and saves 25 per cent on winter heating bills.'

Of course, most of us don't have the luxury of specifying the shape and character of our bricks and mortar, but we often have much more control over the inside of our homes. Michelle Ogundehin, in her book *Happy Inside*, draws on the insidious effects of indoor air pollution (sources of which includes mould spores, pollen, bacteria, viruses, dust, cigarette smoke, pets, cleaning products, air fresheners, stoves burning solid fuel and kerosene, and paraffin candles). Toxins inside the home are often invisible – unlike much of the city pollution we are desperate to get away from, which we can often see, taste and smell. But there are steps we can take to remedy our interiors, and the more we learn about the ethical, health and environmental impacts of everyday household products, the more we can embrace compassionate products that are designed to last and enhance the home. According to the latest market data, the green household-cleaning products market is expected to grow from US$17.90 billion in 2017 to US$27.83 billion by the end of 2024. So, the appetite is clearly there – we all want to live in places that not only shelter us from the storms of life but also actively make us happier and healthier humans who feel able to contribute to an inclusive urban future.

BELONGING

The whole question of housing could take a dramatically different turn if we reframed it to focus on the 'home'. The concept of home is deeply personal, and the impact of having a safe place to retreat to goes far beyond material comforts. We face a housing crisis in cities because the historic legacy of the institutions that run them has refused to recognise the primacy of belonging. This isn't just a crisis of housing – it's a crisis of home.

Poorly designed neighbourhoods, whether formal or informal, can squash dignity, sideline differences and increase tensions between those moving in and out of the community. Kerryn Fischer, the founder of Frank Features, observed a reality that is replicated across the world: that 'most low-cost houses are so obviously designed for "them" and not "us"'. Referring to driving around the outskirts of South African cities, she reflects on:

mile upon mile of the most soulless dwellings where front doors are abrupt apertures that open directly onto an empty yard with no portico or overhang to define the threshold and offer respite from sun and rain – let alone a tree. The simple addition of a small pergola or covered outdoor area can transform a box into a space that acknowledges climate and the lifestyle that comes with it. Low-cost housing budgets should have landscaping built into them. A tree in every garden – how hard is that?

How neighbourhoods are designed often depends on who is living in them and, when it comes to migrant experience in cities, we often end up with situations where migrant communities are relegated or siloed to ghetto-style areas because the tensions around the paucity of space in neighbourhoods can make any 'incomers' seem like a threat. This reflects what happens when the housing conversation becomes too arm's-length – we can fail to see cities as the organic, complex organisms they truly are. In reality, there is nothing unusual about being a migrant – one in every seven people on the planet is one – and our cities owe their cultural richness and complex charm to their presence.

As an urban migrant, my decision to settle in Hackney was no accident; its renegade history, friendliness and cosmopolitanism made me feel the most at home I'd felt since arriving in the UK.

The borough is bursting with makers and artisans. It's a hub for emerging restaurants and food businesses across the city, whose test kitchens nestle under railway arches or in warehouses, and it is home to markets like Ridley Road that are like a warm, welcoming hug from the parts of the world that have, for now, been left behind.

Feeling a sense of community can have a profound impact on our daily lives. It can be the difference between a bad day and a great one. In my neighbourhood, it's entirely normal to encounter familiar faces – clients from the gym, friends, old colleagues, local shop owners – on a daily basis. Walking the well-trodden paths from station to home, home to high street, high street to park makes connection to place part of my daily routine.

However comforting that sense of connection can become, establishing new roots in any city is hard. Doing so often hinges on where we land and how our neighbourhoods welcome us. Are they prescriptive, welcoming only the familiar parts of us, or do they embrace us as a whole, even when we might have left pieces of our heart in different places along the way? I've been able to find my sense of place in cities many times over because I've found ways of identifying with the elements I've left behind – through food, art, nature and movement, all of which create new social networks. Cities can also help things along by being proactive and visible in the way they choose to celebrate their migrants, and the Superkilen estate in Copenhagen is one example of how design can be deployed in a deliberate act of hospitality and celebration.

BIG architects worked on a project in Nørrebro, Copenhagen, to celebrate the neighbourhood's global identity through a combination of art, street furniture and landscape architecture. To engender a sense of dual belonging, in both home and adopted communities, each piece is accompanied by explanatory plaques describing the object and its significance in Danish and in the language of its origin. Showing the value of local intelligence, BIG asked residents what, for them, would make this new community of housing feel a little more like the homes they had left behind. Some sixty different cultures and countries were represented in this public space and a wander through it is a remarkable and proud display of Copenhagen's cultural diversity. This project shows the importance of thoughtful design and recognition of the global fabric that makes up many cities. It is stimulating, artistic, and a practical and symbolic representation of the melting pot of cultures, all packaged up in one big playground for all. BIG noted that you come across 'neon signs from Russia and Qatar, picnic benches from Armenia, a Thai boxing ring, a slide from Chernobyl, climbing frame from India, swings from Iraq, a Texan line-dancing pavilion and a Moroccan fountain'. This playful and thoughtful use of space challenges the mono-ethnic characteristics of many public spaces found in some of the world's most culturally and ethnically diverse cities.

Putting social activity at the centre of community life is also evident in Superkilen, where an outdoor square acts as an extension to the existing indoor community hall and hosts sports and cultural activities. It's both a garden and an 'urban living room' where 'locals meet around the Moroccan fountain, the Turkish bench, under the Japanese cherry-trees ... permanent tables, benches and grill facilities serve as an urban living room for backgammon, chess players etc.' Emphasising local activity at the heart of our neighbourhoods is a potent unifier and can benefit public health and wellbeing by helping us to make room for lightness and fun in our daily lives, promoting mental health and child development, and encouraging social gatherings and healthy competition through sport and games.

Making the City Ours to Dwell In

What we know about cities is that they are never static. They are their own complex ecosystems, responding to evolutions in planning, demographic shifts and other factors that affect the city's entire mood. The trend of rapid urbanisation, left unfettered, can risk rendering a community soulless and homogenous, where once there was a patchwork of co-existing people, places, cultures, beliefs and hobbies. Embracing diversity and valuing the wealth of skills, economic contribution (both from paid and unpaid labour), languages, religious and other belief systems, and cultures helps us create resilient places. Viewing the city as an ecosystem is one way that we can start to build up an appreciation of the nuanced networks, and to understand that pulling at one lever may result in unintended consequences. Another example from the wilderness springs to mind; in *Wilding*, Isabella Tree speaks evocatively of the anatomy of a hollowed-out ancient oak. The oak is made more resilient by the ebb and flow of different species living in its hollows, where more biological processes take place which then allows for more diverse species to move in. The analogy with cities is that we should allow our communities to be developed gently, by and for people.

The time it takes to build up a village feel in a new area of development can be significant, as many of us can identify with when walking through a site of shiny new buildings. They might look great but they seldom have the welcoming feel of an established community. Not only are many of our newer buildings high density and uninspiring, they also seem sterile and quiet in the absence of neighbourhood chatter. In our bid to create new places worthy of the next generation of urban living, we can risk sweeping out the old, established community networks. These may not be glamorous establishments but they are all the better for it. I think now of the Victory Pub near my home – a dear East End drinking hole of some notoriety (a local of the Kray brothers) that has established itself as a de facto community centre. It keeps entirely unconventional hours, which are based around the needs of local workers and residents. Or, up the road, a tiny patch of green by the canal that houses a community centre, garden and basketball court and is a lifeline for residents of the block (but earmarked for redevelopment). We have a better chance of understanding the value of these places if we have more neighbourhood voices at local authority level and administrations that have open ears, minds and hearts when it comes to making decisions about their future. Community-based action is an example of citizens identifying what is really needed in their community, mobilising the resources they have to hand, inviting others to get involved and choosing to look out for one another.

In Porto Alegre Brazil, the CaSanAT centre shows the potential for community action to change urban power dynamics, even when pitched against a formidable central government. The Transformative Cities programme has referred to CaSanAT as a 'micro-utopia', where social activists and volunteers get together to champion environmental, social, economic and gender justice, and the rights and aspirations of their own community (all this while being threatened with closure by the Bolsonaro government). The centre converted a derelict site using natural and recycled construction materials and clean energy. It now produces its own food, hosts a local farmers' market, houses a library of material on Brazilian environmental movements and the history of the *gaúcho* people, and distributes food and hygiene products to families falling through the cracks in the government's welfare system. Experiments like the CaSanAT centre show how city dwellers can reclaim their ownership of the city, even in hostile political environments. Isadora Hastings from the Atlas of Utopias evaluation committee reflected that those involved in the project have 'through the advancement of local control and participatory democracy ... generated an economy to promote sustainable societies, without exploitation of the working class or livelihoods'. It is a really powerful and humbling example of what can be achieved, and one that could be replicated in cities across the world, if the will is there and even when politics are tricky.

In Mississippi, Cooperation Jackson is shaping a more regenerative future in the west Jackson neighbourhood through its community-led programmes grounded in equity, solidarity and mutual aid. The goals of the project are bold; it aims to make Jackson a zero-waste and zero-emissions city, which depends on community production of local goods and services. In doing so, the initiative has established co-operatives for housing, construction and waste recycling, as well as a community land trust. It is also improving electoral diversity by supporting independent, progressive candidates to municipal offices, and has set up a human rights institute. According to Transformative Cities: 'From community energy centres to the creation of three eco-villages, within the next five years the project will retrofit 100 homes (making them completely off-grid) and build the capacity to produce 10% of Jackson's vegetables on urban, solar-powered farms.' It's a testament to the strength of neighbourhood.

The reason communities can be so powerful is that the capability for adaptation often resides and is at its strongest at local level. We saw this during the Covid-19 pandemic with mutual-aid groups springing up all over the world. The reserves of social capital available will dictate how neighbourhoods bounce back from tough times. Aga Otero commented to me that those with strong community structures, realised through neighbourhood or faith networks, for instance, tend to fare better than those without those social structures, even if their socio-economic status is broadly similar. Protecting and creating this bank of resilience will be especially important in a post-Covid-19 world, where the projections suggest that we will be dealing with a significant period of economic fallout. As these shockwaves pulse through society, it's the resilience banks created by initiatives in the community that are the key resources to keep people healthy, safe, connected and strong. Aga's Energy Garden (which we first encountered in the Wilderness chapter) is a brilliant example of how to create this resilience dividend. While the main driver is solar energy generated in, for and by the community, the project also adds in improvements to health through physical activity and social connection, and ecological knowledge via locally grown produce and wildlife habitat. Very quickly, we can see how creating these multi-layered benefits helps communities survive and thrive. The key to empowering city dwellers is to think globally but act locally; as Aga said, cities may yet get a little less easy to live in with increased unemployment and more demand for city services, but being intentional about things like community gardens, knowing our neighbours and being ready to connect with each other can help us weather these storms.

All too often, those in authority see gentrification as a way of improving the neighbourhood. A perpetual political and social hot potato, its intricacies are too numerous to set out in these pages. But it is worth saying that gentrification is nuanced and highly contextual. It can be both held up as a beacon of urban success and become the road to dislocation and disenfranchisement of communities, often in the same breath. With the interplay of market forces, government policies and neighbourhood characteristics, it comes with positives and negatives, as do most things. As ever, we should be cautious about binary assumptions. When I spoke to Michael Berkowitz, founding principal of Resilient Cities Catalyst, he cautioned that gentrification is complex and not always the enemy. He explained that the worst impact of gentrification, which can be seen in enclaves where property is almost exclusively owned by Russian and Chinese oligarchs or rented out permanently as holiday lets, is that wealth is brought in but nobody actually lives there, and the interaction with the community at a grassroots level isn't there. 'For communities to thrive,' says Michael, 'we need real people living there year-round.' Organic gentrification, which supports a mix of inbound, outbound and static populations without losing the area's social fabric, can be good, but tension arises as improvements for the existing community are played against development that will introduce new waves of residents from a higher socio-economic background and upset the balance. It's a complex set of levers to pull. In some cases, controls like tenant protection can help, and certainly most cities would benefit from a rebalancing of tenant–landlord dynamics. In the 2021 mayoral elections in London, Mayor Sadiq Khan emphasised the measures he would like to take to alleviate the strain on renters in the capital, which include getting rid of 'no fault' evictions, arbitrary rental fees and uncapped deposits – something that many cities are experimenting with and which we should continue to ask for.

Ultimately, cities are restless places where people come and go and communities shift constantly. It is this ebb and flow of migration that makes them so vibrant and stimulating. For us to retain a sense of rootedness, we need to prioritise developments that not only look or feel like home but are also actively lived in, with residential networks that enrich the community.

THRIVING PLACES

By including the softer values of the home in the housing conversation, we can champion homes that are designed to offer us solace and nurture our most fundamental at-home needs: rest, comfort and play. I think Kerryn Fischer's words are worth amplifying here, as someone who spends her life observing, capturing and reflecting the qualities that make homes special. She says, 'Dignity is not just a roof over your head. Quality not quantity of space creates a sense of humanity in a home.'

A huge part of being able to thrive in the city depends on something that we've been convinced we should be allergic to: rest. Modern city life gives us an endless list of tools for comparing busyness, which effectively harangue us into perpetual activity. Maria Eleftheriou, whom we heard from in the Movement chapter, commented: 'I find it really hard to switch off. I'm on the go 24 hours a day, 6 or 7 days a week and when I sit on the sofa, I feel like it's something I shouldn't be doing.' Much like Maria, millions of city dwellers are working on changing their relationship with rest. Our collective fascination with it is certainly growing; we want to know how to do it, why we should do it and what good resting looks like. As Michelle Ogundehin puts it so beautifully in *Happy Inside*, we must recognise that 'to stop is to succeed'. The pauses in life, the ebbs in the hubbub, matter. This is when we recuperate, reflect and recharge.

Claudia Hammond's comprehensive research into the top ten most popular restful activities in *The Art of Rest* should reassure us that, whatever our preference, there's a style of rest to suit us. It can be energetic or sedate, solo or with others. What works one day may not work the next, and we should be non-judgemental in how we approach it. Thinking of my friends' raised eyebrows when I insist that climbing is a form of relaxation, I was reassured when Claudia found that even intense physical activity 'allows the mind to rest'.

The main characteristic of rest, though, is that it is something other than the usual ritual (Michelle refers to this as 'otherness'); it holds no obligation or judgement. The top ten most restful activities,

178

according to Claudia's findings, are: reading, spending time in nature, being alone, listening to music, doing nothing in particular, walking, a hot bath, daydreaming, watching TV and mindfulness. Interestingly, in Claudia's study, what we really want from our rest is time alone. The role of our homes in allowing this to happen can't be overstated. We may live with others but, even then, we still need to be able to create that space or sense of privacy that lets us retreat into our own world, free from external distractions and other people from time to time.

But there is another, more obvious manifestation of rest: sleep. Perhaps unsurprisingly, sleep (or 'sleep hygiene' – a term I personally can't stand) has started a booming industry. While there are reams of scientific studies on sleep, nobody needs a lab coat to recognise that a sleep deficit is bad news. If we don't get enough sleep – and 'enough' differs from person to person – we tend to end up cranky, unfocussed or emotional. We might crave sugary or salty foods and up our coffee intake which makes the inevitable crash even worse. For me, lack of sleep invariably leads to a catastrophic sense-of-humour failure, and, for that reason, I protect sleep above all else. There are medical implications, too, including elevated blood pressure, increased risk of type 2 diabetes, heart disease, stroke, metabolic and mood disorders, and on the list goes. Whatever our symptoms, when we're tired, life is less fun for us and we're less fun to others. To protect the sanctity of sleep in the home, there are a few truths that are worth recognising: rest deserves to be honoured; FOMO, particularly relating to work outside of working hours, shouldn't be a thing; taking a digital break an hour or so before bed, and maybe for longer at the weekends, creates an atmosphere of rest that sends the right kind of signals to the brain and body.

I won't harp on about the ubiquity of the screen because we all know how pervasive they are, but – beyond the benefits to our sleep health – every now and then it can feel very empowering to switch off our devices and exist in the home without the incessant push-pull of the outside world. The liberation of disconnecting, even temporarily, can remind us of what it's like to be in our own company, our own minds and our own bodies. We don't need long – we can find restfulness by thriving without interruption for fifteen minutes.

We rebel against our internal hardwiring by constantly champing at the bit to 'get stuff done'. I'll admit that this applies to me; in my current home, I didn't sit on my sofa for the first four years of owning it. On the one hand, this was a plus because I was never in any danger of the 'sitting disease'. At the time I was working at St James's Palace and, if I wasn't tearing up and down the endless medieval stairs from garret to basement and back again, I was sprinting across London to get to the fitness studio in time to jump on the spin bike or coach clients. The flip side was that my body was permanently tired and I felt that, if I sat down, I'd never be able to get up. I was right – we can only trick the body for so long.

When, finally and following a burnout, I made this change to embrace rest, my home's minimalist style went out the door; I replaced my ever-so-chic, barely there (and therefore barely comfortable) sofa with the kind of deep-backed, heavily cushioned variety that invites you to stop and stay a while. I bought a television (something else I'd long had an aversion to) and lamps; my kitchen dresser was revamped to become a space for recipe testing and food prep, with all my cookbooks set out so that, whenever I'm in the kitchen, I'm tempted to linger, to flick absently through a cookbook over a coffee. My walls went from bright white to deep, forest green and the artefacts and art from my travels, many harking all the way back to childhood, went up on my living room walls. This also had an unexpectedly grounding effect; I was less restless about not being in South Africa, for example, when I was surrounded by objects and symbols that helped me keep my connection with it from afar.

Our living space should perhaps instead be referred to as a thriving space. In shaping our homes, we need to make them conducive to relaxation, which has become something of a global struggle as they've been co-opted into offices, gyms, schools, studios during the Covid-19 lockdowns. Far aside from our homes' immediate function as shelter, we need them to help us live and thrive. Our behaviour inside them needs to find a balance of discipline (keeping it clean and uncluttered) and indulgence (making space for relaxation and time spent free from obligation).

Ilse Crawford, designer, academic and creative director, reminds us of the physicality of behaviours in the home. It is here, in our private spaces, that we return to the nearest version of our primal selves, where our lives at home centre around activities that have greater vulnerability to them, like resting, bathing or loving. In a short film, *Wellness & Wellbeing – Ilse Crawford* by VOLA, Ilse says: 'I believe our senses are another intelligence.' She reminds us that having a connection to our objects can ground us in the moment (think about the tactility of curling up in your favourite blanket in a quiet nook in your home, for example, or clutching your favourite mug as you take your first sip of tea in the morning). By treating our spaces as backdrops to our lives and curating our objects, Ilse says we can transform normal everyday moments into 'habits and rituals' that make life more special. Then, when we recognise our objects are attached to ritual and habitability rather than just being 'stuff', we delicately nudge ourselves towards better behaviours. Living at breakneck speed blocks our capacity and desire to dwell.

The Right to the City idea urges us to shift 'the focus of our cities away from being playgrounds for capital and profit, and towards being living social, political, and indeed economic entities. By reclaiming urban spaces as collective places for people, by people, we can prevent the marginalization, criminalization and expulsion of large sectors of the population from our cities.'

In embracing the opportunities for rest and play that our homes can offer us, they become spaces of solace and regeneration. When we consider the projections of recessions, possible next waves of Covid-19 and the likelihood of a lingering nervousness in the public psyche, we're likely to keep turning to our homelife for support. Reaching out to change the elements of life that are within our grasp can help us to navigate more challenging external circumstances. For those with the means to do so, Covid-19 has caused many city dwellers to consider moving out of the city to places where they can pursue greater quality of life in the long term. But a great many more will remain, out of choice or necessity, so making cities liveable for the long term, for all stages of life, should be our most important mission for planners, policymakers and neighbours alike.

If the concept of being still is one of the most appreciated aspects of lockdown, then creating more opportunities for gentle activity and time and space to dwell should be high on the list as we renegotiate our city lives. While we may not be able to see behind the closed doors of master planners and developers, we can stay active and engaged in the spaces that allow us the all-important breathing room. New and existing developments of all scales should enhance locally significant biodiversity, and recreational spaces that stand to enrich our physical and mental health.

Ultimately, as renters or buyers, planners or policymakers, we have a shared identity as city dwellers, and we have to keep asking ourselves what kind of places we want to inhabit. We don't need to be property owners to feel invested in our spaces or to recognise that our neighbourhoods are an extension of our homes. If we subscribe to the view that diversity of skills, landscapes, life experience and identity adds hugely to our sense of wellbeing in the city, then these are the types of neighbourhoods we should embrace. Our challenge now is to take an active part in the conversations about how we care for the dwellings of today while planning those of tomorrow, so that we co-create dwellings that allow us to thrive.

6

IMAGINATION

Imagine a city where graffiti wasn't illegal, a city where everybody could draw whatever they liked. Where every street was awash with a million colours and little phrases. Where standing at a bus stop was never boring. A city that felt like a party where everyone was invited, not just the estate agents and barons of big business. Imagine a city like that and stop leaning against the wall – it's wet.

Banksy

IT'S SIMPLY NOT enough for cities to be functional and liveable – they should be lovable too. Art and culture are some of the most powerful tools we have to help us understand and fall in love with our cities. A city that supports our wellbeing will have a slice of creativity to suit the penchants of everyone; according to UNESCO's Creative Cities programme, there are seven major sources of urban creativity: crafts and folk art, design, film, gastronomy, literature, music and media arts.

Writing this chapter in the midst of the Covid-19 pandemic was a challenge, as our creative industries were shuttered and our deep social attachment to them was left without an outlet. With comedy, rhythm and melody shut out of city centres, this was a sure-fire way to burst the bubble on urban life. If nothing else, their absence – profoundly felt and mourned – reminded us that the creative life of cities is what makes them worth being a part of. It seems that our period of yearning to be back jostling at gigs, galleries, festivals and cinemas has built up an enormous groundswell of support. They need our enthusiasm more than ever if we are to encourage our artists back into the city because, as the Knowledge Transfer Network reminds us on their website, 'Long before there were smart cities, there were creative ones'.

Urban creative expression offers us the chance to ground ourselves in our neighbourhoods. The pause brought on by marvelling at an artwork, relishing beautiful design or soaking up the atmosphere of our favourite venue can calm us, impart stories or open our minds; all these experiences put a stamp on our urban identity. As well as inspiring our souls and guiding our leisure time, the size of urban creative economies is formidable and deserves close attention, particularly as creative industries have been the most beleaguered while the pandemic raged. Caroline Norbury, chief executive of the Creative Industries Federation, was quoted in a press release in June 2020 as saying:

Our creative and cultural sectors bring communities together, they employ millions and are at the heart of our soft power. These are the industries of the future: highly innovative, resistant to automation and integral to both our cultural identity and the nation's mental health. We're about to need them more than ever.

According to the Creative Industries Federation, prior to the pandemic the contribution of the creative industries to the UK was £115 billion. To put these statistics in perspective, this is more than the combined contribution of the automotive, aerospace, life sciences and oil and gas industries. In America, the National Assembly of State Arts Agencies puts the figure at US$919.7 billion. This is 4.3 per cent of the US GDP and is worth more than the construction, transportation and warehousing, travel and tourism, mining, utilities and agriculture industries put together. The South Africa Cultural Observatory pegs it at R63 billion, which is 1.5 per cent of the South African GDP and, across the African continent, creative industries are estimated to be worth US$4.2 billion in revenue, employing in the region of 500,000 people, according to *Getting Creative about Development* report by Aubrey Hruby of the Atlantic Council's Africa Centre.

Urban areas are both magnets and amplifiers for creativity, and the industries they spawn are inherently localised, which makes them a vital source of economic and social resilience in turbulent times. In the World Cities Culture Forum report, *Culture and Climate Change*, culture is 'valued' as a platform for provocation as much as celebration. In a 2021 event, 'Can Art Save the Planet?', run by Tortoise Media, climate justice creative Suzanne Dhaliwal spoke of three ways culture impacts us: it illustrates the world around us; it is at the forefront of innovation; and it elevates stories. Speaking in the same panel, Alison Tickell, founder and chief executive of Julie's Bicycle, a not-for-profit that supports climate action by the creative community, emphasised that art often harnesses values and action, and the two can't be decoupled. It is not uncommon for artistry to reflect, provoke, tease, challenge and celebrate the status quo, and it can be directed at those with the hard power, the marginalised and the everyday unsung heroes.

Almost irrespective of its underlying motive, the presence of art and culture fundamentally lifts our spirits and it is part of the unique DNA making up many communities. The benefit of having creative capital inextricably woven through our urban networks is that it can ignite interest in our neighbourhoods and cause us to connect with the people and places around us. The opportunity for this is made greater in cities because they multiply the chance to share art in all forms, in large volume, with others. When we squeeze our way out of a live music gig or theatre, for instance, and find ourselves in a gaggle on the street, there is a collective buzz that comes from having had a shared experience with complete strangers.

We are sensory beings. We might at times lose the strength of our vital connection to the wild, but creative forms can rejuvenate feelings of awe, joy and discovery – allowing us to find new meaning or enjoyment in everyday rituals right on our doorsteps. Art and culture can lift our neighbourhoods, helping us encounter new things even on the days when life may seem at its most banal.

BUILDINGS WITH IMAGINATION

Creative expression is transformational; it can elevate our life experience, so we need to understand how we can help create the conditions for these experiences to thrive. The reimagination of existing urban space is part of this; we often don't need to build something new, as we'll see when we get to festivals later on in the chapter – we need different eyes to see the potential in the parts of our cities that are lying fallow, and this is where residents can help. In cities across the world, vacant high-street shops, decaying post-industrial areas, blank walls and dormant real estate should remind us that spaces are waiting to be reimagined into inspiring places of artistry. Contrary to traditional ideas of creative expression, it doesn't all need to be concentrated in a designated 'culture district'. When I spoke to Lee Bofkin, founder of Global Street Art, he suggested that, at their healthiest, cities should have space for many different kinds of expression: small and large scale, authorised and unauthorised, and of varying levels of skill.

Charles Landry, author of *The Creative City*, suggests that culture transcends our traditional idea of 'art'. It's as much about our activities as physical form and reflects the 'lived experience of a place and time'. Reading University, drawing on Landry's work, suggests that culture includes:

> artistic or archaeological history, built form, landscape and landmarks, attractiveness and legibility of public space, indigenous and recent ethnic traditions, local products and craft skills, quality of retail, leisure, sport and entertainment, sub-cultures, civic traditions, festivals and rituals, traditional arts and new cultural industries.

This shows us that there are ample opportunities for city dwellers to lean into, and support, our urban cultural life forces.

Nurturing our makers and creative industries will be critical as we seek to shape cities that are beautiful, welcoming and sociable. Rather than art being added as a gloss over the top of our city experience, creativity is embedded in the very fabric of our communities and buildings, often without us realising it. So how do we know if a city is artist friendly? While there's no fixed formula, public investment in the arts and affordable living for the people who make it seem to be a couple of the dealbreakers. Between them, the BBC and *Format Magazine* consider some of the most artist-friendly cities to be Sante Fe, Lisbon, Copenhagen and Barcelona. Of course, artistic communities fluctuate as much as cities, and while our traditional centres of art are still on the scene, they are now sharing the limelight with cities like Sharjah, Belgrade and Mexico City, whose alternative histories have spawned the emergence of strong, modern and non-Western artistic communities. This creative expression can be seen in the very buildings that surround us.

Cities aren't all about cement monoliths and glass walls; there are innumerable examples of buildings that stop us in our tracks with their beauty, boldness or flamboyance. St Basil's Basilica in Moscow, Angkor Wat in Bangkok and the Casa Mila in Barcelona, for instance, can stir awe in even the most casual passer-by. This is the value of design: it can disarm, inspire and provoke, and so often it involves the use of colour, texture and shape which combine to bring a vibrance and atmosphere to the area.

Design can also provoke thought by focusing our attention on the local environment. At a planning level, cities tend to concentrate on the physical and psychological comfort of a building's inhabitants, but a building also needs to complement and draw out the best in its landscape. In the early days of the Covid-19 pandemic, I escaped via Zoom to Africa and a world of luxury thanks to Deborah Calmeyer's assembly of some of the finest designers behind luxury lodges in South Africa, Botswana and beyond in her 'Power of Design' event. At this point you might question what relevance this kind of luxury and landscape has to do with our cities. Granted, retreating even virtually to the floodplains of Botswana is a privilege for the few, but there are still lessons that apply to how buildings settle into their place in the urban jungle. In the depths of nature, lodges begin from scratch, with no infrastructure or services and with stringent environmental controls and limits on materials (often no concrete or cement, for instance). Botswana has a strict development brief in place to protect the integrity of its wilderness and is an example of how design-led development can create versatile and thoughtful places that enhance the spirit of people and place without compromising on performance. In the webinar, Anton de Kock, reflecting on his latest project, the Xigera lodge in the Okavango Delta floodplains, observed the deeply powerful inspiration that can be harnessed from the bush. 'If we draw from nature,' he says, 'design is timeless and elegant.' Thoughtful design means creating something that is meant to be in its place; this means that every element – each piece of metal, stone, wood or textile – needs to be thought out in terms of form, function and life cycle. The idea is that buildings are there in perpetuity, nestling deep into the landscape and enhancing the spirit of the place. This is surely something we want to emulate at a city level.

Utopic as it sounds, taking some of these principles of thoughtful design can help us dial up the energy behind beautiful places. The UK *Living with Beauty* report, co-authored by the Prince's Foundation, offers three pieces of advice on development design: 'ask for beauty, refuse ugliness, and promote stewardship.' If beauty versus ugliness sounds a little fairy tale, beauty for the report's authors means 'everything that promotes a healthy and happy life, everything that makes a collection of buildings into a place, everything that turns anywhere into somewhere, and nowhere into home'. Ugliness, on the other hand, refers to buildings that violate the landscape in which they are placed. Ugly buildings are those that 'destroy the sense of place, undermine the spirit of community, and ensure that we are not at home in our world'.

Of course, in all of this, beauty is in the eye of the beholder and the aesthetic sensibilities of those with hard power often fail to clock the deeper riches in urban communities that underpin the unique, creative character of cities. In our transition towards good design, we need to be conscious of creating so-called 'ghettos for the rich'; Hudson Yards in New York, HafenCity in Hamburg and Canary Wharf in London are a few examples of well-intentioned schemes that have been accused of trumping socio-cultural capital and exacerbating localised inequalities. Making space for creativity doesn't mean 'out with the old'. Rather than focusing on creating new cultural and social spaces, our cities must recognise what already exists so vibrantly within our diverse communities, be they hipster, squatter, migrant or indigenous. Simply put, the social versatility of our places increases when they are nice to be in.

We've seen throughout this book that social and environmental wisdom woven into the fabric of our communities supports places that people can thrive in. For this to be true, we need to dispense with the old-fashioned idea of 'consultation' with communities (usually passive, light-touch and aimed only at narrow groups of residents or businesses) to genuine co-design. Co-design hinges on democratic participation at the local planning level. As the *Living with Beauty* report suggests, local plans need to become much more visual and reflective of community views. They should be seeking to share a full picture of the local vision in lived-experience terms rather than being overly technical or hard to access, which can obfuscate aspects that might be contentious. This is a critical lever for protecting and valuing local beauty, community, history and landscape.

Whether or not a city is 'liveable' hinges on the lived experience of city dwellers – those working, living and spending time in the urban environment. This is far more critical than the transient experience of visitors. The desires, needs, preferences and ability of city residents to access arts and culture are often different to those who are visiting. It's a balancing act because the contribution of tourism to major cities is immense. The World Travel and Tourism Council's 2019 report, which studies seventy-three global cities, found that travel and tourism directly accounts for 4.4 per cent of city GDP (US$691 billion) and 17 million jobs. In 2018, Shanghai, Paris and Beijing had some of the largest travel and tourism economies globally, while tourism accounts for 7.9 per cent of GDP in Cape Town, 30.2 per cent in Marrakesh and a whopping 49.6 per cent in Cancun. But much like runaway residential gentrification, the ecology of our urban environments can be substantially changed by tourism and the imagination that is already inbuilt in our cities can be trampled to make space for manufactured tourist precincts.

In spring 2021, I was working in Lisbon as the Covid-19 pandemic restrictions in Portugal eased. The city was completely empty of tourists but full of Lisbonites enjoying their city. It's the only time I've ever seen a European city devoid of international visitors during what would usually be the beginning of the peak season. It occurred to me while running through Barrio Alto one evening that one of the gifts we have been given in the past twelve months is the chance to think deeply about what we really need from our cities as locals, and not as tourists.

There are examples of cities winning the battle on this, as Kerryn Fischer reminded me when we spoke; in 2020, Greece's Central Archaeological Council ordered a newly constructed luxury hotel in Athens to remove its top two floors, which had blocked neighbourhood views of the Acropolis. The mayor of Athens, Kostas Bakoyannis, was quoted in *The Architect's Newspaper* saying, 'The Acropolis is our heart and our soul, an essential part of our cultural heritage. It's very important that everyone can enjoy it.'

Often the physical heart of our cities can feel a little empty, belying the generations of transformation that have come before. The real heart and soul of our cities can't be confined to a tight geographic locale, and such neatly delineated spaces are seldom representative of the depth of a city's personality. In fact, these spaces are often the sites of a profound cleansing of history – the faceless architecture of mass retail that now defines many an urban high street, as well as the museums and galleries that house art and artefacts that themselves have often been lifted from their original intended context.

In reality, the heart of our urban centres is more disparate and all the better for it. We are as likely to find it in Buttes-Chaumont over the Hôtel de Ville in Paris, Hackney Wick over Trafalgar Square in London, or Greenpoint over Times Square in New York. Luisa Bravo, of the University of Bologna, in her report *Public Spaces and Urban Beauty* puts this down to the fact that the urban heart of many of our cities no longer offers us the opportunity for public and social relationships. In becoming 'en plein air museums, a postcard for tourists', they have also become places that citizens actively avoid. Most city dwellers will be able to identify the place in their city that fits this bill: a network of monuments, museums and places, connected by a predictable mix of luxury retail and souvenirs, where consumer messaging trumps the more thoughtful ways of living in the areas away from mass attention, and where products and services that meet transient needs are prioritised over the everyday. Bravo comments that the 'need to preserve historical values of designed public spaces, for a large consumption of their beauty, for many years [has] frozen any possibility to enhance emerging needs and desires to enjoy public life inside the city'.

SELECTIVE STORYTELLING

All too often, the historical values being preserved in our cities are not the ones that reflect the true histories of the people living in them. In Demi Ademuson's essay 'Finding Modernity Through History' on the Nigerian architect Mariam Kamara, she reflects Kamara's belief that 'Colonisation led to the destruction of architecture around the world, which occludes the imagination of people so much so that we often cannot imagine what existed before. And if we can't trace our history it is hard to picture a modernity that stems from us.'

Meanwhile the collective reckoning of multiple and layered voices in city narratives has increased the value of creativity and innovation in cities in the global south. Reflecting on Accra's experience, Ghanaian architect Alice Asafu-Adjaye noted that, as more opportunities become available for creatives, emerging artistic talent no longer feels the need to leave the continent for cities in America, Europe or beyond.

Growing interest in architecture and design is happening alongside better access to, and celebration of, the creative prowess of diaspora communities. Asafu-Adjaye, for instance, has observed a return to domestic planning in Accra, where social and environmental uniqueness are underpinning new developments. Speaking to the art magazine *Elephant* in May 2019, she says, 'Until a few years ago all the houses looked like something you'd find in Texas. Everything was just built on a huge scale, as opposed to designed, but now people are seeing the value in working with an architect, to create something that responds to the environment, and feels truly Ghanaian.'

This goes to the core of how we choose to tell the story of our cities. Our persistent focus on the most recent version of history has perpetuated a city narrative that periodically but heavily edits out its roots and, in the process, erases access to alternative visions of the future. Returning to Mariam Kamara, in an interview with *Elle Décor* in January 2021, she eloquently comments that how we narrate yesterday determines how we imagine tomorrow and observes that

'Our focus on relatively recent – and often expertly edited – Western histories is at best a missed opportunity. The future presents challenges like the climate crisis, rapid urbanization, and demographic explosions for which we cannot consider real solutions until we decolonize our point of view.'

Kamara's practice is based in Niamey, Niger, where she invites teenagers to contribute to her participatory design process. In Demi's essay about Kamara she reflects on how, when the architect invites young people to visualise their dream home, they tend to draw not a single dwelling but a community of dwellings, which is testament to the importance of community in African life. Also, the buildings are usually accompanied by trees, again testifying to how, even from a young age, Nigerians value the way nature increases the liveability of their surroundings, particularly by offering shade from the punishing 45°C temperatures of the Sahara Desert.

What would it be like if we got our young people in every city to draw their dream homes or to photograph the parts of the city that mean most to them? I'm certain that we'd understand the complexity of our urban populations more. In Durban's Narratives of Home project, Russel Hlongwane reflected in 2019 that many of our assumptions about designing a home don't reflect the nuances of different cultures. He says, for instance, 'South African Black families aren't nuclear ones consisting of two parents with one or two children. Instead, we're constantly surrounded by and cohabit with what we have come to call "sister cousins" or "cousin brothers" and family friends who have come to etch a life in the brutal city.'

If architecture and design can exclude communities, though, they can also be used to include them. Inviting variety and places co-designed by communities is a powerful way to dilute the dominant top-down approach to city design. Done right, urban regeneration makes it fun to unpack our places and understand the lives that have come before us, and it can inspire us by showing us the kinds of crafts that are woven into our buildings and products.

In the sweet spot where architecture meets artisanry, Kamara is working on Artisans Valley, a project in Niamey, Niger, that is a marketplace-cum-craft studio-cum-open-access gallery. Rather than consign local artisans to the tourist quarter, Artisans Valley puts them at the heart of local activity. The project transforms a down-at-heel part of town, provides a place for artisans to display and sell their products, and gives voice to local craft-masons, weavers and metalworkers who will build the space. This mixed-use area will be full of life at all hours: in the waking hours it will be peopled by artisans and shoppers, who are invited to relax and play in the surrounding space, and at night it supports food vendors and entertainment. According to Kamara's architecture practice, atelier masōmī: 'The goal is to inject traditional building forms into the rapidly urbanising city, to integrate artisans and create common ground between the "haves" and "have nots" on opposite sides of the valley.'

This approach to architectural design shows how we can build imagination in and, by doing so, connect with others and create a sense of community in the city. This can be replicated across the world. But the indoors is only one part of the equation and, if we head outside, it's clear that the city offers us a multitude of living canvases.

PAINTED CITIES

A couple of juxtaposed truths exist when it comes to creativity in cities. The greyscale monoliths that have emerged from outmoded planning systems and skewed policies sit alongside the inextinguishable posse of independent artists, performers, designers, artisans and creators whose passion is a potent source of energy. I wanted to highlight outdoor art in this book because of its openness and accessibility, and during the Covid-19 pandemic, it was the primary source of 'live' visual art for many of us. Behind closed doors, beneath railway arches, in multi-storey car parks, on building facades and often under the cover of the night, a network of artists and renegades are rewriting how we interact with our cities. From Invader's pixelated Spider-Man in Paris and Banksy's

'Girl with Balloon' in London to South African artist Faith47's 'The Progress of the Truth of Men' in Vancouver and MadC's '700 Wall' in Berlin, street art has become an iconic part of city landscape and often sits alongside built landmarks.

The space we make for art – indoor or outdoor, sanctioned or unsanctioned, free, affordable or elite – will help us activate creative expression worthy of the twenty-first century. As cities recognise the uniqueness of their local artists and designers, and there is less talent flooding out of emerging cities to the west, there will be more demand for artistic spaces that are embedded in their cultural landscape. The Southern Guild Gallery in Cape Town, for instance, is one of a few spaces that celebrates African designers and artisans. Trevyn McGowan, co-founder of the gallery, reflects that in Africa we haven't historically made room for dedicated spaces to celebrate our own artists. Southern Guild supports work that is produced with longevity and increases awareness of the level of talent available on African soil. In an interview with the *Financial Times* in 2019, Trevyn observed that the people are becoming more open-minded to the contribution of other cultures, particularly set against deepening civic and political fractures in cities of the global north. As art, artefact and inspiration flow back towards their creative roots, the traditional gallery spaces have a chance to reimagine what and who they exhibit, and how.

Classical art is often housed in a space that is frozen in time while contemporary art tends to be shared in ultra-modern, sterile galleries that don't always invite us in, and we don't always feel much when we do go inside. One evening in winter 2020, I sat in with my beloved neighbour Heidi Kreamer-Garnett, gemologist and co-founder of Gem X, nursing some wine and setting the art world to rights. Thinking back to the days of gallery visits in New York and Paris, we reflected on the strange phenomenon of crowding so many fine works together. In some ways, too many paintings clustered together may devalue the art and the effort behind it, and often tends to be aimed at an old 'been there, done that' model of tourism that seeks to fuel the rush of ticking things off. What we get from this 'drive-by' art viewing, to borrow Heidi's words, is limited.

As Heidi pointed out, 'it takes time to experience beauty', and the savouring of it is what creates our memories. In democratic terms, our urban galleries have traditionally been exclusive, made most welcoming to the elite, though there are signs that this is changing – Frances Morris, director of Tate Modern, refers to her gallery and others as being 'in conversation with people'.

The idea that the average city dweller has the time or inclination to make purposeful visits to 'see art' or 'do culture' is outmoded and misses the beauty of the modern city and ignores the demands on our time and energy. While our grand opera houses and museums hold a dear place in our hearts, they can't always quench our thirst for artistry day to day. Instead, we get this through a gentler and more democratic process of participating in pockets of creative activity as they flare up in our neighbourhoods. Juliana Engberg, programme director for European Capital of Culture Aarhus in 2017, observed in *The Guardian* that the modern city dweller prefers to 'meander about in districts characterised by warehouses, and the hole-in-the-wall operations of nascent pop-up culture – cafes, start-up galleries – which themselves breed the next gen of outlets: bookshops, grassroots and recycle boutiques'. Engberg's suggestion resonates with lots of our post-industrial cities, where the transition to a service economy has led to factories and warehouses lying derelict and dormant, quietly waiting for a *Doctor Who*-style regeneration.

Artists and creators are fundamental to seeing this potential and catalysing fresh starts; co-operatives and other community-based models have shown their clout by triggering the reinvention of forgotten parts of our cities, reclaiming social pride in these areas. Copenhagen's Kødbyen (meatpacking district) is one such example. As the industrial meat businesses moved out, they left a cluster of large warehouses, primed and ready for the artists to move into, followed by trendy restaurants and micro-breweries able to make the most of the space. From these humble beginnings, districts can change their identity, create civic pride and attract a new demographic of residents and businesses who add another layer to the story of place.

A recent study by Gerald Carlino of the Federal Reserve Bank of Philadelphia and Albert Saiz of Massachusetts Institute of Technology examined the connection between a city's beauty and key growth indicators. Their findings pinpoint a new type of neighbourhood that catalyses a return to the city for young, smart, creative residents. They call it the Central Recreational District: 'The CRD, not the CBD, is the magnet for the back-to-the-city movement, as more affluent and educated people are drawn to the urban center's abundant amenities and beauty.' This research is interesting because it also flags to us something we've already seen with areas like Shoreditch in London or Redfern in Sydney (each at different points on the 'hipster' scale). While these places are beloved to both cities, they also remind us that even the process of reimagining spaces needs to be approached at a landscape level (like Tilly Collins' approach to mapping green areas that we explored previously). Otherwise, we run the risk of repeating old habitats by doing a full 180, shunting capital and investment in one direction which can strip the area of its heart, soul and people – the very reason it became so interesting in the first place. We can also take a more varied approach to urban regeneration by focusing on the uniqueness of an area and the local spirit; it doesn't mean only following the coffee–craft beer prescription. A connected, imaginative city will embrace repurposing of spaces and work out how they can nestle into and reflect their neighbourhoods with renewed relevance.

The presence of art and culture can debunk the myth that cities are unresponsive to their surroundings. When it comes to changing how we interact with our places, sometimes our hardwired busyness can only be disrupted by the visual equivalent of a slap in the face. Street art is one such art form. Like it or loathe it, street art helps return the people power to cities and gives us something beautiful, different or even challenging to look at along the way. By its nature, it tends to be more temporary than traditional arts and may respond to the propensity for a neighbourhood to be in flux or to change over time.

Our urban physical environments are traditionally harsh landscapes: physically they give us hard lines, muted colour palettes and imposing structures; politically and institutionally they can be fractured and behind the times. It's no wonder then that we need bold imaginations that tear up the rulebook and give us the chance to enjoy our urban lives in new ways.

Otto Schade (aka Osch) is a Chilean-born artist of international acclaim living in London and painting the streets of the world. He described it to me like this: a lot of the time, street artists are painting for fun and the most attractive and risk-light options for this type of vandalism is the archetypal abandoned building. He reflects somewhat drily on the reality that artists are often painting alongside groups of people injecting hard drugs. Once the street art settles into an area, the tourists arrive, then the area gets cleaned up and the housebuilders move in. When I asked him about why street art has become so ubiquitous in gritty inner-city centres, he paused for a moment, before reflecting that 'when we have no landscape to show, we have street art'.

I didn't know Otto prior to this, but for about a year I had walked past a building he'd painted (a piece called 'Aquarium'). Taking a fairly nondescript block opposite a wholesale supermarket and on a street with considerable illicit activity, Otto transformed it into an aquarium scene. The tentacles of a squid now reach across the building, tropical fish blow bubbles beneath residents' windows and a crab scuttles to the left of the front door. This was commissioned by the owner of the building, although sadly the amount of paint needed to cover the whole block was considerably more than budgeted for and Otto had to make a personal investment to bring the piece to life. But, he insisted, he was so passionate about the merits of the project and bringing the wall to life that he saw it through and he speaks with great pride about it.

When I asked Otto what he felt was necessary for us to be able to live among open-access art in our cities, his response was thoughtful. The main thing we need, he said, is for our councils or local authorities to connect with artists. There was one suggestion I particularly loved, which was that each city could have a map that details the potential points for street-art activity, private or public.

Administered by a mayoral or council team, communities would have access to a pool of artists either based in the city or internationally and would be able to nominate and crowdfund artwork. Otto also reminded me that, as community members, we are entirely able to commission our own works of street art for far less than the cost of an annual membership to a museum, for instance. I asked him how much of this had happened so far. None of it yet, he admits, but as a veteran in this space, he is optimistic that the future is bright for painted cities. Street art is relatively nascent in its role in urban development but has emerged as a popular, visually appealing and cost-friendly way of bringing art to the people.

To dig deeper beneath the skin of street art, I had an animated exchange with Lee Bofkin, founder of the creative agency Global Street Art. Bringing up the concept of dwell-time (the time we feel inclined to linger in a space), Lee reflected on the power of street art to alter the speed at which we walk through an area. Generally, when we aren't paying attention, our urban autopilot mode propels us through our streets and buildings without a second glance. However, irrespective of whether we like the pieces or not, just the act of noticing street art triggers a part of our brain that is often otherwise rendered passive while we hustle from place to place. The bold and refreshing mission of Global Street Art is to enable us to 'live in painted cities'; at an immediate, sensory level, street art injects colour and variety into our well-trodden grey paths. I asked Lee for his thoughts on any connection street art might have with nature, and he said:

> There is no mural as beautiful as being in a forest. I wonder if in some ways, street art is a cry for help in an attempt to create a more variable environment that approximates some of the beauty of being in nature ... The idea of being in a monotone, grey environment of monoliths is banal and gets us down.

His take on cities is that they are often 'retrofitted accidents' and, in trying to insulate us from some of the risks of nature, they can also deprive us of its joys at the same time. Street art's vibrant colour, then, is perhaps a way to give us that sensory immersion that we're unconsciously missing in the concrete jungle.

Lee noted that the very presence of street art sends a signal to us about what kind of interactions are permitted or encouraged within the local environment. Essentially it signals to the viewer and visitor that 'art is welcome, creativity is normalised and that people are able to paint in the area'. However, Lee also draws a distinction between 'what street art currently is versus what it could be'. Inadvertently, we can create an unbalanced approach to urban zoning where we associate street art with exclusively young, cool neighbourhoods full of coffee boutiques, co-working spaces and hipsters, while our more 'conventional' areas end up with very little. In fact, the reality could offer us so much more and Lee talks about the possibility of neighbourhood programming that provides a level of street-art curation. This is similar to Otto Schade's suggestion. Supporting the street-art community – both artists and viewers – is important because this type of art is free and accessible at volume. The UNESCO Creative Cities programme itself observes that culture and creativity are woven into the everyday life and practice of local city dwellers and, in the street setting, artworks are at their most vibrant and contemporary, giving us real-time reflections on city life. Dismantling the customs that box arts and culture into specific times and places will require us to lean into artistic practices that are available and affordable to anyone living in the city. Art that walks the streets, as it were, is infinitely better suited to the practical needs of the living, breathing local population – it can sustain our imaginations and remind us of the primacy of creative expression to our sense of fun.

What artists can offer our cities derives from how they treat the city as a frame of reference. With an eye for the things that few of us notice, they can keep the currency of forgotten spaces alive and amplify the voices of communities who feel unseen or unheard. For city dwellers, the beauty of it is that we tend to stumble upon a piece rather than seek it out. Indeed, street-art tourism is now also a common feature of cities from Johannesburg to Valparaíso, and the lessons from it are valuable.

A few hours of immersion in the local street-art scene attunes us to the neighbourhood dynamic. Dorian Lynskey, writing about the renowned Hackney-based artist Stik, reflected that on his tour of Shoreditch with the artist it was like he suddenly had x-ray vision – 'you see things you would otherwise miss'. Stik has two works on my street, so his iconic figures are now also something I associate with home in London. But we also find them throughout New York, Jordan and Berlin (including his pieces: 'Migrant', 'Liberty' and 'Holding Hands'). As Dorian so aptly reflected, Stik's 'doleful, defiant figures are an emblem of resistance, symbolising Londoners who refuse to be rendered invisible'. Stik's understanding of the local community demonstrates more than just a drive to publicise his art; there is a kindness, intelligence and empathy to where he locates his work which comes from his desire to give back to the community. In an interview with Christie's, Stik said, 'It was squatting and eventually social housing which enabled me to gain a foothold and get back to a decent standard of life. Street art was my way of giving back to the people who helped me.'

Much of his work looks at the issue of roots and upheaval in urban communities but is also positioned in a way that gives ownership to the local community through its connection to the local context. In 2020, his self-funded sculpture 'Holding Hands' was unveiled in Hoxton Park. Describing the work in an interview for the website GraffitiStreet, Stik says:

> It is a subtle reminder of what it is to look at the world from other people's perspectives as relevant today as it will be in 100 years. The 'Holding Hands' sculpture is being installed at a poignant time in our history when holding hands is not always possible but is a symbol of hope for what has always been and what will be again. The sculpture is intended as a timeless and inclusive meeting place for all regardless of race, sexuality, gender, faith, or social status.

Artistic disruption, commented Lee Bofkin, gets us to appreciate things at a range of scales from the very close range (miniature art) to the far off (murals that stretch across whole buildings). This variation is a healthy aspect and encourages us to expand our gaze beyond our normal field of vision. One of my favourite examples of this is by street artist Ben Wilson whose exhibition space is the grimy London pavement, and his canvas, the ubiquitous feature of most city pavements – chewing gum. Walking across Millennium Bridge in London can very quickly cause neckache but it's worth it. Ben has transformed hundreds of wasted blobby masses into miniature paintings with a mind-boggling level of detail. His art does a couple of things: once you've discovered that the bridge is a gallery and waste is art, any self-consciousness about how silly you look walking with your head craned towards the ground is soon overtaken by curiosity and the joy of discovering each miniscule, brightly coloured world. Invariably, because you aren't watching where you're walking, you bump into others who are either doing the same thing or looking at you like you're a loon. If the latter, a simple explanation usually turns scepticism to curiosity and suddenly you've had a conversation with a stranger and set them off on their own street-art trail, when really all they had started out to do was cross a bridge over a river. In cities we often aren't paying attention and so we aren't necessarily incentivised to slow down. But, as Ben's work shows, the smaller-scale stuff can keep us engaged in a certain area and the likelihood of us hanging around, or returning, increases.

At the other end of the scale, there are murals that are so expansive that they occupy entire walls or buildings, often emblematic of urban change. The Silo mural in Nashville, for example, looms large over the Nations community as it slowly but surely transitions away from its industrial roots. Painted by Australian artist Guido van Helten in 2017, the piece brings to life the story of a community in flux; on one side of the disused silo is a portrait of a local man, Lee Estes, then 91 years old, who had lived in the neighbourhood since the late 1920s. On the other side of the silo is a portrait of two local children drawing – a symbol of the next generation of city guardians.

Once we've noticed everyday art in the city, we start to seek it out and this act of noticing our surroundings in a different way leads us to see other things too. I've even witnessed this in my parents, who now investigate street art wherever they travel – something they'd never have done a few years ago. On a recent trip to southern America, there was no stopping them – from the Gulch in Nashville to Treme in New Orleans, they were off – and recently when my dad visited London we made a point of seeking out the new David Speed pieces together. Not only does this art appreciation make us less passive but it also empowers us to find our own relationship with the places we live and visit.

Thankfully, the passion and love for community expressed by street-art creators is also shared and amplified by its viewers. It's a great testimony to the open access of art, as it reaches across physical and virtual worlds, mostly by social media. This is surely as valuable as being tucked behind private doors or constrained on a plinth. As Lee noted, this sharing then spawns more creativity and yet more large-scale murals to pop up all over the world. At a planning level, cities also have a growing interest in this agenda, with some being adamant that being or becoming boring simply doesn't have a place in their future. For instance, in Copenhagen's 2025 vision for the city, one of its three pillars is being 'a city with an edge'.

Mickey Kavanaugh of Unseen London Bike Tour (and a neighbour and dear friend) works in finance but juggles a few creative side hustles – DJ'ing alongside the Bike Tour. He has harnessed his local knowledge of working in London's Square Mile with a seemingly built-in radar for hidden art and history. He has a remarkable knack for spotting a new work of art on a wall almost as soon as the artist has downed their tools – as he says himself, 'we weave between ancient Roman ruins tucked away in the finance district and the regenerating creative east where the walls are still wet'. The tour was born from his passion for art, love for his neighbourhood and the chance to show locals and visitors alike an area that he has lived, worked, lunched and drunk in for well over a decade. I asked Mickey for his take on street art in the city. We were each travelling at the time and, in lieu of a conversation over a beer at the Victory, he sent me some thoughts over email. Mickey so authentically sums up the reality and possibilities of an imaginative city that I have included his thoughts in full here on the effect street art has upon a city and its inhabitants:

In 2014 I travelled extensively through Asia and cycled from Vancouver to San Diego. During my travels, I noticed I could always easily get on with people I met while attending bicycle tours of cities and countryside – from Tokyo, Manilla, Bangkok, Vancouver to name a few. I figured it was because cycling was something of a shared endeavour and the easy way of chatting to the people around you. Bike tours more than walking and coach tours encouraged people to chat to one another. Bikes also took you through neighbourhoods rather than around them and I saw more of the everyday life of a city – be it the way people interact in the street, the business working and people relaxing and embracing. There was also a tendency to get away from the big sights – which I found to be typically very constrained and didn't gain more insight about a country by looking up close at a landmark than I would by seeing it in a tour book. I liked getting the dirt on my shoes (or between my toes with flip flops).

After returning to a fast-paced corporate role in banking and business consulting, I decided to take a sabbatical and combine my enthusiasm for bike tours with a long-standing love affair with London. The elements of London I know about are the City (financial district) and the East End where I lived. When I began this was also an area that was going through the turn of gentrification so was under serviced and had a bad reputation despite, in my opinion, being far more interesting than the over-developed West End and stale images of London palaces, black taxis and the Tower of London. My London was exciting – it had Roman walls with craft coffee shops built into them, unknown tunnels from the cold war, legends re-told the world over, and hidden angels in the architecture. It also never got dull because the walls were refreshed weekly with new street art which always had something to say about the world.

Banksy and his peers had some of his formative years in the East End, and there is a legacy of street art now where the biggest names in the world come to London to paint. Like many people with an interest in street art, for me it began with Banksy's subversive and humorous pieces placed guerrilla fashion and then embraced. I learnt where all the Banksy's were and the context of the story behind them. This led to discovery of many more 'local' heroes who just went out on their day off from work and created eye-catching work, for example, 'Floating Concrete' the married couple with grown-up kids creating concrete Lego-men, Subdude, who used to write for the financial press and now made subversive puns with simple imagery, and the infinite number of messages about politics.

The street became the backbone of my bike ride; it was not the big names (though everyone loves a Banksy), but the subtle, personal pieces placed in perfect position – that could light up anyone's face and give them the buzz of discovery. We might find a marriage proposal spelled out in colour block tile by Regents Canals, painted fibre-glass mushrooms masking as climbing holds (placed there by a rock climber-cum-artist) or bits of chewing gum that have been painted. It's incredibly egalitarian.

Ultimately, everybody likes the feeling that they are walking through a door marked 'Private' and disappearing backstage. Taking people on a bike tour away from the big sights is taking them behind the scenes on a AAA pass to the city navigating to hidden corners to view little-known creations that will deteriorate within days/weeks/ months is a privilege and builds lasting memories.

For me, the loose term street art adds colour to dull parts of the local environment, builds a sense of community and ownership with shared impressions of the same artist, and dilutes much of the advertising and branding that dominates elsewhere. The East End now has part of its identity from world-leading street art, but equally from the enthusiasts and amateurs who don a hoodie, take to the walls and talk to the world.

THE CITY OF THINGS

As urban consumers, we are becoming more invested in the value of buying less and buying better, which could be a good-news story for the future of creativity in our cities. When artisanry is valued, being a maker becomes an empowering and attractive career prospect. Cities can give voice to human ingenuity by providing us ample opportunity to build creative networks, create communities based on shared enjoyment of art forms and offer routes to market for the work of artisans, as exemplified by London Craft Week, for instance. Our creative industries combine to improve our quality of life by offering us an outlet for rest and relaxation, and a source of joy and discovery. Alongside the trend towards shareable art is affordable luxury, and we as consumers are actively seeking craftsmanship from our products. Running counter to fast fashion and its kin are the trail-blazing retailers emphasising high-quality, ethical production, connections to businesses and artisans with a story to tell, and products that are designed to be classic and collectable, rather than disposable. David Droga, speaking at the Cape Town Design Indaba, delved into this heightened consumer consciousness and explained that people want to get behind things that have belief systems: 'Linear and logical people make the world go round, but it's the creative people who make it worth living in. And that's the world I wanna be in.'

Evidence for changing consumer habits and emphasis on creativity is already available and Gen Z (those born between 1997 and 2012) is showing us this better than anyone. Impulse purchasing is no longer in vogue and, according to Facebook, 45 per cent of Gen Z'ers of spending age value sustainability more highly than the cost of a product. *Vogue* article 'From Activism to Sustainable Fashion, Here's What You Need to Know About Gen Z' tells us that the new mantra is 'community first, catwalk second' and that Gen Z shoppers will interrogate the life cycle of a product and the brand's ethics before they choose to part with their money. This is significant for anyone in the business of retail as young shoppers account for 40 per cent of the spending power in the USA, Europe, Brazil, Russia, India, China and South Africa. In a retail world that promotes wellbeing of people and planet first, craft skills, vintage, resale and rental are all part of the mix. Far from being a barrier to access, these emerging rental and resale markets make design more inclusive. There is also something to be said here about fashion, jewellery and other decorative objects.

When I spoke to Heidi Kreamer-Garnett, she observed that, when so much of our lives have been taken online, jewellery and fashion 'anchor us to the physical world' as they are designed to be worn and connected to our bodies. The currency of objects and art forms that have been manipulated by hand is increasing, and we are becoming more interested in connecting with our designers and unpacking the story of our everyday items.

In this vein, we talked about the different ways of viewing our cities – we can think of them as a package of politics and policies with challenges and limitations; or we can think of them as physical spaces where we can fulfil our desire and appetite for experiencing beauty and craftsmanship, the very essence of human activity. Reflecting on her native New York, infamous for its non-stop-ness, Heidi spoke about the possibility for creative pieces to slow us down and unite us in collective admiration. The growth of GemFlix, a curated programme of talks on jewellery that Heidi creates with her New York co-founder, is testament to the value of these kinds of communities where awe and decadence become accessible to anyone with an interest and an internet connection. She points to the 'bonding experience of shared enjoyment' of creative enterprise and its importance in cities. In galleries, clubs, theatres and bars, we are rarely alone, and even solo outings allow us to share in something communal, possibly even making friends along the way.

In my conversation with Heidi, we also discussed that luxury designers are now recognising the need to make themselves relevant to contemporary people and culture. She observed that for many this has meant reaching out by developing capsule collections that bring luxury down to an affordable price point. Taking art and design 'off its pedestal' enables it to take root within communities of people who may have previously been excluded because of unaffordability or lack of representation. By putting creative products out to the general public, communities get to know their artists and start to invest in them.

Opening the doors to art and design by making it wearable and shareable shifts how we access creativity. We want to live in beautiful places and, while we may have limited control over the physical appearance of our outdoor spaces, we have far more autonomy over what adorns our homes and bodies. Our ability to exchange and share in art across digital platforms has democratised access to it and allowed for the expanding role of beauty and creativity in our lives. The more art forms we can support, the more artists we can commission, and the more we amplify the contribution of creative industries to the local economy and the feel of our cities. As Glenn Adamson, historian and author of *Craft: An American History*, points out: 'Craft, at its best, preserves the good in what has been handed down, while also shaping the world anew.'

With increasing public appetite for ethical production methods, circular design (meaning, for instance, the use of recycled fibres) and connection with artisans, the days of passive ask-no-questions consumerism appear to be numbered. Aga Otero and Michael Berkowitz refer to this as 'prosumerism'. A prosumer is the type of purchaser that is informed, curious and actively out to engage in society. Discerning customers are essential for the growth of small businesses, which are, in turn, the social lifeblood of urban communities; they employ locally and help us access small-scale producers, products from beyond our shores and high-quality items that we might not otherwise happen upon.

This dilution of the homogeneity of large-volume retailers doesn't just make our purchasing power more targeted, it also makes our streets more interesting. A street lined with independent retailers is rarely less interesting than one populated with carbon copies of every high-volume retail brand. When I met with Leo Johnson he confirmed that 'hyperlocalism' is one of the biggest trends shaping our urban futures. The spanner that this throws in the works of the 'mass era', to use Leo Johnson and Michael Blowfield's words from

Turnaround Challenge, is significant and welcome. Musing about the future of our iconic city high streets, Leo and I dreamed for a moment about what Oxford Street or Fifth Avenue might look like if they prioritised and celebrated local designers and artisans.

Our major high streets tend to be dominated by the craft of fashion, and fashion capitals like Milan and Paris have typically emerged alongside artistic hotspots, where innovation, design, production, retail and advertising coalesce to support clothing as a big business. While fashion is rooted in craft and design, the volume that we consume in cities has become worrying. According to the World Economic Forum, 85 per cent of all textiles end up in landfill annually (for context, WEF helpfully highlights that that's enough to fill up Sydney Harbour every single year); textiles make up 10 per cent of our global carbon footprint and they are the second largest consumer of water. As city dwellers learn the benefits of slowing down, we can also help to shape the impact our fashion has, too. Instead of increasing the number of collections that come out annually, we can use our buying power to buy better, less often. Looking at the shift in consumption patterns as *Vogue* observed above, this is a great opportunity for us to influence what our fashion brands offer us, and emerging emphasis on provenance and slow fashion is a hopeful sign.

ALIVE AT NIGHT

City infrastructure should be able to support us whether we're morning larks or night owls. A hefty amount of urban activity takes place between dusk and dawn, and yet our conversations about liveability are dominated by conventional hours of sun-up. Not only is this strange considering a lot of our leisure time is consigned to hours of darkness but, in weighting our conversations about city liveability towards only half the day, we risk neglecting the vast portion of our urban populations whose livelihoods are rooted firmly in the night-time economy. Leni Schwendinger, founder of the International Nighttime Design Initiative, reflects that 'Night is a time, but it is also a place'. On the initiative's website, she reminds us that 'depending on one's viewpoint, the night can be poetic or dangerous, romantic or lonely, rowdy or sleepy'. Whether using the night for productivity or leisure, or even just for sleep, our cities should be designed to allow us to thrive at all hours of the day and night.

NewCities, a global non-profit taking a 'whole-city' approach to urban futures, talks about the need for many cities to 'humanize the night' so it becomes something to be embraced and enjoyed rather than avoided. A working group of urban leaders is on a mission to do just this. Mayor Horacio Rodríguez Larreta of Buenos Aires talks about the city's Museum Night (La Noche de los Museos), which converts the city into an open-air museum. It involves some 280 museums, galleries and cultural institutions opening from 8 p.m. until 3 a.m. Public transport is free for the evening, helping as many city dwellers as possible – nearly a million in the one night each year – visit places that they may never otherwise go to, let alone at night.

Reflecting on Sydney, Clover Moore, Lord Mayor and also a member of NewCities, offers some figures to put the contribution of the night into perspective. Sydney's night-time economy is valued in excess of A$4 billion, employs 35,000-plus people and touches approximately 5,000 businesses. When I was at university in Sydney, I was lucky enough to benefit from the Lord Mayor's 'small-bar revolution', which totally transformed the shady back alleys of the Central Business District. Once-foreboding backstreets woven between shops and offices became pathways to city-tailors-cum-cocktail-bars and new basement venues for live music and comedy. It was exciting, new and, sadly, short-lived. In a deeply misjudged and much-lamented move, the New South Wales parliament put a cloche over Sydney's internationally acclaimed nightlife with its draconian 'lockout laws'. Although intended to curb nefarious activity in King's Cross, the laws stifled the night-time economy as a whole, penalising small and independent businesses, their workers and patrons, and making it much less fun to go out.

There is a happy ending, though. After years of campaigning for their repeal, the laws were put to parliamentary review and, in March

2021, were officially lifted. The painful lessons of the seven years of lockout laws are that proportionality and listening are often absent from discussions about remedies to very nuanced urban problems. In a *TimeOut* article in 2021, it's estimated that this legislative snub was catastrophic both reputationally and economically, and is said to have cost the city more than A$16 billion in revenue.

THE FESTIVAL OF THE CITY

Aside from our more permanent scenes of arts and cultural activity, festivals have become an integral part of our urban landscapes and there are few cities in the world that can't boast of one. They revere everything from murals, beer and jazz to sex, light and tomatoes. No matter the subject for celebration, they are convivial anchor points that help to reveal the personality of a city.

Often not without underlying community tensions, their place in the ideal city make-up should be upheld; they ultimately serve to expose a mass audience to different stories, traditions and world views, and even courting controversy gets these issues out into the public domain and creates the opportunity for a conversation.

All festivals have in common their mission to celebrate the links between people and places. As natural hubs for social and cultural crossover, creative resources and supporting infrastructures, cities allow us to make a party out of just about anything. They can help us to see our home cities in new ways, encourage us to explore further afield in pursuit of influences we don't necessarily get in our own backyard (like the jazz festival in New Orleans or the beer halls of Munich) and, most importantly, celebrate communities that may have been overlooked in mainstream cultural channels.

The opportunity to amplify tradition, culture, heritage or creativity on our urban streets can help to ground us in our neighbourhoods – it can solidify belonging and cohesion for those connected with the subject of the festival, expose those less familiar to different narratives and put an alternative spin on how we identify with our homes.

Festivals offer alternative versions of our neighbourhoods: walls become canvases, parks become amphitheatres, streets become dance floors. They can also be a way of healing divides and reviving social resilience when it gets damaged. They can be a highly public spectacle, offering visual and audible reaffirmation of the value of urban areas that may have had major setbacks like natural disasters or terrorist attacks. Galvanising creativity in this way, often born from passion and love, can be one of our most heartening shows of defiance, survival and adaptability in the face of existential threats.

The Covid-19 pandemic heralded a move to more outdoor art and events and we need our public spaces more than ever. Public spaces, though, shouldn't equate to 'touristy' spaces. Where creativity counts and is most equitable is when it can be accessed by those who may not have the means to travel into tourist hubs, which are often also quite expensive. The Infect the City festival in Cape Town (recoined Un-Infect the City in 2021 for obvious reasons) has a mandate to do just that. The programme aims to give voice to the mood of the city – in 2021, to the social and psychological stressors brought by the pandemic – and has been a platform for artists to explore issues like local food security or displacement in ways that all Cape Townians have access to.

There is a difference between the impermanent festivals and those that stimulate permanent structures like the Olympics, for instance. Always boasting the promise of economic opportunity, skill development, jobs and platforms for creative industry, our major sporting events still court controversy. When the FIFA World Cup came to South Africa in 2010, the decision to relocate informal settlement dwellers to build the sporting infrastructure was at times deeply unpopular, particularly with the residents whose homes and livelihoods were directly affected. This points to the challenge of investing in buildings first, rather than people. Big-ticket, commercial events and festivals like the Olympics can lose their local sheen when they uphold economic return as the ultimate prize. Like any capital venture, building projects – especially the publicly funded variety – have a knack for overrunning, draining the public purse and being underwhelming in their real impact. Writing for *The Conversation*, Jonathan Wynn of the University of Massachusetts considers buildings less equitable creative investments. Festivals and their kin should be the preference because they don't monopolise space or absorb resources that will be felt on the balance sheet long into the future. Our tendency to invest in buildings over people is also a reflection that empathy has started to ebb from the city centres. But what makes our landmark artistic and cultural institutions special is not how impressive they are on the outside. Even our most iconic landmarks, like the Sydney Opera House, Guggenheim or the Louvre, are only as good as the art they contain and the imagination they stimulate.

The very nature of a festival's here-today, gone-tomorrow composition is valuable: they give us a concentrated window to focus our celebrations and allow for more diversity, at greater frequency. Compared to building programmes, festivals are resource-light and allow us to celebrate human creativity rather than the bricks-and-mortar assets that are really only the vehicle for it. While their footprint in terms of space, time, and human and physical assets is small, the impact of festivals can be profound. They are to contemporary culture what our museums are to the past. This is not to say that they just happen, of course, and the cities with strong festival heritage understand that they need to provide the enabling conditions – we need to be able to apply for licences and road closures, for instance, without being blocked at every turn. In a similar vein to what Lee Bofkin spoke about in the street-art context, if we want art, we need to be able to make it happen and, to do that, sometimes we need to be bold enough to ask for it.

As with all these things, there isn't necessarily a perfect event that can be everything to everyone, but this is because of the wonderful variation of tastes and preferences inherent in our cities. But, certainly, the things that seem to work best take root in the communities they seek to celebrate and are cautious about branding and commercial sponsorship that might separate the festival from its original roots.

Cities that cause imagination to flourish can breathe life into the spaces between our buildings and give colour to the lives lived within their walls. There are countless forms of creative expression, of which this chapter has touched on a few illustrative examples. But creativity isn't just limited to the artists and we all have a stake in its future. When we're on 'urban autopilot mode', we often brush past the extraordinary and assume it just happens. We seldom pause to question how or to ask what we might be able to do to keep it as part of our 'normal'. Shaping the future depends on the dreams and mastery of all city dwellers: architects, engineers, scientists, teachers, small businesses and councils alike – we just need the right enabling conditions. Together, we can set the conditions that encourage us to slow down and appreciate the beauty of the city, forge social bonds and create connection to place. In the city – back to that concept of dwelling – our collective imagination is one of our greatest strengths.

7

LOVE

Cities need ... love more than most of us care to imagine. Cities, after all, for all their massiveness, all their there-ness, are acutely vulnerable.

Junot Diaz

BEFORE WRITING THIS chapter, I returned home to South Africa, where I unplugged from everything life had thrown at us over the past year or so. As usual, it took a good few days to detach from city mode. I disappeared back into the bush and slowly I started to shed my urban trappings: watch, phone, jewellery, shoes ... Standing in a shuka with a cold beer by the Olifants River, dusty and watching the sun dip behind the Drakensberg Mountains, I could admit that this is where I feel the spirit return to my body. But having just spent such an intense, concentrated period in the city, I wasn't quite ready to dismiss it. By chance or design, the urban jungle had become almost as intrinsic to my identity as the wilderness. For everything from relationships to work to learning, my city home is just as much of a bedrock and in many ways is the gateway that lets me return to the bush when I need it. The truth is that both these versions of home are necessary for my life to work, and so they exist in parallel pockets of space and time. The same is true for city dwellers across the world: the place of binary assumptions about where and how we live our lives is receding. How or where we feel at home isn't as simple as where we were born or where we live. In truth, for many of us it is a complex and dynamic feeling that changes across our lifetime. This is the story of our cities; they are never static, never simple.

Differences aside, the main point of common ground for city dwellers is our shared urban experience and desire to be able to enjoy our lives beyond mere survival. We share the good, the bad and the ugly with our neighbours, often in very close proximity, but we know that the joys and trials aren't always equally felt or distributed. The role of leadership can't be overstated, but beyond the institutional level, the reminder that so many urbanites coalesce around one or more of the pillars in this book should give us courage, because beneath the veneer of bustle is a compassionate heart.

There is an interesting shift in language around city living. Where previously words like love, joy, happiness, dwelling and compassion would feel like outliers, they are being increasingly used in conversations about our urban lives. This is entirely appropriate and welcome, because they sit at the core of what makes our places feel like home. Compassionate Communities frames the concept of a compassionate city as:

> A thriving, resilient community whose members are moved by empathy to take compassionate action, are able to confront crises with innovative solutions, are confident in navigating changes in the economy and the environment, and are resilient enough to bounce back readily from natural and man-made disasters.

Whether or not our cities get everything right, it is important that we recognise our stake in, and rally for, the places we spend our lives in.

URBAN HOMELANDS

Our relationship with cities is complex and evolving, and over the past year or so, we have been on something of an emotional rollercoaster with our urban homelands. After successive and ever-tightening lockdowns that curtailed our city freedoms, we've become grudgingly familiar with a cycle of frustration and cabin fever, yearning for something other than the city – for family and friends on the other side of the world – anger and anxiety, grief and hope ... sometimes all before breakfast. Going through this myself, I found it curious that I always returned full circle to rediscover my love for the city even in its dark days. Taking London as an example, I found it sad to see this magnificent beast of a city empty and mute, and I hoped that we would all stick around to see it come back to life. I think we owe ourselves and our cities that. When speaking to my friend Will (an ardent countryman), he chuckled and likened this to not wanting to break up with a partner while they're going through a hard time, which I found amusing but had to agree.

When we grant ourselves permission to take root in our cities, even temporarily, we start to see the urban landscape as a habitat, not just a short-term set of conditions we need to endure. Rather than resisting the concept of the city as a home, we would serve ourselves better if we lean into our neighbourhoods to make it so. Then, instead of focusing on the benefits of escaping, we can turn our attention to the benefits of staying. If we find it's not meeting our needs, we can help be part of the solution.

Understanding our personal critical levers – the things we really need to feel a sense of equilibrium and contentedness – will help us to live our lives in a fuller way. The Covid-19 pandemic presented us with an opportunity for introspection and re-evaluation of the way we live our lives; the UN Habitats 2020 *World Cities* report noted that the pandemic has spurred health-focused innovation in cities that make them fundamentally more liveable, such as closing streets to cars and opening them up for al fresco dining, walking, cycling and playing, all of which we've seen examples of in the previous pages.

There's no shortage of escape-planning services to coax disillusioned city dwellers to throw in the towel and skip town. We've been told some convincing tales about the utopia of life in the country or by the sea, and yet these seldom major on the other hard realities that come from living away from the city. A different kind of life is certainly possible, but we don't always need to leave the city to get it. The city itself is not the problem; it's often the enabling conditions that don't quite add up – like poor working patterns, insufficient infrastructure, absence of nature and lack of time to enjoy it, and so the list goes on until we feel it might be easier to accept defeat and walk away. While this might immediately triage our own quality of life in the short term, it doesn't help to reprogramme the city systems because we remove our influence once we leave, and leaving certainly isn't an option available to vast numbers of urbanites. Beyond the city bounds, we can stand to lose out, particularly as we age, on opportunities for more accessible essential services, regular social interaction, and the stimulation and connectivity of our urban environments.

To fix this, we need to flip the way we consider our place in the city; if we feel we have an impact on our communities and an immediate, meaningful stake in the future, we are more likely to stick around and, in turn, the city will evolve in response to the needs of its residents. Otherwise, we have a perpetuating cycle whereby the outmoded systems will continue as the wealthy jump ship when they reach 'peak city'. If our cities became worth living in for the long term across all generations, we can start to normalise vocations that give us purpose and meaning, prioritise nature and regenerative systems, and we are more likely to see urban centres as incubators of creativity and enterprise that make them places worth living in forever.

Young people have underpinned the great urban revival over the past few decades and a study in the *Journal of Regional Science* found that the preference for central urban neighbourhoods, with high density of amenities, is increasing from one generation to the next, and as such 'youthification' is transforming our cities. But we have to be careful to nurture the longevity of this relationship. Cities are not just the home of the young, and policies and social infrastructure need to balance intergenerational needs. We cannot afford to create urban dens that spawn a new generation of transient city dwellers who, when fully formed, flee the city, leaving an urban wasteland behind them.

Ultimately, cities need to knit home and heart together so that we see their value as places to dwell in and their potential to create an enriching home life.

MAINSTREAMING EMPATHY

When it comes to our own health and happiness, we tend to care greatly about what affects us personally but, in the context of city systems, empathy is often selectively applied. These blind spots drive inequities in our cities as the rich get richer and more powerful, and the poor and marginalised get poorer and pushed out to the fringes. Look at the experience of our low-paid essential workers during Covid-19; those who could afford to leave the city fled to their second homes in the country or overseas. The result was that disadvantaged city residents were left behind, many in difficult and cramped conditions that made it easier for the virus to spread, and many carried on working because they were either classed as essential workers or were in the informal economy. The story seemed the same the world over. Speaking to urban friends around the globe, our conversations often centred on the irony that the city encourages people to live and work there but, as soon as the shit hits the fan, those who can afford it turn tail and bolt off to the country.

As we've seen throughout this book, cities that actively address the lived experience of under-represented groups stand to benefit the population as a whole. The rising popularity of terms like fairness, inclusion and respect shows that, more often, individuals, communities, organisations and governments must be prepared to be held to account if the apparatus for urban inclusion fails to deliver. It's interesting here to look at the experience of our ageing urban populations. Alongside the macro trends of overall population growth and an expanding young population, we are also living longer than ever before. The World Bank, in *World Population Prospects: The 2019 Revision*, estimates that by 2050 one in every six people will be over the age of 65. At the moment, cities aren't always easy places to age in and the World Bank cautions that urban inequalities can cause older people to be locked out of 'spaces, services and society'. So how, then, can caring for an ageing population be reframed as an opportunity rather than a resource drain?

In many ways, this feels like an odd problem to have – we all have skin in the ageing game and, at least on an individual level, we care deeply for our elders; it's conceivable, too, that we might hope to grow older ourselves and be looked after when we do so. Rather than worrying about the drain that different segments of the population might be on scant urban resources, our ageing urban residents are an incredible source of knowledge, tradition and heritage. We can learn from some of our religious and spiritual institutions here, where age is looked up to as an asset. As WHO's *Global Age Friendly Cities* guide highlights, urban faith communities in the global north and south hold their elderly members in the highest esteem. In general, faith communities are welcoming and inclusive, 'facilitating participation by people who may be at risk of becoming isolated' and their regular schedule of worship, pastoral care and social activities connect elderly members with the rest of the community. In turn, this exposes others to the life experience, wisdom and storytelling of those who have had a few more years on the planet. The point still stands that if we look after our most vulnerable populations in cities, everybody stands to benefit. WHO points out that age-friendly cities that make streets, buildings and homes open and accessible are also more welcoming to children and those with disabilities. When we prioritise care for older generations, we also reduce the burden of stress on families who otherwise have to juggle care for elderly relatives. This often falls outside of the city or requires someone in the family – primarily women – to leave the workforce to provide this care.

Intergenerational living can also counter the stigma of ageing and open city dwellers up to a world where to be urban is not necessarily to be young. I had first-hand experience of this with my late grandfather, for example, who used to rollerblade from Paddington to the Houses of Parliament, bought a scooter, learned to ski and took the helm of a family hiking trip all in his much later years. If mobility and health allow, older people can also assist with care of others, including children and ageing spouses. Economically, they are also incredibly valuable urban spenders. The Brookings Institution reported that, by 2030, it's projected that the over-50s will be spending just under US$15 trillion. Oxford Economics puts the figure at £500 billion in the UK.

In Asia, urban developments in Singapore, Japan and South Korea have shown examples of integrating active ageing in the design of housing and infrastructure. According to City Monitor, 12 per cent of Singapore's population is over 65 and the city's Admiralty development includes 100 homes for older residents, equipped with extra safety features like non-slip surfaces and alarms, medical and care centres within the complex and public transport just downstairs. In Seoul, a high-rise social-housing complex has created a 'memory lane' – a brightly coloured path in the common recreation area

– designed to assist those experiencing cognitive decline. Being coloured (green), the intention and hope is that residents are less likely to get lost or disorientated, and benches have been installed at regular intervals to allow for rest. The Seoul Institute, commenting on the City Monitor website, observed that even this relatively simple step resulted in a 16 per cent increase in elderly residents heading outside multiple times a day. The humble bench makes an appearance in many emerging intergenerational developments to encourage people to socialise outside the home.

In Harare, Zimbabwe, Dr Chibanda has found a way of harnessing the combined power of benches and grandmothers (another example proving the weight of our urban matriarchs, as Aga Otero pointed to) to address a spiralling mental-health crisis. The Friendship Bench was founded in 2006 to bridge the gap in available mental-health treatment in Zimbabwe, where only twelve psychiatrists work throughout the whole country and the population is 16 million. The scheme trains a voluntary network of grandmothers in 'evidence-based talk therapy', which they deliver to patients on the Friendship Benches scattered throughout communities. Commenting in a BBC article in 2020, Dr Chibanda recalled his initial reservations that the grandmothers had no prior medical or mental-health background and, in many cases, very low levels of education. But what they had instead was far more valuable – the ability to reach people because they understood their neighbourhoods. The article notes that this meant abandoning Western medical terms like 'depression' and 'suicide' in favour of 'culturally rooted concepts that people can identify with'. Perhaps most interesting of all is Dr Chibanda's observation that the grandmothers, despite having lived through the traumas of the Rhodesian War and Matabeleland Massacre and other tumultuous events, remain on a remarkably even keel. He reflects, 'What we see in them is this amazing resilience in the face of adversity. We're exploring why this is, but what seems to be emerging is this concept of altruism, in which the grandmothers really feel that they get something out of actually making a difference in the lives of others.'

Reaching over 30,000 people in 2017, the grannies have even shown their methods to trump those of conventional mental health-care, in a study done in 2016. So successful has the initiative been that the Friendship Bench has expanded to Malawi and Zanzibar, and even to New York City. As the Centre for Global Mental Health points out, this shows the value of adapting solutions from low- and middle-income countries to high-income countries. The Friendship Bench reflects the depth of impact that modest yet compassionate and practical solutions can have if they are deeply rooted in the communities that depend on them. The humble bench has proven its worth as a fixture in the urban landscape, as a powerful tool for health and social care, and as a potent manifestation of the power of dwelling.

DO WE CARE?

The future city narrative should be characterised by the goal to generate as much of our happiness as possible by contributing to the happiness of others. Lord Richard Layard, director of the well-being programme at the London School of Economics, suggests that this should be the basic ethical system for the twenty-first century. Everybody can identify with this goal – it is a secular ideal that speaks to those from all walks of life. But to be able to care for others, we also need to take care of ourselves. I mean this not in the fad-ish 'self-care' way but in a very real way that recognises the impact of the pressures we experience and helps us prioritise the things that affect our quality of life, like mental and physical health, the quality of our relationships and our communities. Not all relationships are romantic ones, of course, but I thought it was interesting that both Maria Eleftheriou and Rod Buchanan, who we met in earlier chapters, each reflected that, when it comes to finding love, the list of urban pressures means it often takes longer to meet partners. When we do, it can be more challenging to grow healthy relationships because of the level of stress most of us are experiencing as 'normal'.

Again, the value of slowing down a little and living more fully in our immediate neighbourhoods may play a part in this. The more we lean into neighbourliness and co-create charismatic local communities and social support structures, the happier we will be.

Fortunately, almost wherever we look amongst our neighbourhoods there are heartening displays of neighbourliness. Not being able to get to New York in person, I sat down for a FaceTime with Hetty McKinnon, food writer and cookbook author, to discuss what it means to belong in the city. Hetty's legendary salads at Arthur Street Kitchen, which she founded in Sydney, wound their way into the hearts of Surry Hills locals. Hetty reflects on the experience of being a migrant, which strikes a chord with me; we talk about how we often want to belong, but we don't quite. Hetty, who has Chinese Australian roots and now resides in New York, observed that being a migrant, voluntary or otherwise, can give us the chance to restart – to reinvent ourselves and what we can offer. She posed the question: 'What happens when we are lifted up and placed into different contexts?' I think there is real beauty in this. She is driven, as so many urbanites are, by the desire to connect with people from other parts of the world, with other world views and life experiences. Reflecting on the strength of her connection to the Surry Hills community in Sydney, she says, 'I saw the people in Surry Hills as my family and viewed the neighbourhood as an extension of my dining room table.'

The connection to place and people in cities can be intense and these types of relationships are a testament to the fact that cities are not places for the rootless but rather the rootful, and often those roots are deeply tied to community. Describing her time in Arthur Street Kitchen, Hetty says that she felt she belonged to the people of Surry Hills and it was magical: 'I was a home cook feeding people in my community. It was pure joy. It filled my soul to be able to feed people and nourish people, many of whom started off as strangers and became close friends.'

Cities are melting pots of people and life experiences, and arguably the dominant images of the bustle and aloofness are too reductive to really capture the truth. Like the proverbial iceberg, our urban centres are so much more than meets the eye. There isn't a city I've come across that isn't deeper, warmer and quirkier than it appears at first sight. Their true character often sits out of immediate view and we need to get beneath the surface to understand them.

A HAPPIER HUSTLE

To create cities that unify rather than alienate will require us to rethink how we value success. The prevailing culture in cities has entrenched the goal of personal, rather than collective, success. This needs to change because, as Lord Richard Layard explains, it has traditionally been set up as a zero-sum game, meaning that someone always has to lose out, and this is why stress becomes the lifeblood of the urban rat race. For urban dwellers especially, it is all too easy for a lifetime of sanctioned stress to begin at a young age in schools and carry through until retirement.

As the conversation shifts towards regenerative urban centres that take care of people and planet, our next steps will be as much about the pauses as they are the action. The hubbub of the city is magnetic and keeps us hooked on urban life for very good reason. But there is a difference between this vibrancy, which comes from social connection, leisure and creative expression, and the pervasive, adrenaline-fuelled stress propped up by the currency of busyness.

Office culture has, for cities, been a prime driver of our 9–5 pattern of life and is worth a mention here, although of course urban life depends on the contribution of a great many other work forms. As we digest the challenges presented to us by the Covid-19 pandemic, it's evident that the primacy of conventional office working has been turned on its head. We now know that we can work from anywhere and it has been interesting to see the response of organisations as we've pursued a return to some semblance of normalcy. Some have forfeited office spaces, recognising that there are savings to be had and acknowledging the resistance from staff to return to a working model that leaves them with less time in their day and increases their risk of exposure to disease. Others have changed their travel policies and implemented more permissive practices like hybrid and flexible working, founded on trust, respect and autonomy. Some organisations are still grappling with these mild innovations; even when most have proven that productivity continued – or even grew – some persist in their pursuit of a return to full-scale, rigid, business as usual. I think it's clear that, for those who have had a 'quality of life epiphany', the shape of office work has undergone a huge, permanent shift.

The implications for a city less based on office culture seem significant; are we at risk of empty skyscrapers and dead streets if people are no longer moving in and out of the city every day en masse? The Covid-19 pandemic has certainly given us cause to question the aspiration of the linear and conventional city lifestyle, which funnels us through fairly homogenous experiences of education, work, family structure and so on.

It's worth stepping back to take a look at this. Are we in fact still in a digital revolution or have we moved on to the next stage? Are we witnessing the birth of a quality-of-life revolution? The pandemic has invited us to be thoughtful and provocative in this respect.

The gathering momentum behind wellbeing is worthy of note. While we are so caught up in the experience and rhetoric of survival and coping in the city, we can also become divorced from other experiences essential to the human condition. The Wellbeing Economy Alliance, for example, was established by a group of world leaders – many of them women – in pursuit of swapping GDP (never intended as a measure of health and not fit for it) for human and planetary health, and putting happiness firmly in the frame as a laudable and necessary goal. Unpacking this, the incentives for public spending need to give people what they need; and this is about leadership at all tiers.

A city that is built by and for humanity will be alive with stories of behaviour change, compassion and practical, creative solutions. Beyond the vacuum of multilateral or institutional chambers, this change is happening in real time on our streets, in our homes and across our neighbourhoods.

EMBRACING THE DYNAMISM

I've talked a lot about slowing down in this book but that isn't to discount the energy that cities give us. We often assume that the stress and freneticism is inevitable and negative, but actually it isn't all bad. Hetty reflected on the fact that this energy and tension brings people together in such a dynamic way. 'Yes,' she observes, 'it's challenging to live 24/7 within this framework, but the flip side is that we can stand to gain a lot from the experience of not feeling relaxed.' She points out that the buzz of New York, for instance, fuels an intangible drive to create. Agreeing that it is an addictive feeling, she adds that cities can push us to reflect, do more and produce great work. Rod Buchanan says that he, too, gets off on the stress of city life; so magnetic is the city's power that it compelled a teenage Rod to move from Blantyre, Lanarkshire, to New York City (and straight to the Bronx) to dance. He's been in the thick of the urban buzz ever since and reflects that the city's vitality not only helped his creative career, but also his recovery from a period of illness and subsequent venture in the fitness industry where he co-created Psycle's barre programme with Maria Eleftheriou.

With millions of people brushing shoulders at pace, the idea of community in urban places can also feel a bit remote at times. Far from pretending that we are all friends in some kind of twee way, community is as much about the intangible, subtle shared experience of living among others. There is often an openness to city people, perhaps because we are so accustomed to change and to moving among such large groups. Hetty and I agreed that this was a feature of all cities we'd lived in. Hetty mentioned that, when she moved to New York, she was so astonished with the number of New Yorkers who reached out to welcome her and who offered to share their parts of the city with her, especially given the (unfair) reputation that New York City has of being brusque.

As we settle into a different rhythm of urban life in the aftermath of the Covid-19 pandemic, Hetty suggested that we'll have to relearn how to be with one another. Interestingly, as London geared up again after a third lockdown, the transport network was full of signs imploring us to be patient, kind and respectful of others, as though we all need to be reminded how to be good citizens and neighbours again. Perhaps we do. Hetty's perspective here rings true and resonates far beyond New York: 'New York is a tough city, it keeps you on your toes. It's busy and overcrowded but that's part of its joy. All of the difficulties of the city are indelibly linked to why we live here.'

SOCIALLY SMART CITIES

Over the past decade, the rhetoric around future cities has often turned on this idea of 'smart'. 'Smart' always sounds alluring doesn't it? A city that is so connected by the so-called 'internet of things' that it knows enough about the human experience to be able to adapt accordingly and help us live better lives. But while smart buildings may be able to tell us if the occupants are too hot or too cold, they can't tell us about their emotions or subjective experience. In my view, it's nothing but positive that the 'smart'-only rhetoric is being called into question. As valuable as our data is to helping us identify patterns, it's no substitute for the human experience and shouldn't lead the process. Charles Montgomery, in his book *Happy City*, aptly says that 'the most important psychological effect of the city is the way in which it moderates our relationships with other people'.

While tech is always going to be part of the solution, we need to be mindful of putting it on too much of a pedestal. As we know from our digital-based lives over the Covid-19 pandemic, while technology has helped us to continue with some sense of normalcy by connecting us with others, most people agree that in no way is it a neat swap out. Aga Otero agrees that 'smart' city interventions aren't necessarily the most human, commenting: 'Crusading for smart cities must stop. We must develop socially smart cities. This starts by sharing who the heroes growing home are and how they do it.'

Aga is the type of urban leader we want for our future cities. His ability to nestle into and enhance his neighbourhoods (much like Anton de Kock's Xigera Lodge in Botswana) has shown the possibility of creating rooted, flourishing communities even in our adopted cities. His projects, from Edible Bus Stop (a precursor to Energy Garden) and Repowering London (an energy co-operative) to Energy Garden, are successful because they unite city dwellers in creating and shaping their bare necessities. He brings his entire lived experience to city challenges, as an artist, architect, dancer, survivor (he beat cancer twice before 30). It's this tenacity, sense of care and deep listening, and ability to find the real leaders in the urban landscape that we can all learn from.

Leo Johnson agrees that 'we don't want to be overdependent on the inputs like tech; we can either have a digital or an organic human version of the city'. And the latter is just the version of the city I met him in. One crisp autumn day in 2020, we met for a brisk walk in the park. Dodging the prams, scooters, dogs and toddlers, we fell into stride as we compared notes on the reasons for optimism when looking at the future of our cities. Hope was in the air (this meeting came just days after the 2020 US presidential election in which democracy, for now, had won) and I breathed a sigh of relief when I heard Leo affirm that there was still reason to be positive. We spent the rest of the walk talking about the irrepressible 'cool stuff' going on in cities across the world.

The cool stuff, it seemed, was everywhere. As city dwellers, our preferences are changing and, when it has counted most, we've chosen to deepen our connections with one another. We've seen this by way of the rise of the barter economy (exchanging stuff for stuff) and parallel currencies (like time banks and local currencies). In many ways, Leo suggested, these initiatives 'help us to wear our hearts on our sleeves when it comes to sourcing goods and services'. When we are transparent about what we need, we can often go straight to the source – locally. Of course, this benefits us directly because we get what we need but it also comes with the value-add of kind, visible and person-to-person exchanges.

The Covid-19 pandemic, too, has caused a surge in demand for self-sufficiency and in the popularity of local goods. Leo observed that the presence of local goods on a high street increases footfall, which increases spending in the local economy. With a high presence of social enterprises and small businesses, rooted in the local area, money spent is more likely to be reinvested in the neighbourhood, making room for more locally produced goods and inviting more people to visit. On our final lap around the park and as another layer of mud caked on to our shoes, we imagined what our iconic capital high streets might look like if they turned into hyperlocal markets for nearby businesses, artisanal products and food from urban rooftop farms. Streets like Oxford Street in London, Fifth Avenue in New York and George Street in Sydney have tremendous footfall, and the opportunity to put local makers and artisans front of stage in these globally famous but locally, socially and environmentally inept streets could be transformative. Urban communities would stand to benefit from this local source of economic uptake, a clear sense of purpose, a channel for creativity, a platform for commerce and the ability to generate social capital. We're not quite at a transformation of that scale yet, but it's something worth thinking about as we set our future for urban living. Of the undeniable pulse of neighbourhood activity, Leo said, 'There's stuff happening in the community as well as stuff happening by the community. Ideally, we want both these things to come together.'

Creating a more human city depends on people that care more. Currently, it feels that the channels of empathy are disrupted, often reaching a dead end. Recognising the home truth that our cities are ecosystems will come down to repairing our connection to place. In this vein, when I sat down to talk with George Lamb, who we met in the Wilderness chapter, in our neighbourhood local Jolene, our conversation turned to quality of life in cities, and on this score George went straight for the jugular of the education system. He reflected on the two juxtaposed versions of city life that often co-exist: extreme wealth and extreme poverty. He cited, on the one hand, his friends who have grown up with unconditional love and immense wealth, and whose kids go on ski trips and speak multiple languages; he then compared this to urban children living in poverty, who don't necessarily have family or role models, or know where their next meal is coming from. Pausing for a moment, he reflected, 'It's no wonder the rich kids grow up to rule the world – they've grown up feeling that they can do anything.'

The way the global north approaches educating its children and young people is a prime example of something called 'pathway lock-in', where we become blind to alternatives because the status quo has always been adhered to. Our education systems are so entrenched that, for change to happen, it takes someone to come through and smash the convention to pieces. George pointed out the dangers of stratifying and limiting children from a young age; up to Year 9 (age 13/14), he'd noticed that children were eager to learn about mindfulness, how to grow food, practise breathwork and so on. But by the time they get to Year 11 (age 15/16), he observes that they are so beaten down by a narrow-beam education system that their interest in school is diminished. The current model, he suggests, quashes creativity, denies the value of knowing the self and leaves children and young people ill equipped to grow as human beings. Initiatives like GROW, and many others like it, which encourage children to be inspired, think systemically and know themselves beyond the traditional curriculum, will help to rewrite the rules of our outmoded systems. Emerging from this kind of curriculum, we should see purpose-driven, empathetic young people with the confidence to lead and the drive to make good choices. Growing compassion from the bottom up in this way is crucial for the future of the city, but we also need to reboot our leadership in the here and now, and this is something we can all get involved in.

CITIES FOR ALL

When I spoke to historian and food writer Angela Clutton, she reflected that urban dwellers are often drawn to parts of our cities that feel like a village. Village-feel offers us a small enough landscape in which to be comfortable and familiar. The point about familiarity is especially relevant for culturally rich and migrant communities, because cities can help us maintain our connection to our roots. In 2020, Cherae Robinson, founder of Tastemakers Africa, made a lovely comment that 'as a kid, I travelled to Africa every Saturday. Except Africa was a market in Harlem and my passport was my Grandmother; who insisted on African outfits to Church on Sundays'. City communities can also provide a sense of safety in numbers, and minority groups, especially ethnic minorities, often feel safer in cities than they would moving into the country where they are more likely to stand out and experience racial prejudice. Anecdotally this has been the case for many of my friends. The tolerance, sense of unity and shared heritage that life in cities can offer is significant. According to UN Habitat, international migration accounts for about one-third of urban growth in developed countries and is increasingly transforming urban areas into heterogenous, multi-ethnic, multicultural and multilingual spaces.

In tandem with the enrichment offered by those moving to the cities is the need to recognise the value that comes from restoring lost heritage like indigenous connections. In the Australian context, for instance, the Nature Conservancy reminds us that Australia's cities are first and foremost Indigenous places and some 80 per cent of Aboriginal and Torres Strait Island people are urbanised. In the Greater Sydney Commission's 'A Metropolis of Three Cities', the Commission noted that 'Greater Sydney holds a special place in Australia's history because it is where the first major point of contact occurred between European and Aboriginal people. However, during the making of the city post 1788, the multidimensional nature of Country has never been deeply considered, reconciled or remembered.' Emerging from this is the Connecting with Country Framework project, which aims to integrate Aboriginal cultural knowledge into the city planning through co-design and -development of infrastructure projects, particularly to manage the impact of natural events like fire, drought and flooding, and protect and maintain access to Aboriginal lands, including sensitive sites, and preserve cultural practices so that they can live on.

Retrieving and celebrating indigenous identity and knowledge in our cities benefits all of us. Without it, we are deprived of alternative models for living and interacting with our urban and natural environments. As Nature Australia champions, 'Beyond mere survival, Indigenous cultures – rich in art and cultural practices – demonstrate time for reflection, fun and story-telling.' On this point, I also spoke to Shannon Royden-Turner, South African architect and leadership coach. Shannon observed that what the global north could learn from the heritage of African and other cities is the 'primacy of connection to spirit and social networks'. Speaking about our sprawling, messy cities, she commented that 'our outside world reflects our inside world, and it is this inside world that we have to change. The challenges we face at a city level are a manifestation of what is inside us.' So, reseeding our deeper values back into our city structures and populations depends on progressive and unifying leadership.

ORDINARY, EXTRAORDINARY URBANITES

Resilience is key to our quality of life and is often called upon in cities, which can amplify and concentrate stress (money, job security, safety, conflict and so on). To help us weather these challenges, we need people we can rely on. Our community can help us strengthen our physical and psychological wellbeing by anchoring our sense of identity and social purpose. Community takes many forms: we can find it in our cultural centres, gyms, places of worship, volunteer groups, and among those we share hobbies and passions with. It is mission critical for our physical and psychological health that we lean into community to combat the rising loneliness we're seeing. Kimberley Wilson, author of *How to Build a Healthy Brain*, notes that 'loneliness is a major risk to our brain-health with lonely people 40% more likely to develop dementia'.

As UN Habitat observed in its 2020 *World Cities* report, true 'smart' cities are 'people-oriented' and their leaders will recognise and respond to the realities obstructing or enabling quality of life. The world over, centralised government tends to travel a similar broad trajectory of misaligned incentives and short-term planning. Generally, our governments are in power for a brief time when it comes to effecting real change. No sooner have they got their feet under the table than they are campaigning to remain in power; this is obviously deeply unhelpful as new policy is rushed in a bid to fulfil election promises without being fit for the long-term purpose, or good policy ends up being withdrawn and decades of progress is lost. We witnessed this on the world stage when the former president of the United States of America unilaterally exited the Paris Climate Agreement. So, the stage is set for leadership at a local level to become all the more important. City leaders, both the formal and informal kind, have the greatest visibility and understanding of local needs. Globally, local governments account for 24.1 per cent of public spending, 25.7 per cent of public revenue and 36.6 per cent of public investments, so they have considerable clout to put behind suitable solutions. They also hold the greatest capacity to engage citizens in participatory decision-making. But they also often need help and guidance from city dwellers, as we've seen in previous chapters. If all else fails, urban communities have shown themselves more than capable of stepping in and stepping up, proving that the potential for leadership resides in us all.

Over the Covid-19 pandemic, we've been reminded of the soft power within our neighbourhoods, which can be activated and supercharged in times of extreme need. Levels of volunteering soared during lockdowns, which is perhaps reflective of a recalibration of sense of purpose. The break in the pattern that Covid-19 sparked perhaps allowed us to tap into our morality because what mattered most to us as individuals – our wellbeing – was shared universally. We were reminded of our humanity, and of the fact that cities should be about humanity first. We should take heart that even behind closed doors and possibly behind face masks and Perspex screens, communities are ready to self-organise and resource themselves by pulling together private funding, volunteers and in-kind support to make profound change.

What struck me about my conversations over the course of researching this book was the sheer number of solutions that are dreamed up, championed and led by ordinary humans. They aren't necessarily specialists, but they are sick of waiting around for help and just get on with it. In many cases, the founders of various movements feel irked by the inequities of the city, understand the problem at a local level and have come up with practical solutions. Many have given up their conventional careers to target the problems they see. This is why we have DJs becoming farmers, architects becoming leadership coaches, lawyers becoming environmentalists, footballers becoming food campaigners, dancers becoming teachers, bankers becoming artists. As George Lamb noted when we met: 'All humans have the capacity to be ingenious.' He suggests that the majority of the population has 95 per cent of their bandwidth available and that 'If we could get everyone to care and act so that they use 10–15% more of their bandwidth we could fundamentally shift the world'.

Rashiq Fataar, of Our Future Cities – a platform to promote involvement in urban development in the global south – has commented that improving quality of life for people goes beyond just a physical project. In Cape Town, for example, it has become a sociocultural project to undo centuries of barriers (he points out that for 300 years the city was designed to segregate the population, so all this needs rewriting). With challenges to democratic processes, such as we see in South Africa, social participation becomes all the more vital. Rashiq's 'Young Urbanists' programme invites anyone under 40 to join discussions, field trips and lectures about the state of urbanisation in Cape Town. By creating a network of diverse, engaged Cape Townians, he hopes that, in a few decades' time, the city's leaders will have come up through the programme and have benefitted from the rich cross-pollination of ideas that has come from dialogue with fellow residents.

Speaking at the 2015 Smart City Expo in Barcelona, Rashiq reminds us that, 'If we are to build a new world, we need to start on our own streets and in our own neighbourhoods'. Every city, even in its murkiest days, has heartening examples of human ingenuity and resilience – pockets of determination and compassion that resist even the most oppressing circumstances. In an article in *Roar* magazine, members of Cape Town Together, the mutual-aid group, reflected that Cape Town's segregated past had meant that 'city-wide organising and solidarity' were under-established. We saw this in the 2018 drought, when the city narrowly avoided turning off the water supply – an ordeal for many residents that was characterised by lack of information, top-down decisions and an arm's-length approach. Perhaps something began percolating following this particularly tough period because the pandemic brought a new era of action to Cape Town's residents. When Covid-19 struck, the city became the global mothership of community action networks (CANs), bringing together community members, public-health experts, advocates, artists, chefs and many others who mobilised – usually using WhatsApp – to meet the immediate needs of their neighbourhoods while the government floundered.

The success of Cape Town Together, and the many thousands of CANs that followed it all over the world, is that these groups are 'hyper-local, decentralised and anti-hierarchical'. Free from bureaucracy, inefficiency and corruption, they tend to have a strong moral compass, a focused mission and are receptive to social cues and local realities where centralised agencies may be tone deaf, if well intentioned. Cape Town Together refers to this as 'moving at the speed of trust' – 'moving quickly when things feel right and slowing down, sitting with the complexity and asking "why," when they do not'.

Because CANs hinge on interpersonal relationships, they tend to transcend the boundaries of public institutions and communities. This is an incredibly powerful tool, and Cape Town Together points out a few examples:

When CAN members were arrested for trying to prevent an illegal eviction, they were assisted by public servants who recognised this injustice, and through long-standing relationships could negotiate release with a fine. Trusted relationships with local law enforcement officials have enabled some CANs to continue food distribution efforts under lockdown and other CANs have asked for, and received, protection from local police when delivering food parcels in unsafe parts of their neighbourhood.

This is perhaps one of the brightest and most heartening examples of our power when we are united as individuals, and it is all the more powerful having emerged in a deeply challenged city, in the heart of the global south.

LOVABLE CITIES

Rescuing the language of city life from staunch rationalism is important if we want to know how well our cities are doing, and if we actually love them or not. Interestingly, lovability and live-ability don't always go hand in hand, which an article for the World Economic Forum pointed out in 2016. Our tendency to overengineer metrics and reduce rich, qualitative conversations to indices mis-understands the nature of being human. When it comes to our feelings about our places, there is no substitute for lived experi-ence and emotions; this is the most powerful data we have. A city built for and by humanity needs to recognise that 'perception and attachment' are the critical determinants of our relationship with our cities.

We don't necessarily need to travel out of our cities to have a change of scene. Maria Eleftheriou speaks about falling in love with the city at first sight on a day trip from her childhood home in Shropshire. She recalls, 'My mum took me to London when I was 10 years old, and from that moment, I knew I wanted to live here.' Moving to south-east London from regional England, she reflected on the joy of being able to travel across all corners of the city and be in entirely different worlds – moving from Dickensian-like scenes to the ultra-modern and back again, along the way being able to 'experience new restaurants, new tastes, new theatres, new fitness styles'. Much like Angela Clutton, Maria too reflects on the beauty of the village-like feel in her corner of the city, Herne Hill. By tapping into the lifeblood of our places – seeking out the street art, the local cuisine, watching how the locals live and play, finding the pockets of wilderness – our city homes also provide a source of inspiration and awe, and are far more readily accessible for most on a regular basis than a planned holiday out of town.

Every city offers us an entirely different experience; when we are looking for solutions, what works for one will not necessarily work for another and we need to be cautious of the seductive appeal of simply dragging and dropping ready-made initiatives from other cities. The way we move, eat, interact, play, live and work is shaped by such a nuanced raft of contextual factors that we're never going to get the same urban blueprint twice.

Much of this book has been about the humanness of cities. The challenges facing city dwellers are immense, but so too are responses at grassroots level. Undoubtedly, there's a time and a place for fear and guilt – used properly they can be effective provocateurs for action. But the narrative of sustainable development can be a blunt instrument and can make us feel powerless and depleted. Cities, like us, are always a work in progress – and there is real beauty in this. It's time, therefore, to give ourselves permission to live happily and speak hopefully.

The Covid-19 pandemic has given us an important opportunity to reacquaint ourselves with our urban homes and our quality of life within them. The affection that's bloomed for our houses, streets, neighbours and neighbourhoods clarifies what we need from our cities as the fabric of a people. The ingredients for a life well lived – wilderness, nourishment, movement, connection, dwelling, imagination and love – are what we instinctively long for. They are deeply woven into our city psyche, and living fully within our neighbourhoods will give us a greater chance for happiness, resilience and equality to become intuitive and foundational rather than forced and secondary.

This book brought me full circle. From the early days of frustration and uncertainty brought by the Covid-19 pandemic, I couldn't stay mad at the city for long. When I returned from South Africa to London, I realised I hadn't fallen out of love with it after all. London was here for me. My neighbourhood had my back, and I could feel my heart swell and spirits lift as I saw well-trodden establishments buzz comfortingly back to life as another lockdown eased. On the day I arrived home, my postman waved at me while doing his rounds. At the time, I was several streets away from my building, wearing a face mask and hadn't been home for months. It brought an instant smile to my face (which he, of course, couldn't see because of the mask!). The next day, I happened upon a new mural (still wet, as though he'd just picked up his brush and walked away only moments before) by street artist David Speed. Later, I wandered to Broadway Market at lunchtime and found world-class chef John Javier whipping up street food on a kerb-side grill outside my local fishmonger, Fin and Flounder. In the same week, my hairstylist and long-since dear friend Beth — one of the many thousands of freelance creatives whose businesses had been shuttered by the restrictions — moved her studio to my street. It really felt like the stars were aligning, and was all the sweeter after a year of city life on pause. The realisation settled that this is the profound and soulful way of living that's available to us all once we tune into and get involved in our neighbourhoods.

We often say that life in cities is hard, and it is true. But it's also no less true that it's beautiful. Our dominant narrative tends to focus too much on what goes wrong, rather than what's going right. Institutional degradation, deep social injustices and environmental damage are undoubtedly a reality of city life. But there's another, concurrent reality of the city bubbling alongside it: grit, beauty, resilience, diversity, tenacity, creativity and heart. Which reality do we give more power to and what story do we want to be able to tell? Even amid the turbulence of the Covid-19 pandemic, the sense from the people I interviewed – city dwellers and city experts alike – was one of hope, buoyancy and joy, and recognition of urban life as a shared endeavour.

There's no doubt our urban lives ask us to juggle competing priorities, but this is the nature of life, not the city. In the weeks before I finished this book, my company went through a restructure, my job changed, and a budding relationship turned sour. It had, by any measure, been a shit week. But the city was here to pick me up and return some of the energy I'd lost – I returned to my friend Ahmed's bootcamp in Highbury Fields; I sat working in my local cafes absorbing their vitality; I made my final edits in the sun in London Fields with friends basking on picnic blankets next to me in solidarity. Friends, clients, old housemates and colleagues, also juggling frantic city lives, sent sweet notes of encouragement and love at the points of the day that can feel lonely, especially for a writer. And I finished this chapter where it all began – sat nursing a coffee and a pastry at Pavilion in Victoria Park, enveloped by the canopy of trees and watching the Egyptian geese – themselves London blow-ins – potter about the lake.

Appearances can be deceiving: beneath the frenetic exterior our cities are full of heart and vulnerability, and this is why they feel like home.

As we emerge from a period of life on pause and on mute, this is a beautiful moment to reflect on what makes our city homes lovable and liveable. From my lively conversations with urbanites, experts, creatives and renegades across the world, it's clear that joy goes hand in hand with the challenges. The things that bring us delight in life – wilderness, nourishment, movement, connection, dwelling, imagination and love – also bring people together and, from here, great things happen. The warmth and charisma that underpins urban communities and the practical, empathetic responses they support should give us courage that cities are so very worthy of our enduring love.

For the city dwellers reading this, my invitation for all of us is to:

- Explore wilderness,
- Seek nourishment,
- Embrace movement,
- Find connection,
- Discover dwelling,
- Spark imagination, and
- Fall in love.

SOURCES AND FURTHER READING

BOOKS

Agarwal, Pragya, *Sway: Unraveling Unconscious Bias*, Bloomsbury, 2020

Allen, Joseph G., and Macomber, John D., *Healthy Buildings: How Indoor Spaces Drive Performance and Productivity*, Harvard University Press, 2020

Armitstead, Claire (ed.), *Tales of Two Londons: Stories from a Fractured City*, Arcadia Books, 2019

Blowfield, Michael, and Johnson, Leo, *Turnaround Challenge: Business and the City of the Future,* Oxford University Press, 2013

Criado Perez, Caroline, *Invisible Women: Exposing Data Bias in a World Designed for Men*, Vintage, 2020

Davey, Edward, *Given Half a Chance: Ten Ways to Save the World*, Unbound, 2019

Dobraszczyk, Paul, *Future Cities: Architecture and Imagination*, Reaktion Books, 2019

Ellard, Colin, *Places of the Heart: The Psychogeography of Everyday Life*, Bellevue Literary Press, 2015

Hammond, Claudia, *The Art of Rest: How to Find Respite in a Modern Age*, Canongate Books, 2019

Juniper, Tony, *What has Nature Ever Done for Us? How Money Really Does Grow on Trees*, Profile Books, 2013

Landry, Charles, *The Creative City: A Toolkit for Urban Innovators*, second edition, Routledge, 2008

McKinnon, Hetty, *Community: Salad Recipes from Arthur Street Kitchen*, Plum, 2014

Montgomery, Charles, *Happy City: Transforming our Lives Through Urban Design*, Penguin Books, 2015

Ognundehin, Michelle, *Happy Inside: How to Harness the Power of Home for Health and Happiness*, Ebury Press, 2020

Sennett, Richard, *Building and Dwelling: Ethics for the City*, Penguin Books, 2019

Townsend, Anthony M., *Smart Cities: Big Data, Civic Hackers, and the Quest for a New Utopia*, W.W. Norton and Company, 2014

Tree, Isabella, *Wilding: The Return of Nature to a British Farm*, Picador, 2018

Wales, HRH The Prince of, Juniper, Tony, and Skelly, Ian, *Harmony: A New Way of Looking at our World,* Blue Door, 2010

Wilson, Kimberley, *How to Build a Healthy Brain: Reduce Stress, Anxiety and Depression and Future-proof your Brain*, Yellow Kite, 2020

NEWSPAPERS, JOURNALS, REPORTS AND ARTICLES

Abubaker, Iman, Tuniz, Janene, and Oursler, Anna, 'As the Coronavirus Looms, Can African Cities Become More Walkable and Bikeable?', *The City Fix*, 12 August 2020

Ademuson, Demi, 'Finding Modernity Through History', *People's Stories Project*, 10 August 2020

Alexandra, Jason, 'For Green Cities to Become Mainstream, we Need to Learn from Local Success Stories and Scale Up', *The Conversation*, 8 July 2019

'Alltags- und Frauengerechter Wohnbau' ['Everyday and Women-friendly Housing'], *Stadt Wien*, www.wien.gv.at/stadtentwicklung/alltagundfrauen/wohnbau.html

Alpert Reyes, Emily, and Smith, Dakota, 'New LA Laws Clear the Path for Homeless Housing Projects and Motel Conversions', *Los Angeles Times*, 11 April 2018

Appel, Rebecca, '"A Collaboration with City": Stik and the art of the street', *Christie's*, 4 September 2019

Arnost, Melanie, 'Forest Schools: A Growing Alternative for Parents Wanting Less Screen Time for Kids', *ABC News*, 13 December 2019

'Artisans Valley', atelier masōmī website, www.ateliermasomi.com/artisans-valley

Bakar, Faima, '"The English Countryside was Shared by Colonialism": Why rural Britain is unwelcoming for people of colour', *Metro*, 21 September 2020

Barlow, Nigel, 'Salford City Council's New Housing Company is Launched', *About Manchester*, 6 November 2019

Biloria, Nimish, 'From Smart to Empathic Cities', *Frontiers of Architectural Research*, Vol. 10, No. 1, March 2021, pp. 3–16

Bliss, Laura, '"Slow Streets" Disrupted City Planning. What Comes Next?', *Bloomberg CityLab*, 6 January 2021

Borchers Arriagada, Nicolas, Palmer, Andrew J., Bowman, David M.J.S., Morgan, Geoffrey G., Jalaludin, Bin B., and Johnston, Fay H., 'Unprecedented Smoke-Related Health Burden Associated with the 2019–20 Bushfires in Eastern Australia', *The Medical Journal of Australia*, Vol. 213, No. 6, 2020, pp. 282–3

Bravo, Luisa, 'Public Spaces and Urban Beauty: The pursuit of happiness in the contemporary European city', *European Symposium on Research in Architecture and Urban Design (6th Congress) Proceedings*, September 2012

Browning *et al.*, *The Economics of Biophilia: Why Designing with Nature in Mind Makes Financial Sense*, Terrapin Bright Green, 2015

Building Better, Building Beautiful Commission, *Living with Beauty: Promoting Health, Well-Being and Sustainable Growth*, independent report, 30 January 2020

Burgen, Stephen, 'Two-way Street: How Barcelona is democratising public space', *The Guardian*, 23 December 2020

Campos Garcia, Ana, and Nagar, Ankur, 'Building Sustainable Resilience for Sub-Saharan Africa's Urban Era', *Medium*, 24 June 2020

CAN Activists, 'Cape Town Together: Organising in a city of islands', *Maverick Citizen*, 30 June 2020

Chalaby, Odette, 'How Vienna Designed a City for Women', *Apolitical*, 23 August 2017

Charles, Alice, '10 Ways Cities are Tackling the Global Affordable Housing Crisis', *Apolitical*, 19 June 2019

Cities Economic Impact Report, World Travel & Tourism Council, 2018

Clark, Helen, Coll-Seck, Awa, Banerjee, Anshu, Peterson, Stefan, Dalglish, Sarah, Ameratunga, Shanthi, *et al.*, 'A Future for the World's Children? A WHO–UNICEF–*Lancet* Commission', *The Lancet*, Vol. 395, No. 10224, 22 February 2020, pp. 605–58

Collins, Tilly, and Fletcher, Ellen, 'Urban Agriculture: Declining opportunity and increasing demand – how observations from London, UK, can inform effective response, strategy and policy on a wide scale', *Urban Forestry & Urban Greening*, Vol. 55, November 2020

'Community Gardens, Street, Gardens and Compost Hubs', City of Melbourne website, www.melbourne.vic.gov.au/residents/home-neighbourhood/gardens-and-green-spaces/Pages/community-gardens-compost-hubs.aspx

'Culture and Social Wellbeing in New York City: Highlights of a two-year research project', University of Pennsylvania Social Impact of the Arts Project Reinvestment Fund, 9 March 2017

Culture Health and Wellbeing Eurocities Culture Forum, Tampere, 7–9 October 2020

Cuthbert, Helen, 'Living Streets, Liveable Neighbourhoods, Al Fresco Dining, Parklets and Streateries?', *Planning Potential*, 11 March 2021

Desai, Dhaval, 'Non-motorised Transport: Not just a pandemic strategy but THE way to go in smart cities of the future', *The Free Press Journal*, 23 December 2020

'Design Activism from Africa', Diseño Yucatán, 5 July 2019

Dickman, C., and McDonald, T., 'Some Personal Reflections on the Present and Future of Australia's Fauna in an Increasingly Fire-prone Continent', *Ecological Management & Restoration*, Vol. 21, 2020, pp. 86–96

Ding, D., Lawson, K., Kolbe-Alexander, T., Finkelstein, E., Katzmarzyk, P., Mechelen, W., *et al*, 'The Economic Burden of Physical Inactivity: A global analysis of major non-communicable diseases', *The Lancet*, Vol. 388, No. 10051, 24 September 2016, pp. 1311–1324

Dittmar, Hank, and Falk, Brian, 'The Pink Zone: Where small is possible', *Lean Urbanism Paper*, 4 November 2016

Elbert, W., Weber, B., Burrows, S., *et al.*, 'Contribution of Cryptogamic Covers to the Global Cycles of Carbon and Nitrogen', *Nature Geoscience*, Vol. 5, 2012, pp. 459–62

Ellen MacArthur Foundation, *Circular Economy in Cities: Project guide*, 2019

Ellen MacArthur Foundation, *The Circular Economy Opportunity for Urban & Industrial Innovation in China*, 2018

Ellen MacArthur Foundation, *Cities and Circular Economy for Food*, 2019

Ellen MacArthur Foundation, *Urban Buildings System Summary*, March 2019

Filkov, Alexander I., Ngo, Tuan, Matthews, Stuart, Telfer, Simeon, Penman, Trent D., 'Impact of Australia's Catastrophic 2019/20 Bushfire Season on Communities and Environment: Retrospective analysis and current trends', *Journal of Safety Science and Resilience*, Vol. 1, No. 1, 2020, pp. 44–56

Florida, Richard, 'The Beauty Premium: How urban beauty affects cities' economic growth', *Bloomberg CityLab*, 15 May 2019

Florida, Richard, 'Young People's Love of Cities isn't a Passing Fad', *Bloomberg CityLab*, 28 May 2019

Foodbank Australia, *Foodbank Hunger Report 2020*, 2020, p. 10

Foreground, 'Green Infrastructure and the Creative Future of Carbon Capture', *Foreground*, 26 July 2019

Francis, Adrienne, and Midena, Kate, 'Female-Run Personal Training Service Giving Canberra Muslim Women "a Safe Space" to Exercise', *ABC News*, 21 May 2021

Frearson, Amy, 'Superkilen by BIG, Topotek1 and Superflex', *De Zeen*, 24 October 2012

Freese J., Klement, R.J., Ruiz-Núñez, B. *et al.*, 'The Sedentary (R) Evolution: Have we lost our metabolic flexibility?' [version 2; peer review: 2 approved, 1 approved with reservations], *F1000Research*, Vol. 6, No. 1787, 2018

'Future of Cities', *Centre for Cities* website, www.centreforcities.org/future-of-cities

Goodyear, Sarah, 'Why City Kids Need to Play in the Street', *Bloomberg*, 1 May 2012

Government Architect New South Wales, *Designing with Country*, March 2020

Hernández Olivan, Paola, *Growing Food, Growing Healthy Communities: Opportunities for the European Healthcare Sector*, Health Care Without Harm Europe, December 2020

Hinsliff, Gaby, 'As a Rent Crisis Looms, Councils Have a Plan – the Government Should Take Note', *The Guardian*, 30 October 2020

How to Make Cities Accessible and Inclusive, Disability-inclusive and Accessible Urban Development Network, no date

Hruby, Aubrey, *Getting Creative about Development*, Atlantic Council Africa Center, September 2018

'Incorporating Indigenous Knowledge and Perspectives into the Development of Australian Cities', Australian Housing and Urban Research Institute, www.ahuri.edu.au/research/ahuri-briefs/ incorporating-indigenous-knowledge-and-perspectives-into-the- development-of-australian-cities

'Isle Crawford Discusses Design and Wellbeing in Short Film by Vola', www.youtube.com/watch?v=n_oD9n_GeuU

Kamara, Mariam, 'Western Design has Long Ignored the Work of the Wider World. It's Time for that to Change', *Elle Decor*, 15 January 2021

Kloppenburg, Joanna, '"All of Us Create an Urbanism": How our future cities builds empathy in city-making', *urbanNext.net*, no date

Knudsen, Christine, Moreno, Eduardo, Arimah, Ben, Otieno, Raymond, and Ogunsanya, Ololade, *et al.*, *World Cities Report 2020: The Value of Sustainable Urbanization*, United Nations Human Settlements Programme (UN-Habitat), 2020

Krznaric, Roman, 'The Empathy Effect: How empathy drives common values, social justice and environmental action', Friends of the Earth, *Big Ideas* project, March 2015

Latham, Lucy, Pym, Martha, Tickell, Alison, Crossley, Paul, Badiali, Chiara, *Culture & Climate Change: 14 World Cities Tackling Climate Change Through Culture*, World Cities Culture Forum, 2019

Los Angeles city profile, *World Cities Culture Forum*, www.worldcities- cultureforum.com/cities/los-angeles

McCarthy, Richard, 'Rebooting Food and Community in New Orleans After Katrina, Part Two', *National Geographic*, 12 August 2015

Martin, Taahirah, 'David Droga on Why he is Still Optimistic About Advertising', Design Inaba Conference, 4 April 2019

Max Planck Society, 'Algae, Lichens and Mosses Take Up Huge Amounts of Carbon Dioxide and Nitrogen from Atmosphere', phys.org, 4 June 2012

'Mental Health Matters' editorial, *The Lancet Global Health*, Vol. 8, No. 11, 1 November 2020

Miles, Paul, 'Why Some People are Enclosing Their Entire Home Within Glass', *Financial Times*, 8 July 2016

Musau, Zipporah, 'Lifestyle Diseases Pose New Burden for Africa', *Africa Renewal*, December 2016–March 2017

OECD, *The Governance of Land Use in Korea: Urban Regeneration*, OECD Publishing, Paris, 2019, chapter 3

Parveen, Nazia, 'The BAME Women Making the Outdoors More Inclusive', *The Guardian*, 2 December 2020

Peach, Joe, 'Eight Guidelines for Urban Design: Keeping creativity at the heart of cities', *Smart Cities Dive*, no date

Peddler, No. 6, autumn/winter 2020

Pereira, Audrey, Handa, Sudhanshu, Holmqvist, Goran, 'Prevalence and Correlates of Food Insecurity among Children across the Globe', *Innocenti Working Papers*, No. 2017-09, UNICEF Office of Research, Innocenti, Florence, 2017

Pineo, Helen, and Rydin, Yvonne, *Cities, Health and Well-Being*, Royal Institution of Chartered Surveyors, London, June 2018

Rice-Oxley, Mark, 'Grenfell: The 72 victims, their lives, loves and losses', *The Guardian*, 14 May 2018

Richmond, Riva, 'Paris Mayor Anne Hidalgo on Resilient Cities and Resilient Women', *The Story Exchange*, 29 June 2017

Smith, Oliver, 'Cities Most Reliant on Tourists for their Economies Named: Highest percentage of GDP from tourism', *Traveller*, 24 October 2018

'Sustainable Communities Initiative', cooperationjackson.org/sustainable-communities-initiatives

Technopolis/Oxford Economics, *Silver Economy Study: How to Stimulate the Economy by Hundreds of Millions of Euros Per Year*, European Commission, 2018

'The Friendship Bench', Centre for Global Mental Health, www.centreforglobalmentalhealth.org/the-friendship-bench

The Outward Bound Trust, 'Diversity in the Outdoors', www.outwardbound.org.uk/blog/diversity-in-the-outdoors

The Prince's Foundation, 'Walkability and Mixed-Use: Making valuable and healthy communities', 2020

Thomas, Aaron, 'Havana Urban Farming', WWF, 1 March 2012

Turiel, Rachel, 'Karlos Baca Forages for a Forgotten Paradigm', *Edible Southwest Colorado*, no date

Valletta 2029 European Capital of Culture, 'Living Cities, Liveable Spaces: Placemaking and Identity', *Proceedings of the Fourth Annual Valletta 2018 International Conference on Cultural Relations in Europe and the Mediterranean, Valletta, 22–24 November 2017*, Fondation de Malte, 2018

van Doorn, L., Arnold, A., and Rapoport, E., 'In the Age of Cities: The impact of urbanisation on house prices and affordability', Nijskens R., Lohuis M., Hilbers P., and Heeringa W. (eds), *Hot Property*, Springer, 2019

Vande Panne, Valerie, 'Foraging, and Forging, Connections in Cities', *Next City*, 16 December 2019

Vogue, 'From Activism to Sustainable Fashion, Here's What you Need to Know About Gen Z', *Vogue*, 7 January 2021

'Why Creativity? Why Cities?', UNESCO Creative Cities Network website, en.unesco.org/creative-cities/content/why-creativity-why-cities

'Women Workers Association Builds Tens of Thousands of Homes', *Transformative Cities*, 2018

World Health Organization, 'Physical Activity' factsheet, 26 November 2020, www.who.int/news-room/fact-sheets/detail/physical-activity

Wross, Lawrence, 'How Urban Foraging Became the New Way to Explore a City', *National Geographic*, 18 May 2020

WEBSITES AND ORGANISATIONS

Active Pregnancy Foundation, www.activepregnancyfoundation.org

Alliance for Wellbeing Economy, wellbeingeconomy.org

Cape Town Together, capetowntogether.net

Centre for Cities, www.centreforcities.org

Chefs in Schools, www.chefsinschools.org.uk

Cities for Adequate Housing, citiesforhousing.org

The Conservation Volunteers, www.tcv.org.uk

Cool Streets, www.coolstreets.com.au

Elman Peace, Elmanpeace.org

Energy Garden, www.energygarden.org.uk

Food for Life, www.foodforlife.org.uk

Food Foundation, foodfoundation.org.uk

The Friendship Bench, www.centreforglobalmentalhealth.org/
the-friendship-bench

GemFlix, www.gemx.club

George Clarke's Council House Scandal, councilhousescandal.co.uk

Global Street Art, globalstreetart.com

Iron Bound Boxing, ironboundboxing.org

Kiss the Ground, kisstheground.com

Magic Breakfast, www.magicbreakfast.com

Narratives of Home & Neighbourhood, narrativesofhome.org.za/
resources

National Park City, www.nationalparkcity.org

Nature Australia, www.natureaustralia.org.au

New Cities, newcities.org

Parkrun, www.parkrun.org.uk

Playing Out, playingout.net

The Prince's Foundation, princes-foundation.org

The Prince's Trust, www.princes-trust.org.uk

Project Ethiopia, www.project-ethiopia.org

Outdoors Queensland, qorf.org.au/resources/links-master/women-girls

Right to the City, www.right2city.org/the-right-to-the-city

ROAR AFRICA, www.roarafrica.com

Slow Food, www.slowfood.org.uk

Steel Warriors, www.steelwarriors.co.uk

Tortoise Media, www.tortoisemedia.com

Transition Towns, transitionnetwork.org

We are Grow, wearegrow.org

Women4Climate, w4c.org

World Economic Forum, www.weforum.org

World Green Building Council, www.worldgbc.org

World Resources Institute, www.wri.org

ACKNOWLEDGEMENTS

This book wouldn't have been possible without the perspectives of city dwellers and subject-matter experts from across the world. Warmest thanks to those I spoke to: Deborah Calmeyer; Dr Tilly Collins; Dr Audrey de Nazelle; Hetty McKinnon; Angela Clutton; Leo Johnson; George Lamb; Agamemnon Otero MBE; Sapan Sehgal; Maria Eleftheriou; Juan Lopez; Rod Buchanan; Sally Kettle; Ahmed Jaffer; Ben Bolgar MVO; Grahame Davies LVO; Joseph Daniels; Kerryn Fischer; Michael Berkowitz; John Edwards; Lee Bofkin; Eva Omaghomi LVO; Heidi Kreamer-Garnett; Otto Schade; Mickey Kavanaugh; Shannon Roydon-Turner; Justin Mundy LVO; Ed Davey; Beth Patten; Andrew Day; and Dr Mike Tenant. Your clarity of thought, candour, sense of humour, outrage and wisdom has been invaluable.

Tony Juniper CBE has been a steadfast source of environmental wisdom and thoughtful counsel. Thank you for listening to this alternative view of urban life and so generously penning the words of support to open this book.

Dwellbeing celebrates that the possibility of home lies everywhere, and I owe that to my wonderful parents, Toby and Brigid. It's thanks to you that wilderness, tenacity and adventure is so deeply rooted.

To the Bradburys and my extended family, present and dearly departed, you've shown unwavering love and support across great gulfs in time and distance. I'm blessed to have you.

My delightful editor, Jo de Vries, has helped me to bring *Dwellbeing* to life with warmth and skill. Thank you for your belief, encouragement, kindness and patience (and all throughout a global pandemic). Laura

Perehinec, there for the birth of *Dwellbeing* in the West End of London and the beautiful team at Flint Books – Chrissy McMorris, editorial manager, Katie Beard, head of design, Cynthia Hamilton, head of PR & marketing, and Graham Robson, marketing & PR executive – for stewarding *Dwellbeing* (and me) with such care and dedication.

Katie Read, thank you for your confidence and commitment, and for helping me to bring my thoughts to materialisation.

I'm grateful to Sally Kettle, dear friend, adventurer and powerhouse behind the Active Pregnancy Foundation, whose introduction to the inspirational Roz Savage MBE led me to Jo and Laura at Flint Books.

Antonia Brown, for years you have listened, reflected and counselled; thank you for helping me find the tools to take *Dwellbeing* forward and for barely raising an eyebrow when I took on yet another project.

Thank you to Dick and Teresa for welcoming me home to Africa in 2021 as though I'd never left. The time with you was nurturing beyond all measure.

To all my clients and class-goers who have sweated in some way with me over the years, thank you for your commitment to movement, for trusting me with your bodies and your energy.

My colleagues past and present have championed and challenged me and helped the ideas behind *Dwellbeing* percolate. Special thanks to the Centre for Environmental Policy at Imperial College London, HRH The Prince of Wales, Action Sustainability, the Active Pregnancy Foundation, and Carbon Intelligence.

Finally, my gracious thanks to friends near and far. To Grace, Olivia, Natalie, Pip, Renee, Jared, Bern, Isabel, Angela, Ally, Rowan and Leslie, for your faith and support especially during these strange times; for reminding me to pause to celebrate the wins; for calling or showing up at critical moments; and for every joyous, powerful, or messy moment we've shared. It's in no small part thanks to the incredible Vyner Street crowd that living in London has been such a happy time. Mickey and Phuong, Debbie, Matt and Heidi, Vinny and Lucy, you are proof that good neighbours really do become good friends. Thanks to Penny for your company during editing sessions in the park; Steven, for sanity checks towards the end; Will, for showing up with a bluebell wood in Cornwall at the perfect moment; Sophie for being the ultimate hype-girl; Rosie for that merciful trip down the Wye; Vinny for the photos; and Beth for being bottomless. You make my heart whole, and that's what makes a home.